DEEPER WRITING

DEEPER WRITING

Quick Writes and Mentor Texts to Illuminate New Possibilities

ROBIN W. HOLLAND

FOREWORD BY
FRANKI SIBBERSON

CORWIN
A SAGE Company

CORWIN
A SAGE Company

FOR INFORMATION:

Corwin
A SAGE Company
2455 Teller Road
Thousand Oaks, California 91320
(800) 233-9936
www.corwin.com

SAGE Publications Ltd.
1 Oliver's Yard
55 City Road
London EC1Y 1SP
United Kingdom

SAGE Publications India Pvt. Ltd.
B 1/I 1 Mohan Cooperative Industrial Area
Mathura Road, New Delhi 110 044
India

SAGE Publications Asia-Pacific Pte. Ltd.
3 Church Street
#10-04 Samsung Hub
Singapore 049483

Acquisitions Editor: Carol Chambers Collins
Publisher: Lisa Luedeke
Associate Editor: Megan Bedell
Editorial Assistants: Sarah Bartlett and
    Francesca Dutra Africano
Production Editor: Veronica Stapleton
Copy Editor: Daniel Gordon
Typesetter: C&M Digitals (P) Ltd.
Proofreader: Scott Oney
Indexer: Molly Hall
Cover Designer: Glenn Vogel
Marketing Manager: Maura Sullivan

Printed in the United States of America

A catalog record of this book is available from the Library of Congress.

9781452229942

This book is printed on acid-free paper.

FSC
www.fsc.org

MIX
Paper from
responsible sources
FSC® C014174

12 13 14 15 16 10 9 8 7 6 5 4 3 2 1

Table of Contents

Acknowledgments   vii

Foreword   ix
   Franki Sibberson

Preface   xi

**Introduction: Deeper Writing With Quick Writes
and Mentor Texts**   1
   What Is Deeper Writing?   1
   Why Is Engaging in Deeper Writing Important to You?   4
   How Did We Get to Now?   5
   What Are Quick Writes?   7
   Teachers Writing   9
   Why Use Mentor Texts?   9
   What About Sharing?   10

Overview of the Quick Writes   13

Chapter 1 Knowledge and Memory: Writing Ourselves   17
   What You Know First   17
   What's in a Name?   23
   Where Do You Live?   27
   I Know What I Know   34
   Stones in My Pocket   37
   Whiting Stories and Boasting Poems   42
   For Better or for Worse   46
   When I Was Silent   49
   It Was a Very Good Year   52
   When I Was Magic   55
   What Dreams May Come   58

Chapter 2 Art, Lenses, and Visions: Writing the World We See   63
   Seeing Things and Having New Eyes   63
   Who Wore the Hat?   67
   Head Swivelers   71

Horizons 74
Artful Reading and Writing 77
Snapshots: Capture the Moment 82
Proverbially Speaking: Words to Live By 88
Opportunity Costs 91
The Things They Carried 93
The History We Know 97
The Remains of the Day 101
The Face of Reality 104
Metaphors: Seeing the World in Other Words 107

Chapter 3 Passion, Power, and Purpose: Writing to Change the World **111**
Rites and Righteous Celebrations:
   Celebrating Events in Our Lives With Special Words 111
My Big Words 115
Encounters 120
Secrets 123
The Work of Our Hands 126
Numbering Our Village 130
Watering Our World 137
The Bill of Rights 140
Contingency Plans 144
Of Thee I Sing 147
We Are America 151

Chapter 4 Containers, Craft, and Conventions: Writing in Different Genres **157**
If That's a Poem: Introducing Mentor Texts 157
What Container Will Hold My Words? 162
And I Heard Them Say 165
The Story of My Story 169
Cumulative Poems 171
Where the Action Is 175
Less Is Better 178
Comic Lives 182

Chapter 5 The Creation of a Quick Write: Developing Your Own **187**
Context 188
Content 190
Container 192
Container Lining: Our Lenses 193

References **195**

Literature Cited **197**

Index **209**

Acknowledgments

There are so many people that have supported and encouraged me throughout this process. I have been blessed to have teachers, guides, advisers, cheerleaders, family, and friends along each step of the way.

First and foremost, I must acknowledge my great debt to David Bloome, without whom this book would probably have remained simply a file on my computer full of individual quick writes used solely in my own teaching. I cannot express how much I appreciate his time and encouragement throughout this process, particularly during the initial proposal preparation and submission phase.

Likewise, I thank Melissa Wilson, David's doctoral student at the time, who also met with me along with David. She edited the original proposal, continues to use the prompts with her university students, and has been my colleague on many curriculum-writing teams, and my friend.

This book would also not exist without my involvement in the Columbus Area Writing Project (CAWP). This professional community has provided so many possibilities and opportunities for me. I am forever grateful to the codirectors, past and present, including Linda Kelly and Michele Winship, who facilitated the 2005 CAWP Summer Institute in which I participated, and to my current fellow codirectors: David Bloome, Kevin Cordi, George Newell, and Melissa Wilson.

I am grateful to all the teachers in the CAWP from 2005 to 2012 who have written to these quick writes during the summer institutes, during our writing happy hours, and in their own classrooms with their students, thus helping me weed out the junk and discover the gems.

The initial writing invitations were created for and piloted in the Salem Teacher Writing Project and the Salem Student After-School Writing Project, groups I facilitated in my building as a result of my initial involvement with the CAWP.

Thank you to the Salem teachers who participated in the Salem Teacher Writing Project each year it existed: Tina Carpenter, Cathy Patzer, and Michelle Weber. Additionally, I thank Caroline Egan, Celeste Guglielmi, Stephanie Hawking, Meg Lagucki, Lynn Markle, and Sheila Wilson, who also participated. A huge thank-you is also due to my former principal, Gail Buick, for her participation in the teacher group and unwavering support of both groups.

Thank you to all the students whose work has inspired me and helped me to be a better writer and writing teacher, all of the students who participated in the Salem Student After-School Writing Project, and a special thanks to Ian Tran and Michael Lipster who graciously allowed me to use their pieces.

I thank Katie Brintlinger, Barb Keyes, and Steve Schack for our monthly conversations, continuing support, and most of all for holding me accountable.

I am indebted to those family members and friends who have encouraged me and understood the frustrations and elations of the writing (or not writing) process and listened to my constant updates, including my parents, Elizabeth and Robert Jackson, my sisters, Rhonda Abban and Renee Jackson, and my dear friend Diane Reavling. I also thank my mother for reading every quick write and proofreading both the initial proposal and the first draft.

I am deeply indebted to my husband, Ralph V. Holland Jr., who ignored the constant piles of books and papers on the dining room table, who would say "keep writing" and celebrate any positive feedback with me, and who would encourage me in times of waiting.

I thank Franki Sibberson for her encouragement after reading an early draft and for graciously agreeing to write the foreword.

Finally, I thank the Corwin family for all of their efforts on behalf of *Deeper Writing: Quick Writes and Mentor Texts to Illuminate New Possibilities,* with special appreciation for my editors, Carol Collins for initially seeing something in this book that was worthy of publication, Lisa Luedeke for her support, encouragement, and vision as we moved forward, and Dan Gordon for his meticulous copyediting of each page in preparing this book for publication.

PUBLISHER'S ACKNOWLEDGMENTS

Wanda Mangum, Language Arts Instructional Coach
Suwanee, Georgia

Peggy Semingson, Ph.D., Assistant Professor, Literacy Studies
College of Education, Curriculum and Instruction
University of Texas at Arlington

Sharon Kane, Professor, Literacy and English Methods
State University of New York at Oswego

Foreword

Franki Sibberson

Inviting students to write and to explore their world through writing is one of the most important things we can do as teachers, and *Deeper Writing: Quick Writes and Mentor Texts to Illuminate New Possibilities* is a gift to teachers of writing. No matter the age of your students, Robin Holland's book will help you support them in their growth as writers.

When I think of prompts, I think of the prompts of the past in which we asked children to respond to a fantastical situation or to fill in the page about an imaginary experience. But that is not what these quick writes are about. In *Deeper Writing*, Robin invites students to try new things as writers. The quick writes are not intended to inspire a final draft of writing. Instead, they are intended to stretch the writer in new directions.

The ideas in this book are based on sound theory about writing. As the codirector in the Columbus Area Writing Project (affiliate of the National Writing Project), Robin Holland is perfectly poised to share her insights and strategies for helping students of all ages to engage in deeper writing. Not only is she codirector of the project, but she has many years of classroom experience. The combination of the work she has done with students and adults has allowed her to develop quick writes that support students across various ages and levels.

There are no scripts or have-tos in this book. Instead, the book provides *possibilities*. In addition to an abundance of excellent quick writes, Robin Holland further supports our teaching efforts with booklists and mentor texts for each quick write that help reinforce and strengthen these important writing occasions. She understands the classroom setting and how writing workshops work. She knows the kinds of things that will help teachers move students forward. She gives us solid thinking along with resources that will help us support our students.

This book is organized around quick writes, but throughout the reading, we learn much more about being a teacher of writing. Robin doesn't just share ideas. Instead, she shares ways to make these ideas your own—she shares her thinking, the reasons behind the ideas, and allows her thinking to act as a mentor; it is an invitation to think about how to best use them with your own students.

Robin places a high value on teachers as writers. This is demonstrated over and over again as she shares her own writing inspired by the quick writes. At one point, early in the book, she explicitly talks about the importance of this:

> I rarely give a quick write to which I have not written except for the first time a prompt is ever used, and I write along beside my students or fellow writers. I have written to many of the quick writes numerous times—always producing something new and different from my previous writing to the same prompt. p. 9

The brilliant message of this book is that quick writes invite possibilities. Robin helps us see each of these invitations in a way that is not based on an end product but instead begins a new conversation. As she says, "These prompts are for playing with and practicing writing. For putting the pen on the paper and just going for it."

Preface

This book is about how to get writers engaged in meaningful and reflective writing—deeper writing. By deeper writing, I mean writing that challenges writers to engage in a thorough search of memory, a critical analysis of relationships and situations, and a powerful discovery of themselves and the world.

Deeper writing is writing that digs beneath the surface, underneath the obvious observations and topics, to reveal that which is in the background, unnoticed. It touches both the reader and writer with emotions we have buried or ignored and it surprises us with fresh perspectives of the familiar. The quick writes in this book lead to new writing possibilities, new content, contexts, and containers for our deepest thoughts and feelings.

HOW TO USE THIS BOOK

While the idea of quick writes may be intriguing to you, you may be wondering how this fits in to your already busy daily schedule. Rather than complicating lesson planning, this book is designed to enhance the writing opportunities and instruction that you are already providing for your students and to expand the store of ideas you consider as possibilities for engaging your students in writing. If you and your students are well into the writing workshop process—selecting topics and drafting with ease— these quick writes will challenge you to dig below the surface, to reflect and remember and imagine—to write with deeper meaning.

If you are relatively new to teaching writing or unsure of where to go next with your writing instruction, this book is the perfect place for you to begin. You will find that the quick writes lend themselves easily to your current instructional focus and lead to or enhance mini-lessons in which you are already engaged as well as those you wish to provide, such as selecting topics, choosing appropriate genres, getting started writing, and using writing of other authors or mentor texts, as well as other areas of focus. As you provide mini-lessons in your class to instruct students about necessary writing knowledge, strategies, and skills, consider which quick writes in this book will complement each lesson.

INFORMATIONAL TEXTS

The quick writes contained in this book are not limited to use in writing instruction alone. If you are responsible for content area instruction, informational texts, and nonfiction lessons, these quick writes can provide ways to introduce topics or foster further reflection on particular areas of study, including social justice issues and personal issues. Some of the quick writes can be used to invite students to write not as themselves, but as characters in history, science, or literature, and to deepen understanding of a particular area of study, time, and people. These quick writes can foster the thinking and talking that are so important in content-area studies that can lead to deeper levels of conversation, as well as deeper writing. We are reminded, however, that writing nonfiction or informational texts requires specific knowledge. It is recommended that students have time to engage in reading, discussion, inquiry, and research before being invited to write extended informational texts. Writing, particularly informational writing, does not occur in a vacuum, but relies on content and accurate information as a foundation.

This book is *not* intended to teach you as teachers how to implement a writing workshop or manage the writing classroom, nor is it designed to teach writing basics. Rather, it seeks to support teachers involved in these areas as they search for more authentic ways to engage their students and will complement texts already on your shelves and in your students' hands in these areas.

This book *will* enable you to challenge writers to engage in a thorough search of memory, a critical analysis of relationships and situations, and a powerful discovery of themselves and the world. It will complement your current process for writing workshops and encourage a deeper level of engagement.

Deeper Writing: Quick Writes and Mentor Texts to Illuminate New Possibilities provides a way for you and your students to engage in substantive thinking, critical reflection, and deeper, more meaningful writing.

Introduction

Deeper Writing With Quick Writes and Mentor Texts

How do we get students engaged in substantive, reflective, meaningful writing? The answer is deeper writing—writing which challenges us to engage in exploring our memories, our emotions, and our thoughts that lie below the surface. In the introduction, you will be introduced to what I mean when I say deeper writing, writing that challenges us to do the difficult yet satisfying work of remembering, reflecting upon, and reimagining ourselves, our relationships, situations, and issues in the world. I will also discuss how the quick writes came to be developed and how mentor texts are used to support writing.

You may have picked up this book with skepticism. A book of quick writes? You may be wondering if this is more of the test preparation or scripted writing instruction that we are seeing so much of lately. Although this book will help you and your students write better, which may lead to better test scores, this book is *not* about testing.

This book is for writers—both teachers and their students—to lead them into deeper writing.

WHAT IS DEEPER WRITING?

Deeper writing challenges us to engage in writing that explores ourselves and the memories, emotions, and thoughts that we usually ignore or let lie dormant. It challenges us to do the difficult yet satisfying work of remembering, reflecting upon, and reimagining ourselves, our relationships, and our experiences. It asks us to consider various issues and conditions in the world.

Deeper writing digs beneath the surface and peels back the layers of ordinary understandings and topics in order to look at the underside—discovering truths, revealing an essence, or considering an alternative or multiple perspectives. It is reflecting with the pen and tackling the hard stuff—thinking and writing critically, pushing metaphors to the limit—and searching for relationship and relevance where they are not easily detected. Deeper writing is creating rich texts, leaving the writer as surprised as the reader to see where the writing has led.

Deeper writing and thinking forces us to ask again and again: What more? What else? Why? And so what? We create images and reveal ideas that make us reexamine our taken-for-granted beliefs and long-held mental images to notice connections that we didn't realize existed. In short, we write ourselves to deeper understanding and awareness, to deeper feelings and insights of ourselves, others, and the world.

We may not be able to define it clearly although we all recognize deeper writing when we hear it, when we read it. At the retreat that begins each year's Columbus Area Writing Project Summer Institute, I first experienced a response to deeper writing in the unnerving silence that resulted after reading my poem about a conversation that afternoon with the groundskeeper of the retreat center. I had waited until the end, quite nervous and unsure of how my fellow writers would respond. My poem ended with *I saw him again today because I was looking. He waved to me because I know his name.* I was met with absolute silence. Finally I could stand the silence no longer. Everyone else who had read had received comments and feedback. "Somebody say something," I ventured tentatively. Several retreat fellows explained that the poem had moved them and that they had also seen the man, now that they thought about it, but had taken no intentional notice of him. Deeper writing reveals that which is hidden or unnoticed in the background, forcing it to the foreground and our conscious attention.

At the first afterschool student writing project in my building, Bethany, the lone third grader among a group of fourth and fifth graders, also experienced that silence when she read her short poem about her grandmother who had recently died. She began to cry as she read, finally unable to finish the poem—unable to complete the line *They loved me a lot because I was the only baby around. They never put me down because I was the only baby around* . . . My co-teacher finished it for her. Again silence—and then immediately, students crowded around to hug her. *I loved your poem. My grandma died too. I felt the same way.* Deeper writing causes us to remember and reexperience what we have buried deep in our hearts or simply forgotten. It has power to touch us and free emotions heretofore kept in check or unshared for both the writer and the audience.

Deeper writing resonates in our souls with familiarity and truth but at the same time speaks to us of something previously not acknowledged or recognized. When read aloud in my fifth-grade classroom, deeper writing is met with smiles and silence and sighs of delight—and then a burst of talk, as students rush to applaud a well-chosen word, a particular feeling instigated by the writing, or to confess a familiar chord struck. The response to deeper writing is the same whether the author is a seasoned writer or one of our own classmates.

This past winter, when James, our own "bad boy-class clown" who normally writes of war, blood, tanks, guns, and death, and routinely cheers for the bad guy in every story, read a true story about falling into the lake at his apartment complex and being rescued by an unidentified hand that turned out to be his older brother, the kids were surprised and respectfully impressed. We don't usually see this smack-talking, tough guy as vulnerable and needing help from anybody. He is still wisecracking and shrugging his shoulders in keeping with his "I don't care" attitude, but we all know a different James from the writing he shared that day. Deeper writing surprises us and lets us see a new side of the familiar.

The purpose of this book is to lead writers—you and your students—into deeper writing. The invitations or new writing possibilities offered here open doors, foster more thoughtfulness and reflectivity, and lead to powerful words.

These quick writes will open your eyes and the eyes of your students to new writing possibilities, to see the unlimited opportunities and the inexhaustible content available for writing. This book is about recognizing the myriad contexts in which we write and expanding the variety of containers we choose to hold our writing. It is also about the many lenses each of us wears as we both read and write.

These quick writes are for playing and practicing with writing, putting the pen on the paper and just going for it. Like a pianist practicing scales or noodling around with notes, like a dancer trying out new combinations of steps or rehearsing before the real performance, we can practice putting our thoughts and ideas on paper. We can explore those ideas and let them take shape, leading sometimes to new insights about writing, and other times to a satisfying, finished product. There is great value in writing regularly. Professional writers variously call their daily efforts free writing, diving, AM pages, or 10-minute write. It doesn't matter what you call it. The important thing is doing it yourself and providing time for your students to write as well. Deeper writing is not afraid of authentic subjects. Writing below the obvious surface considerations sometimes fosters highly personal self-examination, discovery, and revelation. Some of these quick writes will undoubtedly lead you and your fellow writers to inner delight and exuberant public celebration, as achievements, goals, and happy events are explored, as well as to murky, dark places, as personal secrets, inner insecurities, relationships, and less happy events are explored.

As we consider our world and all that is right with it, we also consider serious social realities such as war, hunger, and poverty—real issues, real needs, real concerns. Your classroom and your writing groups must be safe places—places where risks can be taken, hearts can be shared, tears can be openly shed, laughter comes easily, and all efforts are supported and applauded by an intimate community.

And finally, these writing invitations are about demonstrating our power to define and change both our private and public worlds—about us personally reconstructing, rediscovering, and re-visioning our world and ourselves—seeing the possibilities not yet written, understanding and defining the worlds in which we live, and seeing new relationships and worlds that we, collectively and individually, have the power to create.

WHY IS ENGAGING IN DEEPER WRITING IMPORTANT TO YOU?

Carl Nagin indicates that "writing is a gateway for success in academia, the new workplace and the global economy, as well as for our collective success as a participatory democracy...." And he further indicates that "learning to write requires frequent, supportive practice. Evidence shows that writing performance improves when a student writes often and across content areas" (*Because Writing Matters: Improving Student Writing in Our Schools* by the National Writing Project and Carl Nagin, 2006, pp. 2, 12).

In my teaching experience and in my own school, this was evident. In 2006, the year we introduced both a student afterschool writing group and a teacher afterschool writing group, our writing scores for the building increased from 78% to 96% on the OAT (Ohio Achievement Test) Writing Assessment, placing us the second highest in our large district in writing. My principal attributed this significant gain directly to the increased writing instruction and writing opportunities provided by teachers throughout the school day, by those engaged in the writing project and also to the additional opportunities and instruction provided by the after-school program for both students and teachers.

According to now-deceased writing researcher Donald Graves, "If you provide frequent occasions for writing, then students start to think about writing when they are not doing it. I call this a state of constant composition" (National Writing Project & Nagin, 2006, p. 22).

Engaging in these and similar quick writes can lead students to this desired state of constant composition: a constant state of wonder and discovery, an ongoing consideration of new ideas, and variations on familiar ones—new possibilities of how responses to life may be written.

The New Common Core College and Career Readiness Anchor Standards for Writing (adopted at the time of this writing by 45 of our 50 states), along with most currently adopted state standards, call for daily or regular opportunities to write for a variety of authentic purposes, using a variety of writing strategies and practicing different types of writing including narrative, argumentative, persuasive, and explanatory writing and literary forms.

Daily practice will build confidence, facility, and fluency. In addition, writing regularly will produce gems or kernels for future use in intentional, more formal pieces.

HOW DID WE GET TO NOW?

When I began teaching in 1975, there were two types of writing—there was writing, *real writing*, and there was *creative writing*. And I don't remember teaching or showing students how to write either type. I only remember *assigning* writing. We took pride in providing the most creative prompts for our students, leading them to produce that so-called creative writing. An excellent prompt back then might have been

> A Martian just landed in your classroom and invites you to return to Mars with him in his spaceship. Write about your trip.

Or

> Your mother ate too many tomatoes and turned red. What will you do?

Or

> You suddenly become invisible. How do you feel?

The teacher stores sold books of similar prompts for what we called daily seatwork or board work. The creativity of the prompt itself, it seemed, was the point. The wilder and more illogical, the better.

Except for the most creative and gifted kids, who did not need my help to write, what the students produced was poor writing—as wild and illogical as the prompts and equally inadequate. Even those of us who wrote, usually unrelated to and outside of our school day, did not write to these prompts that we were asking students to use. These were simply part of the immense amount of work given daily to keep students busy during the morning while we conducted reading groups.

Our district had no set curriculum guide or course of study for writing at that time, although we required writing reports of all sorts: book reports, reports about countries, and elaborate unit projects. Some of us began experimenting with different prompts and other ways to get students to write, with sometimes surprisingly delightful results. But we were simply stabbing in the dark, unable to consistently produce the satisfactory results.

I began haunting the campus bookstores, buying college composition textbooks, scrutinizing the lessons and then modifying the ideas for my second-grade students. I still remember a lesson from one such college text (Augustine, 1975) requiring students to write "existential definitions"— concrete and active words to specify an abstraction, category, or concept. (For example: *Contentment is sitting on the deck with my husband having just eaten Chilean sea bass from Bonefish Grill and being so full that talking is out of the question and completely unnecessary,* or *Ecstasy is lying on a beach anywhere, knowing there are seven more days of sun and sand, snorkeling, and seashells before returning to the cold, ice, and snow of Ohio.*) I still love this existential definition activity and continue to use modified versions of it with both adults and children because it requires us to reexamine our ordinary views and definitions of the world.

In the bookstores around this same time, books about journal writing suddenly became popular. Having kept a diary or journal or some sort of writer's notebook since I was a child, I now began the personal discipline, which I continue to this day, of working through books of writing exercises and in this way discovering writing techniques to share with my students. I also had my students keep journals as, together, we tried a variety of journal activities.

There was a stark absence of books about elementary writing. The focus at that time was on language acquisition and reading theory and reading instruction. But then several things happened that dramatically transformed the writing situation for elementary teachers and students.

First, in 1983, Donald Graves (*Writing: Teachers & Children at Work*) showed us a more satisfying way to invite students to write, freeing us from the false sense of creativity housed in an irrelevant prompt rather than a student's own mind and experiences. *Write what you know* became the mantra of the day. Instead of fantastical topics, we now encouraged students to write about people, places, events, and feelings that were real. We encouraged them to plumb their daily lives for interesting, write-worthy topics—and we gave them time to write.

Next, close on the heels of Graves, Lucy Calkins's notion of mini-lessons provided the necessary instructional scaffold to foster better writing (*The Art of Teaching Writing*). Short lessons could be developed that addressed the needs of the students as they arose, presenting, modeling, and guiding the use of not only conventions, but all aspects of the writing process (topic selection, genre, craft, etc.).

And finally, as I continued to experiment, I discovered the power of intentionally linking literature with writing. As a Title I teacher working with struggling readers, I began to use writing as a way to deepen understanding of our read-aloud and guided reading texts. Through using graphic organizers and key language structures to guide thinking, talking, and writing in response to what we were reading, my students were able to comprehend text more effectively. But something else wonderful happened. As they reflected and wrote in response to literature and content-area reading that we were doing, they discovered connections to their own lives, feelings, and memories. They found their own personal stories and began to write powerful pieces. They were engaging in deeper writing.

As a result of these experiences, I began to develop what I now call *quick writes,* flexible writing invitations supported by mentor texts—literature or content-area texts that could teach us how to write, serving as models for our own writing or fostering new avenues of thinking that also led to writing possibilities.

WHAT ARE QUICK WRITES?

The quick writes or writing invitations gathered in this book are offered as ideas to spark thinking and initiate writing. They are unique in that each corresponds to carefully chosen mentor texts to model and stimulate writing. Unlike the prompts described earlier, these quick writes are not one-sentence story starters or fill-in-the-blank worksheets. Instead they invite writers to discover within their memories, feelings, and ideas the meaning they want to make, the story they need to tell. They cause students to analyze the world around them differently and write to define and affect situations, people, and relationships. Although when presented they seem to arise casually and conversationally, each quick write is intentionally and carefully designed to invite writers to challenge themselves to engage in deeper writing.

Each quick write in this book shares a basic framework:

Background for the Teacher

This is an introduction to the topic or concept that includes a context: a short anecdote, story, information, or comments to introduce the ideas in the quick write. As you present the quick writes to your students, you also will want to share your personal connections and contexts.

The Quick Write Lesson

This section will in most cases include the following:

- Sharing Mentor Texts
- Writer's Notebook
- Quick Write Possibilities

Sharing Mentor Texts

Each quick write includes carefully chosen mentor texts to provide models of possible content and containers for writing. These include picture books, novels, essays, poems, and websites, commercial texts and texts written by the author, as well as students—any written texts that will help enlarge the vision of possibilities for the writers' own compositions.

Writer's Notebook (Not Included in All Lessons)

In some cases, brief instruction or prewriting may be necessary to successfully address the given quick write. In such cases, suggestions are provided to prepare for using the quick write. This may include a discussion along with listing, webbing, sharing, or other ways to engage in pre-thinking and prewriting.

Quick Write Possibilities

This is the heart of each quick write—the actual writing suggestions intended to foster deeper writing. But each quick write is a suggestion only and can be interpreted and modified in many ways by both the teacher and the writers.

The Mentor Texts

This provides a list of texts used in the model lesson.

Additional Resources

This final section identifies additional mentor texts, websites, films, and other resources that may be useful as you prepare for and work with the quick writes.

These quick writes suggest both new ideas and twists on familiar ones. And while they have proven successful with both children and adults, as noted above, they remain *merely suggestions.* It is hoped that as you work with the quick writes, you will make them your own—flexibly, yet judiciously, adjusting both subject and process as necessary for your audience.

I rarely give a quick write that I have not responded to myself. The exception is the first time I give a quick write, and then I write along beside my students or fellow writers. I have written to many of the quick writes numerous times—always producing something new and different from the previous time. If the writing strategies or suggestions are new or less familiar to my students, I may also write in front of them to model before asking them to work on their own.

The quick writes in this book have been tested not only by students over the years in my Title I groups, classrooms, and the Salem Student After-School Writing Project groups, but also by colleagues in the Columbus Area Writing Project and their students, and teachers at Salem School who participated in the Salem Teacher Writing Group and their students, as well as other fellow Columbus City Schools teachers. Together, we have all test-driven and helped determine the current shape of these still changing and growing quick writes.

TEACHERS WRITING

Teachers will find that these quick writes will work well in teacher groups, and I do encourage you to work through the quick writes you will introduce to your student writers. Write with a group of interested teachers, discussing the ways that you each used the quick write to foster writing and ways that it may be adapted, changed, or redesigned to use with your particular group of writers in the classroom.

The quick writes, with only a few exceptions, will work with all levels, Grade 4 through adult. There are several so marked that should only be used with middle and high school levels or above without changing the subject matter—yet even those can be adapted as needed to suit your needs. (See Chapter 5 for more on creating your own quick writes.)

WHY USE MENTOR TEXTS?

Reading is crucial for writers. And reading aloud became critical in my classroom and with adult writing groups, as well. It is through reading what others have written that we are able to visualize directions for our own writing. It is through reading that we are able to learn about writing, to ask what words, structures, techniques, and strategies the writer has used to achieve her desired effect. As we begin to read like writers, deconstructing texts—noticing, identifying, and naming what authors have done, turning the texts inside out—we are able to then easily identify the same features in other books or texts and begin to use those moves in our own writing. We can try on the styles and strategies of the writers we are reading. In this way we are learning to write directly from those who write—the authors of the books and other texts we read.

When using mentor texts, it is helpful to chart with students the techniques and strategies they notice while reading in preparation for writing a particular piece. It is also useful to return to previously read books for strategic purposes. For example, when we are working on writing leads, we might pull out every book we have read so far during the school year to examine only the first sentence or first paragraph and then analyze and list the ways that we could begin, based on what we have discovered. In the case of leads, for example, after investigating multiple texts, our list of possibilities for leads in our own writing may include the following: quote, question, anecdote, surprising fact, memory, and so on.

A mentor text can be a sentence, a picture book, an article or essay, a poem, or a longer work, such as a novel or informational text. It can be any text that we imitate or use as a model for our own writing. These texts are intentionally and carefully chosen. I favor short texts or excerpts because they can easily be used in one sitting, leaving room for several texts to be shared with the feature(s) to be modeled easily identified and discussed, while still having time to write. An appropriate mentor text is well-written, with genre, topic, format, ideas, or structures that clearly model what you are challenging students to do. The ultimate goal is that student writers begin to choose their own mentor texts—that they begin to recognize which texts can help them do what they are trying to do in writing.

For an example of a clear, specific, and structured way to use a mentor text, see the quick write titled "If That's a Poem: Introducing Mentor Text." For using mentor texts in a less structured way, see the quick write titled "Where Do You Live?"

WHAT ABOUT SHARING?

Once your writers have begun to write, they will want to share what they have written. They are entitled to both an audience and feedback. Allowing students to share their work provides an affirmation of their ideas and process, an opportunity to hear what is working in their piece, as well as suggestions for revisions. Allowing students to share also provides models of writing for other students. (You can read more about Read-Around in *Reading, Writing and Rising Up* by Linda Christensen, pp. 14–17.)

In my own classroom, we have several guidelines that serve us well:

- Time may not permit everyone to share, so if you shared the day before we ask you to wait until others have shared.
- You have the right to pass and not share.
- You have the right to receive no feedback or specify the type you would like to receive. (For example, *I would like to hear only what works, or I would like to know if the character description is clear.*)

Prior to our first read-around, I teach language that we can use to respond to writing, model that language extensively, and then guide students' practice. Helpful response language in our classroom includes

- *I like* . . . (words, phrases, sentences, ideas, metaphors, juxtapositions, connections, strategies, etc.)
- *I want to know more about* . . . (call for more details or specificity)
- *I don't understand* . . . (call for clarity)
- *I suggest* . . . (specific suggestion for the writer with examples)
- *I am wondering if* . . . or *I noticed* . . . (general reflection)

Students are encouraged to listen carefully and take brief notes to assist them as they respond to their fellow writers. The entire piece does not have to be shared, particularly with extremely long pieces and limited time. You may want to ask for the best sentence or most powerful sentence or paragraph, or the one that connects to or best follows what was just read by a fellow writer, and so on.

As I mention in my classroom guidelines above, you may want to assure your writers that the writing they produce during quick writes will not be seen by anyone but themselves, unless they choose to share. A technique I have used in the past with students is to fold and staple anything they do not want me to read when I collect their notebooks. This gives them a sense of security. Interestingly, even though it is offered, few students use this option. Most really want you to read everything.

As you begin to use the quick writes in this book, you will develop your own writing community, rules, and rites. The quick writes may be used in the given order or may be chosen based on topic or type of writing. You may find a suggested mentor text that correlates with something you are working on in your classroom and want to use the accompanying quick write to enrich your current work. However you use them, the quick writes are designed to take you below the surface, beyond the ordinary, and into new writing possibilities. They are designed to lead you and your students into deeper writing.

Overview of the Quick Writes

Chapter	Prompt Title	Topic	Genre or Type of Writing	Levels
1	What you know first	Early memories	Memoir, narrative, essay, poetry	4–12
1	What's in a name?	Power and pain of our name	Narrative, poetry, essay, information report	4–12
1	Where do you live?	Home or important place	Description, memoir, personal essay, history	4–12
1	I know what I know	Ways of knowing	Essay, opinion, narrative	4–12
1	Stones in my pocket	Objects we collect	Personal or descriptive essay, poetry	4–12
1	Whiting stories and boasting poems	Family stories and tall tales	Narrative, research reports, essays, poetry	4–12
1	For better or for worse	Good and bad in life	Descriptive or personal essay	4–12
1	When I was silent	Being silent	Personal essay, memoir, poetry	8–12
1	It was a very good year	Judging a year or time period	Persuasive essay	4–12
1	When I was magic	Magic in our lives	Fictional narrative	4–12
1	What dreams may come	Our dreams	Personal essay, poetry, experimental forms	4–12
2	Seeing things and having new eyes	Seeing common objects in new ways	Description, poetry, personal essays	4–12
2	Who wore the hat?	Questioning object to discover the nature of its uses and its owner	Poetry	6–12 (adapts for 4–5)

(Continued)

(Continued)

Chapter	Prompt Title	Topic	Genre or Type of Writing	Levels
2	Head swivelers	Things we have said that have shocked others	Narrative, personal essay	4–12
2	Horizons	Limits and horizons in our lives	Personal or persuasive essays or letters	4–12
2	Artful reading and writing	Using paintings to inspire writing	Descriptive or reflective essays	4–12
2	Snapshots: Capture the moment	Using photographs to inspire writing	Descriptive, personal, or persuasive essay, poetry	4–12
2	Proverbially speaking: Words to live by	Examining traditional proverbs and sayings	Proverbs, essays, information reports	4–12
2	Opportunity costs	Effects of decisions we make	Poetry, personal essay	4–12
2	The things they carried	Essentials in our lives and the lives of others	Personal or persuasive essay	6–12 (adapts for 4–5)
2	The history we know	Misconceptions about history	Expository or personal essay	4–12
2	The remains of the day	Our common objects as viewed by archaeologists	Satire, scientific report, or article	4–12
2	The Face of reality	Reality TV programs	Persuasive essay, editorial columns, or letters to the editor	4–12
2	Metaphors: Seeing the world in other words	Metaphors	Personal or persuasive essay	4–12
3	Rites and righteous celebrations: Celebrating events in our lives with special words	Remembering and celebrating special events	Speech, poetry	4–12
3	My big words	Power of well-chosen words	Letter to the editor, editorial column, persuasive essay, poetry	4–12
3	Encounters	New people or groups coming together	Narrative, poetry	4–12

Chapter	Prompt Title	Topic	Genre or Type of Writing	Levels
3	Secrets	Secrets in our lives and the lives of others	Personal essay, narrative	4–12
3	The work of our hands	Our hands reveal who we are	Essays, poems	4–12
3	Numbering our village	People in our world	Expository or persuasive essays	4–12
3	Watering our world	Water availability and usage	Persuasive essays	4–12
3	The Bill of Rights	Knowing our constitutional rights	Petitions, editorials or letters to the editor, personal or persuasive essay	4–12
3	Contingency plans	Planning for the unexpected	Contingency plans	4–12
3	Of Thee I Sing	Recognizing noteworthy people and actions	Expository essays	4–12
3	We are America	Defining Americans	Personal and persuasive essays	4–12
4	If that's a poem: Introducing mentor texts	Using mentor texts to help us write	Poetry	4–12
4	What container will hold my words?	Choosing a genre	Revising a previous piece	4–12
4	And I heard them say	Conversations in our writing	Dialogue	4–12
4	The story of my story	Origins of a piece of writing	Reflective essay, multi-genre project	4–12
4	Cumulative poems	Improving our sentences	Sentences, poetry	4–12
4	Where the action is	Using verbs	Poems, narratives	4–12
4	Less is better	Writing using short forms	Short forms such as haiku, flash fiction, six-word memoirs	4–12
4	Comic lives	Creating comics and cartoons	Comics, cartoons	4–12

The act of putting pen to paper encourages pause for thought, this in turn makes us think more deeply about life, which helps us regain our equilibrium.

—Norbert Platt

The greatest part of a writer's time is spent reading, in order to write; a man will turn over half a library to make one book.

—Samuel Johnson

1 Knowledge and Memory

Writing Ourselves

What is your earliest memory?

How do you know what you know?

What objects carry your story?

The quick writes in this section challenge writers to examine themselves, their lives, and their beliefs and to discover the ever changing nature of both memory and knowledge. They can be the genesis of a variety of types of writing:

- memoir
- personal essays
- descriptive essays
- persuasive essays
- narratives
- tall tales
- poetry

What You Know First

Grades 4–12

Memoir, Narrative, Essay, Poetry

Early Memories

> • What is the earliest memory that you can clearly recall?

Background for the Teacher

There is a current trend in the literary world to share deepest, darkest secrets and to explore their meaning in our present lives. We call this memoir or memory writing. Books on the display tables of Barnes & Noble share the uphill climb to stardom, the downward spiral caused by a myriad of addictions, the marriage gone woefully wrong, the climb back out of the depths of depression, the search for spiritual growth, the unlikely political or career success story, and on the list goes. We have a multitude of new books sharing every kind of experience imaginable about people's personal lives. Some few recently caused eyebrows to rise as we discovered that the fascinating stories presented as truth were in fact more fiction. Still, we were really no less enamored with the stories. We are all voyeurs at heart. We want to know about the lives of others—the ordinary and the most private and secret. How does our life compare, contrast, compete, and count? We want to know what we are missing. What have we not experienced? Who else has experienced our own secret life? What does our life mean?

Our memories, whether they are accurate or not, play a factor in defining who we are today and who we may be in the future. We shape our todays by events and feelings stored in our memories. If these memories are happy, we probably approach today with a degree of positivity. If we have tragic memories, not properly and tenderly dealt with, we may experience mental anguish in the most ordinary of events as our memories color them.

We all tell stories about our lives—what we remember from earlier in the day and what we remember from earlier in our lives. We greet people with "Guess what happened to me today!" At dinner we share anecdotes about our childhood or college days: "I remember the time I . . ." We often discuss shared memories with friends and family, retelling familiar stories until they almost take on a mythical or liturgical quality. And we don't all remember the same details and truth. My memory of an important event may differ drastically from someone else's who was there. (See also the quick write entitled "I Know What I Know" for more ideas about memories.)

For writers, our memories are the biggest banks of writing ideas we possess. Held safe in our memories are enough ideas to ponder and analyze for a lifetime. As we construct stories, poems, and essays, we can recall details of related incidents, interesting characters, past conflicts, and proud moments from our own lives. These contribute to the fabric of our invented stories, our poems, and other written words, and also undergird our vision of the world and the information texts we are drawn to write.

Our memories are often evoked, unbidden, by smells or sounds: a bar of music, an old swatch of fabric, an unsuspecting moment of déjà vu. We then relax and go back, willingly or unwillingly, to an earlier time that we may be trying to forget.

Memoir writing, which I have discovered I love, is different from autobiography, which I never much liked, in that it reflects on itself. In memoir, memory is twisted and flipped and juggled until patterns emerge and meaning is discovered. Rather than just a recital of *I came, I did, I saw* . . . memoir *interprets* what we did and saw, and may even unintentionally revise a memory, although the truth of the matter is retained. Memory writing helps us discover who we are and what our lives mean.

The Quick Write Lesson

1. Sharing Mentor Texts

Choose one of the texts listed below (I have used each of the texts included for this quick write at one time or another), or choose another book that shares a memory told in first person.

- Ask students to think about why the author chose this particular memory.
- Encourage them to notice how conversation is used.

Ask . . .

- What sensory details are included to help bring the memory alive?
- Does the setting play an important part in the narrative?
- Who is involved? What is the relationship?

You may want to read a second book or several more to compare, asking the same questions.

2. Writer's Notebook

Help your students think about the many ways in which they can call up a memory and then record it. What helps them to remember?

Have them begin to make a list of their memories in no particular order, just recording a note or title each time a memory occurs to them. They can keep this running list available in their notebooks for future writing.

I write when my students are writing and share my writing in the group as they do. Depending on the group, I may also write in front of them before asking them to write.

Here is my sample list:

- Alien (My Dog) Died
- First Airplane Trip
- Learning to Snorkel
- Square Dancing at the Eastside Y in Elementary School
- Cutting My Doll's Hair
- Getting My Braces Off
- My Wedding

3. Quick Write Possibilities

Invite your students to write about an early memory, or ask *What is your earliest memory?*

Students may want to try writing about the memory in present tense, as if they are there now and the event is unfolding before them or around them. This adds a sense of immediacy and may help them better recall sensory details.

They may be encouraged to ask themselves

- Who was there?
- What is your relationship to that person now?
- Did this event affect the current relationship?
- Where did the remembered event occur?
- Is the place significant to the memory?

To deepen the writing . . .

- Ask them to include their present thinking about that past event or situation or impression.
- Are there any patterns, symbols, or insights that surface as they write? Suggest they explore these in their writing.

This quick write can be returned to regularly because your students will never run out of topics in this area.

The Mentor Texts

"Nikki Rosa" and "Knoxville, Tennessee" are two autobiographical poems by Nikki Giovanni that reflect on the memory recounted. Share these poems from Giovanni's *Ego-Tripping and Other Poems for Young People* with your students to show that memories may also be written in poems rather than narratives or essays.

Memories of a childhood home in Columbus and my grandparents' home on the New Jersey shore led to the two poems below. Notice that details include memories but also reflection on those memories.

Our House

Revisiting my house
In Shepard, in my old neighborhood,
Reminded me of the creakiness
The sneakiness
The built-in/live-in
Evil that resided
In our walls
And flushed our toilets
At night and . . .
Breathed on us while we slept
And made us dream . . . bad dreams,
We, awaking screaming,
My sister and I,
The same horrible round face
Emblazoned on the wall of our room
Branded into our brains

We didn't often
speak aloud
About the idiosyncrasies of the house
The normal terror—
Until we left it.

Then a rush of words celebrated our release.
Then a hush of words covered our relief.

I wonder if the new inhabitants
are silent . . . too.

The Sand in Retrospect

The sand
grainy, gritty—salty,
embedded
in the grass
in the carpet
in our clothes
in our eyes.

Sweeping—a duty which eases
our consciences,
but
does not remove
underfoot beads
molded by the sea
that speak of fish
and hundred-year-old coral
with each footstep.

The sand walks
the mile
from the ocean
to my grandmother's yard
and into her house
and up to
my room.

It still calls.
The sand
the warm living texture
is home
to my feet.

Additional Resources

While the books included are not all true memoir, all include first-person narratives that reflect on memories, true or fictional, and will serve as mentor texts for students constructing their own memory writing.

Picture Books

What You Know First by Patricia MacLachlan

Momma, Where Are You From? by Marie Bradby

Saturday and Teacakes by Lester Laminack

When I Was Young in the Mountain by Cynthia Rylant

The Relatives Came by Cynthia Rylant

Grandfather's Journey by Allen Say

Sweet, Sweet Memory by Jacqueline Woodson

How My Parents Learned to Eat by Ina R. Friedman

Marianthe's Story: Painted Words and Spoken Memories by Aliki

Poetry/ Novels in Poetry

Ego-Tripping and Other Poems for Young People by Nikki Giovanni
   "Knoxville Tennessee" and "Nikki Rosa" are both poems included in this book that reflect back on the memory recounted.

Heartbeat by Sharon Creech (pp. 4–5)

Locomotion by Jacqueline Woodson

Sun Moon Soup by Lindsay Lee Johnson (p. 9)

Books for Older Students and Adults

Hunger of Memory: The Education of Richard Rodriguez by Richard Rodriguez

When I Was Your Age: Original Stories About Growing Up, Amy Ehrlich, editor

When I Was Your Age: Original Stories About Growing Up, Vol. 2, Amy Ehrlich, editor

What's in a Name?

Grades 4–12

Narrative, Poetry, Essay, Information Report

The Power and Pain of Our Names

- ## What do you want to know about your name?

Background for the Teacher

In Walter Mosley's novel *47*, the field slaves on Corinthian Plantation were given numbers. If a slave ran off or died, the number was saved and given to another slave when he was old enough to go into the fields. If names happened to be given to the slaves by others, they were never used by the master or the overseer as forms of address or for record keeping. Only numbers were used. When I shared a quote from *47* that explained this practice, my students were horrified and could not comprehend not having a name and being called just a number.

Sadly, we often complain that we *are* just numbers. We are identified numerically by our employers, schools, the IRS, and state departments of education, and of course, everyone, including babies, needs a social security number. But we each were given a name at birth, and names are powerful.

In the opening chapters of *When My Name Was Keoko: A Novel of World War II*, the Korean brother and sister protagonists are discussing how they will be forced to change their names now that the Japanese are in power. My students were equally astounded at the idea that someone could take your name from you and make you use some other name. They are too young to remember the famous scene in the *Roots* television miniseries when Kunta Kinte is beaten unmercifully until he finally acknowledges the slave name Toby.

Every reader of fantasy knows that names in such stories are chosen carefully, often kept secret, and determine destinies. Characters are renamed as they advance in knowledge or quests or levels of testing. In many stories, knowing your name gives power over you to the one holding that knowledge. Many cultures have naming ceremonies with accompanying celebrations; this may be a community affair or a religious rite. Many cultures also give more than one name—based on the day of birth, family names, desired characteristics, or events surrounding the birth.

Roy Feinson (2004) has conducted research related to component letters and sounds of names and found that people with similar sounding names often have similar characteristics and interests. I think there may be something to the sound imparting meaning. When I was a toddler, my grandmother's neighbor used to come out on the porch each day at dinner time and loudly yell for her son, "Sweetmeat," who was usually playing down the street. Even as a toddler, I heard something vaguely forbidden, yet funny in that name. We hear our names called numerous times a day. How do we feel about our names? How did we get them? What do they reveal about us?

This is a fascinating area to explore in writing. There are many emotional, social, and historical responses possible as we explore the origins and meanings, the pitfalls and advantages, and the entire experience of being called by your particular name. One wonderful aspect of this exploration is the necessary interaction with family members who know your name's genealogy and the inevitable discovery of delightful family stories that may have been unknown until this time.

The Quick Write Lesson

1. Sharing Mentor Texts

Read excerpts from either *47* or *When My Name Was Keoko* to begin a discussion about names. Have children make a list of all the things they want to know about their own names. Their list might resemble the one below:

- How did I get my name?
- How do I feel about my name?
- Would I like to change my name? If so, what name would I rather have?
- Do I have a nickname? How did I get it?
- Does my name fit me?
- Do other people in my family have the same name?

Share other books from the list below to suggest additional ways to think, talk, and write about names.

2. Writer's Notebook

Prior to using this quick write, ask students to list all the names they have ever been called in their notebook. This would include actual names, nicknames, endearments, names they like, and names they may not like as much. Also have them begin to ask their families questions about how they got their names, the meaning, particular events surrounding the naming process, and any other interesting facts.

3. Quick Write Possibilities

Ask students to use information collected in their notebooks to write a piece in which their name is important. It may be a narrative or poem. They may also want to try a reflective or persuasive essay. They may refer to the questions generated in the name discussion.

Or

Research and write about the naming customs or naming ceremonies of a particular group of people. Students may include how names are

chosen, who gives the names, and what kind of celebrations are connected with naming in this group or culture. They may also want to
compare these practices with practices in their own family, country, or
culture.

The Mentor Texts

47 by Walter Mosley

When My Name Was Keoko: A Novel of Korea in World War II by Linda Sue
Park

Additional Resources

Picture Books

In these first three books, the protagonists do not like their names and
have experiences that cause a change in feelings about the name.

My Name Is Bilal by Asma Mobin-Uddin

Crow Boy by Taro Yashima

Chrysanthemum by Kevin Henkes

The characters in the books below love their names—the sounds, connections, and meanings.

Quinnie Blue by Dinah Johnson

Poetry

Nathaniel Talking by Eloise Greenfield

Pocketful of Poems by Nikki Grimes

This book contains two partner poems about the name Tiana—haiku
and free verse.

Novel

Bud, Not Buddy by Christopher Paul Curtis

Other

Secret Universe of Names: The Dynamic Interplay of Names and Destiny by Roy
Feinson

Where Do You Live?

Grades 4–12

Description, Memoir, Personal Essay, History

Home or Important Place

- **What do you remember about your home?**

Background for the Teacher

There are many mushy and sentimental adages about *home.* Home is frequently the inspiration for songs, movies, and poems. We have heard that home is the place where they have to take you in, where everybody knows your name . . . and paradoxically that you can't go there again. We all have immediate and imagined, real and relative images of homes in which we have lived or desired to live stored in our hearts and our minds. We all have memories of home that delight us and haunt us.

When we think about home, it may be the first one we can remember, our childhood home. It may be we long for a particular home we later inhabited, a vacation home, or grandparents' house. We probably can access memories of several different homes with a multitude of emotions attached to each one.

When we picture ourselves in the world, we may begin our images in our home—but which one? I have lived in a total of seven homes since I was born and as a child, also frequented two sets of grandparents' homes, and then as an adult, lived for six weeks with my best friend while waiting on an apartment to be ready. Now we are approaching 10 homes. I know that is not a lot compared with some people and probably plenty compared with others. I have fond memories, as well as painful ones, in each home. I don't think I am unusual.

How do I access my memories? One consistently effective way that helps me and my students access images and details with which to flesh out our memories is through sketching—not work-of-art drawing, just quick lines, mapping a place or person, adding as much as we remember. *Just sketching*—not elegant or brilliant painting—but lines to jog our memories and reach into the place where mental photographs and films are stored with no words to accompany them. How do we reach those images?

Inevitably, in the remembering and sketching, more is remembered, and then even more can be sketched. It may be, for example, that I don't remember the small table by the bed in my grandmother's house until I start sketching the room, the bed, and all the other contents that I do immediately remember.

Once the drawing has begun to take shape, memories, objects, conversations, events, people, and feelings can be connected to the place and can be labeled in the rooms of the home. Often, new meanings will occur to me as I sketch, new voices might be raised, and new regrets or joys realized.

Home is where our heart is, and home is where we live, whether in reality or in our minds and hearts.

The Quick Write Lesson

1. Writer's Notebook

Invite your writers to sketch a home or place that is important to them. Remind them that they are not making a work of art but instead using sketching (quick lines and drawings) to help them access their memories of a particular place. You may want to guide them through several stages in the sketching process.

- They may start with a floor plan and then begin to sketch in furniture and other items they remember.
- They can label items or fixtures in the various rooms. They may find they end up focusing on one particular room, and that is fine.
- They will want to add people (remind them to use stick figures, just a face, and so on).
- Quick words or a phrase can be added as they recall interactions, conversations, or events that took place in rooms.

Note: We must be sensitive to the fact that we have children in foster homes and other possibly less than happy and supportive situations. With elementary students in particular, I offer the option to simply think, sketch, and write about an important place, rather than limiting the topic to home.

2. Sharing Mentor Texts

There are so many wonderful books about homes. Books about home constitute one of the largest collections I own that focuses on a particular topic. Not only can we read about homes in a variety of ways; we can also write about our own homes from many perspectives, looking through a multitude of lenses. You may want to share only some of the books suggested below with your writers, focused in a particular way, based on the amount of time you wish to spend and the interest of your group of writers—or you may choose to share all or many of the books, providing lots of models and possibilities for writing.

No matter which selections you choose to share from the suggestions below or otherwise, there are several things you will want to encourage your writers to notice as you share the selected texts:

- The framework or structure which the author uses to share about home
- How the author shares details and feelings about home
- How the home is set in context to the community or larger world

If you choose to share many or all briefly, make sure the books are available for more detailed perusal later—before or during writing time.

You may also want to discuss the genre of memoir writing. Your students are probably familiar with the term *autobiography*, and memoir writing can be described as similar to autobiographical writing in that it is written by an author about his own life, situations, and events—but with one distinct difference. Memoir is written from a distance (for some of our younger writers that distance will be short), reflecting on one particular aspect or incident or several in one's own life—and most important, considering patterns, themes, and motifs that would not have been noticed or considered during the actual experience.

3. Quick Write Possibilities

Invite students to revisit their sketches and notes. They may want time to add to these after sharing several books or other texts.

Invite your students to use a phrase or sentence from one of the texts to structure their own writing about a house (or place) important to them.

For example:

- From *Momma, Where Are You From?* they might use "I am from . . ." as a repeated phrase or refrain.
- From *An Angel for Solomon Singer*, they may want to approach their home or place by describing what it is not, using "My home is not . . ." to describe the chosen location.

Or

Writers may want to record the history of their home or important place. They may

- Choose to take readers back in time in specific increments as in *My Place.*
- Tell the history of their house by considering objects found in and around their home as in *Home Place.*

Or

Invite your students to write about what frightens or delights in their home.

Or

Invite students to select their own mentor text from the selections to discover a framework or structure, an idea or approach, a phrase, or a memory that moves them to write about their own home or important place.

Or

Use other phrases to support remembering and serve as starters:

- *I remember*
- *I wish*
- *I will not forget*
- *I don't remember*
- *I wish I knew why*
- *I will never*

The Mentor Texts

The Specialness of Home

Momma, Where Are You From? by Marie Bradby

Momma answers the title question in poetic prose, listing memories starting with the phrase "I am from . . ." reminiscent of George Ella Lyon's well-known poem, "Where I'm From." (http://www.georgeellalyon.com/where.html)

Let's Go Home: The Wonderful Things About a House by Cynthia Rylant

The author takes us on a tour through one specific house but also makes general statements about components that are contained in most houses.

All the Places to Love by Patricia MacLachlan

Told by Eli, this book tells about all the wonderful places to love in and around his home and includes places that his family members love as well.

Saturday and Teacakes by Lester L. Laminack

A young boy loves to visit Mammaw's house every Saturday where he helps with chores and bakes cookies.

Appalachia: The Voices of Sleeping Birds by Cynthia Rylant

This nonfiction book describes the region of Appalachia in such detail that both the love of this place by the author and the flavor of the area come to life.

The Seven Wonders of Sassafras Spring by Betty G. Birney (novel)

After reading about the Seven Wonders of the World, Eben bemoans the fact that his little town has nothing that could be considered interesting. After a challenge by his uncle, he explores and finds fascinating wonders in his own town.

The House on Mango Street by Sandra Cisneros (novel)

This series of brief vignettes together create a picture of a young girl, Esperanza, growing up in the Latino section of Chicago. This novel details both the joys and heartbreak of living in her neighborhood.

Pictures of Hollis Woods by Patricia Reilly Giff (novel)

Hollis had been to many foster homes and is in danger of being removed from this current one. Each chapter begins with a description of a photograph important to her.

My Mexico—Mexico Mio by Tony Johnston

A collection of poems that describe homes, activities, holidays, and people in Mexico—written in both English and Spanish.

Going Home by Eve Bunting

This book describes a trip home and celebratory arrival in the home town in Mexico of folks who now live in the United States.

The House That Baba Built: An Artist's Childhood China by Ed Young

The newest book in my home collection is a beautiful project detailing the rooms and activities and people that all came to live in the house that Baba built in order to keep his family safe during the war in China.

One Community

Each book in this set deals with the community of Harlem in New York City in a unique way.

Uptown by Bryan Collier

A boy takes us on a tour of his beloved Harlem with metaphors to describe uptown on each page as well as his comments.

Here in Harlem: Poems in Many Voices by Walter Dean Myers

Each poem represents a different resident of his community speaking. Photographs illustrate this unique look at Harlem. A boy takes us on a tour of his beloved Harlem with metaphors to describe uptown on each page as well as his comments.

The Block, poems by Langston Hughes, collage by Romare Bearden, selected by Lowery S. Sims and Daisy Murray Voigt, a Metropolitan Museum of Art Book

This pairing of art and poems creates a vibrant picture of life on "the block."

Frightening, Dangerous, or Not So Wonderful Homes

Something Beautiful by Sharon Dennis Wyeth

Right outside her window a young girl sees trash, broken bottles, and a brick wall. On the street she sees the word "DIE" painted on a door and a homeless woman sleeping on the sidewalk. She sets out to make her neighborhood beautiful.

Life Doesn't Frighten Me, poems by Maya Angelou, painting by Jean-Michel Basquiat

Angelou's defiant, courageous expressions, paired with contemporary art, are poems dealing with the fears we may have in our own neighborhoods.

An Angel for Solomon Singer by Cynthia Rylant

Solomon Singer lives in a hotel for men and does not like it. All of the things the hotel is *not* and all that it lacks that he loves is described.

Looking Back in Time

Each book below suggests a history for a home

My Place by Nadia Wheatley and Donna Rawlins

Starting in 1988, the history of a young girl's home is told by going back 200 years, 10 years on each spread of pages.

Home Place by Crescent Dragonwagon

Finding a chimney made of stone back in the woods means someone once lived there. A family imagines what that family might be like.

The following poem may be used as an additional text to share along with the two poems "Our House" and the "Sand in Retrospect," included with the quick write "What You Know First."

The Loft

The triangular window
reaches to the cathedral
ceiling—to heaven.
White light
warming and
framing
a favorite space.

I curl in the black leather
chair trimmed with wood,
gently swiveling
slowly rocking
as I read the book
by Cheadle and Prendergast
about Darfur.

The black and white marble men
gleam on the smooth checkered chess board
a gift to my husband
before he was that.

My piano sits
within near reach
black and white keyboard
closed,
silent, waiting
promising
accompaniment for this moment.

This sun-framed portrait
discloses a stark contrast
to the hardship,
and hunger,
and death
in Sudan.

I Know What I Know

Grades 4–12

Essay, Opinion, Narrative

Ways of Knowing

- How do we know what we know?

Background for the Teacher

Story is one way we negotiate our world and communicate our experiences in that world.

Different from expository writing with its requisite main ideas and supporting, factual details, and where there is controllable order, story can meander around the facts to arrive finally at deeper truth. Story can be true, whether the facts have been forgotten or stretched, or inadvertently and completely changed.

I come from a large family of aunts and uncles and cousins on my mother's side. My grandparents each had 11 siblings. Most were still living when I was a child. Summer gatherings at my grandmother's house in the country near the New Jersey coast were lively, memorable affairs with plenty of food and laughter, gossip and bragging, arguing and sometimes dancing, and always cousins discovering new ways to have fun and to get in trouble. There were also plenty of grown folks to collectively scold us. We cousins raced tortoises found in the grape arbor at the back of the yard, snuck away to feed ducks at the nearby pond, lit our sparklers at twilight, and begged to stay up longer than usual on these special days. For myself, managing to remain unnoticed on the porch when it got dark was a special pleasure. That's when all the grown folks told the best stories—the ones not meant for younger ears.

My mother and I were having a conversation about one particular Fourth of July gathering. "How could Aunt Edna have afforded to buy each of us cousins an outfit for that picnic?" I asked my mother, puzzled because I knew that Aunt Edna was far from wealthy. Yet, that particular day, each boy had worn a blue shirt and each girl had worn a pink sun dress—gifts that had come swaddled in tissue paper and wrapped in fancy gift boxes for each of us. I can still see the pattern of the fabric of my dress in my memory's eye. My mother replied, "I don't know how she did it either, but all seven or eight of you got one." I was startled. At this point I disputed my mother—*surely* there were 30 or more cousins in the yard, but my mother was adamant about the number being much smaller. There was no dispute about the large number of cousins I actually have—just how many were together at that particular time.

Later that year at my Aunt Lottie's funeral, I had an opportunity to talk with Butch, a fellow clothing-receiving cousin. Of course, I put to him the question of how many cousins there were present that day. He corroborated my mother's memory rather than mine. "Oh, about seven or eight," he said, without even thinking.

I don't care what they say. In *my* memory and in *my* story, my cousins were there in much larger numbers. The real truth of the matter is that the number was *large enough for us to all love each other, enjoy each other, and have a grand party with no one present but family,* and that is the truth that I remember and know. For me the truth lies outside the actual facts.

Tom Romano points out the difference between "narrative thinking or *rendering experiences* as opposed to explaining it, abstracting it or summing it up"—writing and thinking actions we most often call for in our classrooms in expository writing (Romano, 1995). Through story, we can push back from the events and turn them over and over to examine what has happened and what we think about it. Romano suggests that we don't really know what we think about something until we tell a story about it. We need to value narrative thinking as a way of knowing in our classrooms and narrative writing as a way of sharing.

How and why we know what we know is sometimes inexplicable to others. In the landmark book *Women's Ways of Knowing* (Belenky, Clinchy, Goldberger, & Tarule, 1997), the powerful ways of knowing that women have come to value are explored—intuitive, metaphoric ways that sometimes differ from the linear, reasonable ways of our male counterparts, yet are valid just the same.

Using a river as an analogy for all of our life experiences, G. Lynn Nelson suggests two ways to know the river. We can stand by the river on the bank and observe and measure, calculate and analyze, record factual details and numbers, or we can take off our clothes and enter the river, slowly and tentatively, or jump in with wild gusto and anticipation.

Like Nelson, Jallaludin Rumi, the renowned Sufi poet, also recognized two ways of knowing. He wrote of how a child in "school memorizes facts and concepts from books and from what the teacher says," but also of another kind of knowing that is "fluid and flows from within you."

How do we know what we know?

The Quick Write Lesson

1. Sharing Mentor Texts

Read *The Man Who Knew Too Much* to your students. In this folktale, a mother takes her baby to the field with her as she works. When the baby cries, an eagle flies down and tends to her child. This amazing act happens several times. Instead of enjoying this knowledge and the miracle it represented, she felt she had to share with her husband this unlikely behavior of the eagle. He, knowing what he knew about eagles, could not allow an eagle to come close to his baby, and in the end shot an arrow at it—missing—and killing his baby.

Ask your students to discuss the ways in which the man and the woman knew what they knew. Discuss with them other situations in which people "know" in different ways. How do they know what they know? Also ask them to think about how and when they should share what they know and when it is better to keep silent.

2. Writer's Notebook

In their notebooks, have students list ways they know what they know. Sample list items might be

- *Someone told me (name)*
- *I read it*
- *I saw it on TV*
- *I thought of it by myself*
- *I dreamed it*

You may want to encourage them to discuss advantages and disadvantages of each way of knowing. How does each way inform their writing?

3. Quick Write Possibilities

Invite your students to write about something that they know for sure but may not be able to explain how and why they know. They may want to start with the words *What I know for sure is . . .* or *I know I know . . .*

Or

Ask them to write their own story of a time when they knew what other people did not know or when the truth did not seem to be in the facts.

Or

Invite them to write about what they feel is the best way to know something. They should support their way of knowing with reasons, examples, and other evidence.

The Mentor Text

The Man Who Knew Too Much: A Moral Tale From the Baila of Zambia retold by Julius Lester

Additional Resources

Teaching With Fire: Poetry That Sustains the Courage to Teach, edited by Sam M. Intrator and Megan Scribner

This book includes the poem "Two Kinds of Intelligence" by Rumi, which is also available at http://allpoetry.com/poem/8534695-Two_Kinds_of_Intelligence_wbr_-by-Mewlana_Jalaluddin_Rumi.

Writing With Passion: Life Stories, Multiple Genres by Tom Romano

Women's Ways of Knowing: The Development of Self, Voice and the Mind by Mary Field Belenky, Blythe McVicker Clinchy, Nancy Rule Goldberger, and Jill Mattuck Tarule

Writing and Being: Taking Back Our Lives Through the Power of Language by G. Lynn Nelson

Stones in My Pocket

Grades 4–12

Personal or Descriptive Essay, Poetry

Objects We Collect

> ● What objects hold your life?

Background for the Teacher

As a child, collecting the most glittery, interestingly shaped or otherwise unusual rocks from our gravel driveway was a constant pastime. And *What kind is this?* was my constant question to my dad, who has a master's degree in geology. I would wait for him to identify the newly discovered treasure with an exotic name. Most often, my treasures were not exotic, except to me—I picked up lots of granite, shale, and slate, found in abundance over most of Ohio.

I have graduated from driveway stones to semiprecious stones, but I still collect rocks. In Grand Cayman, as my friends were buying jewelry made of pale bluish larimar, unique to the Caribbean Sea, I purchased a small, smooth, chunk—unrefined and unset—to add to my red velvet bag of stones. While on the beach in St. Thomas at Easter time, I stumbled upon a small flat stone with a crooked cross naturally etched on one side.

There is something mystical and magic about holding a stone in your hand, feeling its history, and imagining all that it has witnessed. So naturally, rosaries also make sense to me, as I hold my prayers in my hands. (BEDE is the old English word for prayer.) I collect rosaries too. Instead of buying T-shirts and I-have-been-here-and-here's-the-proof souvenirs that I won't use when I return home, I buy unusual rosaries and pick up stones as I travel.

For me, it is stones, for my girlfriend it is teapots, for others I know it is elephants or fancy boxes or masks. We mark our lives and times by what we collect, by what holds the memories, jubilations, and worries of our journey. What holds your life? What marks your path? What guards your story? What do you collect?

The Quick Write Lesson

1. Sharing Mentor Texts

Share one or more of the books about stones listed below with your class. Invite them to discuss the variety of ways that the topic of rocks is approached and connected to our lives. You may want to notice and chart the following:

- Kinds of rocks
- Ways to find rocks
- Uses for rocks
- Reasons we need rocks
- How rocks were formed

You may also choose additional books about different objects, based on the interests of your writers or related classroom studies, to read and notice how these objects are addressed and related to the lives of the authors or characters.

2. Writer's Notebook

Invite the students to list items they collect or that are important to them. Beside each item, ask them to make a brief note about why they collect this particular item. The lists can be shared noting both similarities and differences in their lists. As they are sharing, students may be reminded of other items they want to add to their own lists.

3. Quick Write Possibilities

Ask students to choose an item from their list to explore in writing.

- Why is this item important?
- Do other people feel the same way?
- How and where do you find it?
- How do you use it?
- How does the item affect your life?

As the students write, they may discover more about their chosen object and more about themselves as well.

The Mentor Texts

This poem was written in response to this quick write and may serve as an additional mentor text. I believe that rocks are not only uniquely and individually appealing, but in all times have proven to be collectively and universally significant.

Stones in Our Pockets

From the beginning
We erected stone pillars—
altars along the way
for sacrificing
life for life
to honor the One
Who gave
Life

Stones emerging
from rivers
and seas

Like the ones taken
from the Jordan
stacked in remembrance
of the 40-year walk

framed on each end
by passage through water

Like the small stone
Denis Horgan found lodged
in a windshield at the foot
of the World Trade Center
carnage
and kept.

We carry them
in our pockets.

It is popular now to
impose
paint
carve
words on them
faith
courage
grace
strength
truth.

Touchstones remind us
what is solid and real.
Worry stones hold our fears.

Monuments
to mark the dead
and honor the living
stones memorialize events
and never let us forget
our losses.

We measure our space
—a stone's throw away.
We used to measure the man
—how many stones?

We delight in the stone
found on the beach
the right size

and shape
to give us strength

We hold
and finger small stones
on a string.
The mere touch
takes us deeper—
silent conversation
reverent contemplation.

We carry the stones
that make us real
in our hearts
in our pockets.

If You Find a Rock by Peggy Christian (author), Barbara Hirsch Lember (photographer)

Poems enumerating the many types of rocks children are likely to encounter: wishing rocks, skipping rocks, throwing rocks, and so on.

Everybody Needs a Rock by Byrd Baylor

Everybody needs a rock, and in poetic language, the narrator provides individual rules for just how to find yours.

The Pebble in My Pocket: A History of Our Earth by Meredith Hooper (narrative nonfiction)

As she re-creates the story of a single pebble in a little girl's pocket, the author tells the history of the earth as well.

Additional Resources (Other Objects)

Flotsam: A Life in Debris (Essays) by Denis Horgan

Each essay deals with a specific object on the author's desk, including a rock found lodged in a car on September 11, 2001, at the World Trade Center.

Show Way by Jacqueline Woodson

A quilt made by one of the author's ancestors tells her history.

The Wall: Growing Up Behind the Iron Curtain by Peter Sis

The wall was both a physical and metaphorical boundary cutting off the rest of the world.

My Name Is Bilal by Asma Mobin-Uddin

Bilal and his sister deal with reactions to her hijab in their new school.

The Polar Express by Chris Van Allsburg

A reindeer's bell is given to a young boy. It can only be heard by young, believing ears.

Wilfrid Gordon McDonald Partridge by Mem Fox

A young boy collects many objects to encourage an elderly woman to regain her memory.

Whiting Stories and Boasting Poems

Grades 4–12

Narrative, Research Reports, Essays, Poetry

Family Stories and Tall Tales

- What stories does your family tell?
- How much do they embellish or exaggerate?

Background for the Teacher

My grandmother's children and grandchildren were the best, excelling in everything. It didn't matter what was being discussed or compared—playing the piano, grades in school, extra-curricular activities or quotable quotes. Grandma's family members were the elite of the "my children stories." Grandma, the eldest of 11 siblings, proudly entered into conversations that related to accomplishments of offspring, near and far, what honors were being received, what degrees were most recently bestowed and which president of which country had just entertained her son. She kept programs and booklets from ceremonies and newspaper clippings and photos, not only to remember the event, but for quietly boasting, as well. She proclaimed whatever had just happened to her children "grand!"

In my immediate family, stories that have this brag-on-me-and-mine quality have become known as Whiting stories, in honor of Grandma

Whiting. We still call each other to share the good things that happen to us—anecdotes that may sound like boasting to those who do not recognize a proper Whiting story when they hear one.

After an article I had written appeared in the local newspaper, in true Whiting style, I called my mother to read her the e-mails that I had received praising the article. *"And this one is from a man, I don't even know who . . ."* and read his rather impressive credentials and favorable remarks. And also over the Christmas holidays, I enjoyed sharing how, while I shopped in a store with olive wood articles from Jerusalem, the owner walked through the store with me chatting and carrying the items I was buying for friends. At my mere mention of wanting something for myself, he insisted—*Go ahead and put that one in your purse, you may have it*—and then, when my sale was completed, offered his son to carry my bags to my car. I was at our newest, largest mall, potentially parked a mile or more away! Perfect—for a Whiting story!

Do the stories grow a bit? Sure! Do the responses of others to us become bigger and better? Of course! Do they take on a warmer glow with years of telling? Definitely! Are we also telling the truth? Absolutely!

It is just a slight left turn to veer from a Whiting story into a tall tale. And there is language that is appropriate for both Whiting stories and tall tales alike. It is the language of hyperbole and superlatives and gush. As my students read tall tales from our fifth-grade reader, they rolled with astonishment and amusement at the statements our "tall" heroes made: *I can rope a river, ride a tornado and use a cactus as a napkin,* boasted Pecos Bill. Later, all of them remembered this quote and loved saying it in unison. *I am the Hercules of the sailors and I arm-wrestled that ole octopus until it cried for mercy,* proclaimed Stormalong. Paul Bunyan and John Henry both provided further linguistic entertainment.

The Quick Write Lesson

1. Sharing Mentor Texts

We had so much fun with exaggerated phrases and claims that I thought my students would surely enjoy the poem "Ego-Tripping" by Nikki Giovanni. I promised to dig it up for them after lunch. Later, we read it and discussed how the boasting language was similar to that of the tall tales but was poetry instead of narrative and written in first person. Also, since we were in the midst of writing descriptions and learning how to include sensory details and precise nouns and verbs, we carefully noted how the poet used these.

You may also want to read the tall tale written by Ian Tran, one of my fifth-grade students (see below in Resources). He chose to write his tale in third person.

- How might this be different from the same tale told in first person?
- How would his ideas work as a poem?

Sharing More Mentor Texts

Tall tales are based loosely, or not so loosely, on real people. When investigating with my students how a real person became a legend or who the legendary person actually was in reality, one of the legends we dealt with was John Henry, the hammer-wielding African American who was immortalized in song. He raced a steam drill to bore through a mountain. After reading two versions of the legend, one by Ezra Jack Keats and the other by Julius Lester, we shared a third book—*Ain't Nothing but a Man* by Scott Reynolds Nelson and Marc Aronson, in which the authors set out to find the origin of the legend, the real man behind the heroic myth. My students were fascinated with the amount of research conducted in this pursuit. Share these three books with your class or locate a similar set about another legend in which your group is interested.

2. Writer's Notebook

Invite your students to make a list of personal qualities and abilities and then to exaggerate those listed, as well as adding unlikely but desired ones to their list. They can help each other think of more qualities and abilities to add to their list.

It may also be helpful to teach a mini-lesson on similes and have them add similes to their list (*as tall as a . . . , as strong as a . . . , as hungry as a . . .*). These will be helpful as they begin to write hyperbolic descriptions of their tall tale selves.

3. Quick Write Possibilities

Remembering "Ego-Tripping" and other poems, as well as any tall tales that you have read to them, allow your students to write their own boasting poem, using first person and describing their own remarkable traits and fantastically tall feats. Encourage them to use sensory details and similes to show, not tell, their readers just how fast or strong or smart they are as they write about themselves.

Or

Invite students to select a favorite legend to research or investigate. What characteristics of this person and incidents in his or her life led to the legend? They may want to write about how this occurred or the reasons that people admired this person. Are there lessons that we can learn from either the real person or the person as legendized?

The Mentor Texts

Books About John Henry

John Henry: An American Legend by Ezra Jack Keats

John Henry by Julius Lester

Ain't Nothing but a Man: My Quest to Find the Real John Henry (A National Geographic Book) by Scott Reynolds Nelson with Marc Aronson

Hip Hop Speaks to Children: A Celebration of Poetry With a Beat edited by Nikki Giovanni

This book includes several poems perfect for this lesson. The accompanying CD includes each of the following poems read by the poet:

- "Ego-Tripping" by Nikki Giovanni
- "Allow Me to Introduce Myself" by Charles R. Smith Jr.
- "Ladies First" by Queen Latifah

The poem "Ego-Tripping" by Nikki Giovanni is also available at http://nikki-giovanni.com/page_51.shtml.

Additional Resources

Nathaniel Talking by Eloise Greenfield

The title poem of this book also works wonderfully with this lesson, especially for elementary students. Nathaniel raps and reflects about himself.

American Tall Tales by Mary Pope Osborne

Nine of our best loved "tall" folk heroes are featured, including Paul Bunyan, John Henry, Stormalong, Johnny Appleseed, and Sally Ann Thunder Ann Whirlwind.

The Tale of Ian Tran

Once, a bad storm happened. It went on for days until the last lightning bolt hit the ground. It was big as a mountain. It crackled and banged until after a while. Then crying started happening. The town's people looked at the baby that came from the storm. The baby was named Ian . . . Ian Tran.

The boy could run as fast as lightning and could punch the ground and make craters. He could suck in a tornado and blow it in a different direction.

The people all knew Ian, but Ian wanted the world to know his name. So he walked for miles nonstop. He walked through storms—snow storms, sand storms, wind storms and much more dangerous weather. But that didn't stop him.

Ian got to many places. At the end of each trip, the people in that place knew who he was. They said, "He's so smart he could teach a monkey manners."

Soon the world knew his name. The world never forgot him until after the end of the universe.

Source: © Copyright 2009 by Ian Tran.

For Better or for Worse

Grades 4–12

Descriptive or Personal Essay

Good and Bad in Life

- • What are your best times and your worst times?

Background for the Teacher

It is the end of the year. The newspapers and magazines will publish their annual "best and worst" issues, and television stations will all produce shows that count down the best and worst of everything. The media will list for us what we loved and chose to support and what we totally ignored and hated. We will be able to find out who was the worst dressed, which books were the best, and whose movies were the worst of the season. We will, perhaps, even vote ourselves to help determine these lists locally— the best restaurant, the worst sandwich, the best college, and so on.

So often we examine life in dualities, pairing the good with the bad. We have been taught by pop psychology to list the advantages and disadvantages, the assets and the detriments of each decision or venture in our lives. In this way we weigh the costs of our living. Our lives, however, rarely fit neatly in these columns with one side clearly the winner. More often, we are faced with nearly equal parts—good and bad.

We understand Dickens's opening statement in *A Tale of Two Cities.* We know what it means to realize a particular time was the worst time of our life and, at the same time, the best time of our life. In the film *Just Wright,* Common's character, Scott McKnight, a basketball player recently recovered from a torn ACL, expresses this same sentiment as he tells how trainer Leslie Wright, played by Queen Latifah, made the worst time of his life the best time of his life. We experience the good, bad, and ugly all at once—not separated into the hypothetical good and bad columns.

Whether the end of the year, the end of each month, or the end of a day, taking stock of what was valuable and positive, as well as what was hurtful and disappointing in what has occurred to us is a human activity. We tell our journals or our dinner companions or our therapists. Sometimes it is someone else who is able to more easily see the positive in the bad that we see or the negative where we see only good.

What we do know is that all manner of events will befall us, and in our lives, as in our marriages, we continue for better or for worse.

The Quick Write Lesson

1. Sharing Mentor Texts—Grades 6–12

Share the opening two paragraphs of *A Tale of Two Cities* by Charles Dickens. Discuss with your students how he describes this time period (1775).

- What techniques did he use?
- How do the paired opposites affect the reader's perception of the time period?
- How does this description relate to our own time period? What is similar? What is different?

Also share the opening paragraphs from Chapter 2 of *Twilight* by Stephanie Meyer. The main character is describing the second day at her new school. How is her description different from that given in *A Tale of Two Cities*?

Encourage students to make as many comparisons as possible, considering both the writing craft and content.

Sharing Mentor Texts, Grades 4–5

The above choices will be too difficult for elementary students. You may want to share *Fortunately* by Remy Charlip or *Alexander and the Terrible, Horrible, No Good, Very Bad Day* by Judith Viorst with them, allowing them to analyze and compare in a manner similar to that suggested above.

2. Writer's Notebook

Ask the writers to make notes by quickly listing or creating a web of a specific time period of their lives. Encourage them to make brief notes beside each item—identifying the worst and best aspects of each time.

Allow time to share individual responses. You may also want to have students collectively list specific time periods that they have shared as a group.

3. Quick Write Possibilities

Invite your students to write about a specific period in their life that was the best and worst of times. Encourage them to use paired opposites to describe the events and feelings of that time. Also ask them to give concrete details and examples that will illustrate their best and worst times.

The Mentor Texts

Excerpts From Novels

A Tale of Two Cities by Charles Dickens is available at http://www.online-literature.com/dickens/twocities/1/.

A Tale of Two Cities by Charles Dickens

Chapter 1: The Period

It was the best of times, it was the worst of times, it was the age of wisdom, it was the age of foolishness, it was the epoch of belief, it was the epoch of incredulity, it was the season of Light, it was the season of Darkness, it was the spring of hope, it was the winter of despair, we had everything before us, we had nothing before us, we were all going direct to Heaven, we were all going direct the other way—in short, the period was so far like the present period, that some of its noisiest authorities insisted on its being received, for good or for evil, in the superlative degree of comparison only.

There were a king with a large jaw and a queen with a plain face, on the throne of England; there were a king with a large jaw and a queen with a fair face, on the throne of France. In both countries it was clearer than crystal to the lords of the State preserves of loaves and fishes, that things in general were settled for ever.

It was the year of Our Lord one thousand seven hundred and seventy-five.

Twilight by Stephanie Meyer

Chapter 2

The three opening paragraphs of Chapter 2 from *Twilight* by Stephenie Meyer (2008) can be found on pages 29–30, or go to http://www.amazon.com/Twilight-The-Saga-Book-ebook/dp/B000QRIGLW/ref=kinw_dp_ke#_and click on "Look inside the book" to find the excerpt at the beginning of Chapter 2.

Note: Edward is the vampire antihero in this book.

Picture Book

Alexander and the Terrible, Horrible, No Good, Very Bad Day by Judith Viorst
Many situations occur to make Alexander's day the worst ever.

When I Was Silent

Grades 8–12

Personal Essay, Memoir, Poetry

Being Silent

- When do we not speak up?
- What happens when we are silenced?

Background for the Teacher

Sometimes we witness something so terrible, so tragic, so traumatic, that we cannot talk about it. When that terrible thing happens to another person or a group, what do we do? What do we say? Or are we silent? Pastor Martin Niemoller, a Protestant minister, reminds us of the danger of keeping silent as others are persecuted or suffering injustice in an often quoted poem from his 1946 speech addressing the German church.

When the Nazis came for the communists,
I remained silent;
I was not a communist.

When they locked up the social democrats,
I remained silent;
I was not a social democrat.

When they came for the trade unionists,
I did not speak out;
I was not a trade unionist.

When they came for the Jews,
I remained silent;
I wasn't a Jew.
When they came for me,
there was no one left to speak out.

Source: Martin Niemöller 1946 speech delivered for representatives of the Confessing Church in Frankfurt, Germany. Retrieved from http://en.wikiquote.org/wiki/Martin_Niem%C3%B6ller.

Keeping silent allows injustice or wrongdoing or violence to continue unchecked, sanctioned, tacitly authorized by our very inaction or nod of silence. Many families harbor secrets that can't be told or even acknowledged in private thoughts. The silences, often begun to protect someone or everybody, are usually revealed eventually with devastating results. Untold stories or secrets can destroy relationships, demolish trust, and change lives.

My family saw the movie *Precious* over the Thanksgiving weekend. This movie, based on the novel *PUSH* by Sapphire, tells of a young girl raped, abused, and degraded unmercifully by her parents. In the telling, finally, came the power. As she learned to read and write she became empowered. As she wrote her own story, with the encouragement of the teacher, she became present to her own body, her circumstances, and her possibilities. Her silence had imprisoned her and stripped her of her present and her personhood.

Elie Wiesel's words, spoken as he accepted his Nobel Peace Prize for his writings, encourage us to speak up, speak out, and speak truth to power:

> "And that is why I swore never to be silent whenever and wherever human beings endure suffering and humiliation. We must always take sides. Neutrality helps the oppressor, never the victim. Silence encourages the tormentor, never the tormented." (Elie Wiesel, © The Nobel Foundation. http://www.nobelprize.org/nobel_prizes/peace/laureates/1986/wiesel-acceptance.html).

Sometimes it is someone else who silences us—they do not want us to speak up, speak out, speak our truth. It may be at a meeting, or funeral, or reunion, or program. Why do they not want us to be heard?

Silence in the Western world makes us nervous. We rush to fill it with nervous talking; we consider silence a bad thing. In "Keeping Quiet," Pablo Neruda calls us to consider a different kind of silence—one in which we agree to be silent together, to stop moving, to do nothing in order to live, in order to "interrupt this sadness." He considers silence healing and good.

The Quick Write Lesson

1. Sharing Mentor Texts

Share *Terrible Things: An Allegory of the Holocaust* with your students. Invite them to share responses to the story. They may include

- How they think the events could have happened
- What they would have done in a similar situation
- How the story made them feel; connections to their own lives
- How to make certain these events do not occur again

Be sure to include a consideration of the role of silence.

2. Quick Write Possibilities

Invite your students to write about a time when they were silent. How did they feel keeping silent?

- It may be a time when they witnessed something that they decided not to tell, were told not to tell, or were afraid to tell.
- It may be a secret kept for a friend.

- It may be something that happened to them personally or to someone else.
- Have they ever finally broken that silence? What were the results?

The Mentor Text

Terrible Things: An Allegory of the Holocaust by Eve Bunting (picture book)

Additional Resources

Mississippi Morning by Ruth Vander Zee

A young boy realizes his father is a member of the Ku Klux Klan.

Novel

Speak by Laurie Halse Anderson

A teen who has been raped and who refuses to speak about this tragic event or at all journeys through the help of art to reclaim her voice. A poem written by the author Laurie Halse Anderson commemorating the 10th anniversary of *Speak* is available at http://www.teachervision.fen.com/tv/printables/penguin/speak_dg.pdf. The poem is composed largely of responses from letters written to her about *Speak*.

Poetry

"Keeping Quiet," *Teaching With Fire: Poetry That Sustains the Courage to Teach* edited by Sam M. Intrator and Megan Scribner

A better known version of Martin Niemoller's poem can be found at http://en.wikipedia.org/wiki/First_they_came . . .

I Never Saw Another Butterfly: Children's Drawings and Poems From Terezin Concentration Camp 1942–44 edited by Hana Volavkova

It Was a Very Good Year

Grades 4–12

Persuasive Essay

Judging a Year or Time Period

- What makes a year good or bad?
- What gifts did this year offer?

Background for the Teacher

For my friends' milestone birthdays, I like to find those books or cards that are made especially for their birth year and contain all kinds of fun facts and fascinating tidbits about that year—newspaper ads, time lines, products used then, popular songs, radio or TV shows, and so on. They make nice keepsakes to celebrate that special day and year and also remind us of how much times have changed.

When you look back in your life, which year was the best? Which year would you identify as a very good year? Frank Sinatra made famous a song by Ervin Drake in which he looks back over his life from "the autumn of his years." He proclaims several specific years—17, 21, and 35—very good years.

Looking back over time has always been important to people. We often accompany our backward glances of remembering by commemorating and memorializing important moments, special events, and influential people. We do this on an individual level by periodically looking back over our own lives and that of our family. We also do this collectively as communities, states, nations, and as the global village. We build remembrances in concrete and stone, we carve them in wood and we etch words to enable future generations to continue to look back.

The year of the 10th anniversary of 9/11, we did all of the above as we remembered the day, the people who lost their lives, the people who saved lives, those who were touched by both, and the places where it happened. We sang songs, we held memorial services, we observed moments of silence, and we remembered.

What makes a year stand out? How do we determine it was a very good year?

We often talk about the good old days and speak longingly of that "better time." Were those days really better than today or some other time? Given a chance, would we really return to those days gone by? I hear a chorus of yeses. I hear often repeated refrains—we talked to each other more, the kids played outside and were in better physical shape. We relied less on the latest technology and relied more on our face-to-face family and friends. But as we go back we also remember that African Americans were slaves and then later segregated, that women couldn't own property or vote, and that war and the depression clouded our days.

What *was* good about bygone years? What in those years made us better people? More able people? More compassionate people? To what year would we return if we could?

I have always found students to be fascinated with any text that allows them to look back in time—particularly texts with lots of specific facts and details to support their looking. Books with complicated time lines fit the bill for this fascination and cause my students to pore over them with continual interest.

The Quick Write Lesson

1. Sharing Mentor Texts

Invite students to elect a specific year, perhaps the year of their birth or a year of current studies in history or science, and identify events that occurred during that year. You may want to use Timelines.com to help them generate a timeline for a year they would like to consider.

- What important events occurred?
- Is there a pattern that your students notice among the events that occurred (or did not occur) that year?

You may want to share one of the texts below with your students. These suggested texts won't be read aloud in the traditional sense. Instead, they may be shared with emphasis on their format and structure. Be sure to allow time for students to linger over the texts to see how times and events were recorded.

You may also want to share speeches or song lyrics that deal with particular events in specific years selected for discussion.

2. Writer's Notebook

Invite your students to make a list of "very good years" in their lives. Beside each year they may list an event or two, or reason that the year was good. They may want to compare their list with others, noting which years and events included are the same or different. Do they notice any patterns among the lists or particular uniqueness in their own lists?

3. Quick Write Possibilities

Invite your writers to choose a year in time and to write a persuasive essay about why this particular year was a very good year. They should include an initial thesis statement along with supporting *Facts, Reasons,*

Incidents, *E*vidence and examples, and other specific *D*etails—what many writers and educators call *FRIED* information.

In choosing a particular year, writers may consider

- What years in your own life were very good years?
- What years in the history of your community, your state, your nation, or the world would you deem to be very good years?

Or

Writers may want to select a year that your group is currently studying in history—why was this year good?

Mentor Texts

Timelines.com provides a variety of timelines organized by type of event and current events; it also allows you to search by specific year to create your own time line.

Additional Resources

Each text below allows us to travel in time considering the events of a place or a life.

Imagine That! by Janet Wilson

My Place by Nadia Wheatley and Donna Rawlins

A Street Through Time: A 12,000-Year Walk Through History (A DK Book) by Dr. Anne Millard

In Short: A Collection of Brief Creative Nonfiction edited by Judith Kitchen and Mary Paumier Jones

    Borrowed Time by Paul West, pp. 96–97

    LZ Gator Vietnam, February 1994 by Tim O'Brien, pp. 60–61

When I Was Magic

Grades 4–12

Fictional Narrative

Magic in Our Lives

● What would happen if we had magical powers?

Background for the Teacher

Flying is the stuff of myths and science, dreams and technology, movie magic and NASA. Our heroes—Superman, Batman, and a host of comic book do-gooders—all fly. Peter Pan and vampires and dragons all fly. Angels and fairies take to the air on gossamer wings. We want to fly, too. Our favorite circus acts include trapeze artists and men being shot from cannons. Man has always wanted to fly. From Icarus to the Wright brothers, our myths and history are full of attempts to aviate. I often fly in my dreams—a most exhilarating experience. Dreams of flying express our desire to leave the earthly realities and routines to be free as a bird and as powerful as gods. According to dream experts, flying indicates both intelligence and soaring ambition—and always freedom (Bently, 1994).

In Virginia Hamilton's *The People Could Fly*, slaves possessed the ancient magic words that enabled them to fly away to escape bondage and return home to Africa and freedom. Several such traditional slave tales of flying gave hope and strength to those who could not literally or easily fly away from their earthly plight.

Tall John arrives at the Corinthian Plantation in *47*, a novel by Walter Mosley, possessing power and the gift of time travel and flight, as well as other "conjure" abilities. He reminds us of the legendary and mythical High John the Conqueror, who is variously a powerful god, a magical person, and still, at present, a healing root. Similarly, in Julius Lester's *The Old African*, the title character uses his abilities to lead hopeful slaves into the sea to walk home, again recalling the power of magic to release us from the mundane and set us on the path to freedom.

Whether it is flying or reading minds or healing, magic powers come with responsibilities and choices about how we will use them.

- Will we use our powers for good or evil?
- Will we help only ourselves or our larger community?
- Will we hide our gifts or flaunt them?
- What rules govern their use?

The Quick Write Lesson

1. Sharing Mentor Texts

Share one of the selections below with your students. Discuss the role of magic or special powers in the story. Did the power change the characters in positive or negative ways? After reading several stories or excerpts, comparisons may be made and insights gained about the variety of ways that power affects us and characters in our stories.

To further support thinking about magical powers in stories, you may want to revisit some of the more traditional folktales and fairy tales with which children are usually familiar, such as *Cinderella, Sleeping Beauty, Rapunzel, Jack and the Beanstalk, The Fisherman and His Wife,* and other like tales.

As they immerse themselves in such stories, they will begin to notice patterns, such as good winning over evil, the rule of three (three wishes, three chances, three characters, etc.), and the role of powerful helpers (fairy godmothers, animals, etc.). They may want to incorporate some of these traditional aspects in their writing as they begin to tell their own stories.

2. Quick Write Possibilities

Invite students to write about a time when they had magic powers or wished or dreamed that they did.

- What was the power?
- How did they get it?
- Was it fun to have or a burden?
- What happened to them because of their powers?

Or

Ask them to write a story telling about themselves and one of their magical adventures.

Mentor Texts

Novels Based on John the Conqueror

The People Could Fly: American Black Folktales by Virginia Hamilton

The Old African by Julius Lester

47 by Walter Mosley

The Magical Adventure of Pretty Pearl by Virginia Hamilton

Using Magic Gifts and Powers: Novels

Gifts by Ursula K. Le Guin

Messenger by Lois Lowry

A Wizard of Earthsea by Ursula K. Le Guin

Fade by Robert Cormier

Other Magic: Picture Books

The People Could Fly: The Picture Book by Virginia Hamilton, illustrated by Leo and Diane Dillon

This is a picture book version of the title story of the above book by the same name.

Wings by Christopher Myers

What Dreams May Come

Grades 4–12

Personal Essay, Poetry, Experimental Forms

Our Dreams

> ● How can we use our dreams to foster writing?

Background for the Teacher

We dream at night—adventures beyond our wildest imagination and hopes, tragedies more sorrowful than the Greeks ever wrote, and sometimes horrors that inspire more terror than the creepiest films created in Hollywood. At night we lie in our beds waiting to enter a world not accessible except through the door of slumber. Some sleep worlds we enter eagerly, welcoming the rush of color or vague people we know only with our eyes closed. Others dreams we dread, and they may recur night after night.

I have a recurring dream in which I am on vacation and after checking into my hotel and initially finding my room, can never find it again. I spend my dream time on those nights roaming less and less familiar hallways and beaches, moving farther and farther away from where I am supposed to be, becoming increasingly frantic, as I try to find my way back to my hotel and traveling companions, always waking up before I do. On other nights, I am looking for my purse, which is continuously misplaced in my dreams.

And then there is my worst fear—I am being chased by someone or something really bad, but not seen. In these dreams, I usually run and run, terrified, until I reach my grandmother's front porch. Only then can I turn and face the horrible specter that is after me. Only then, when I am on the porch of my father's mother, am I safe from whatever still unseen monster or horrible human is pursuing me.

Some people I have talked to say they don't dream at all and others insist they dream only in black and white. I consider myself fortunate—I dream nightly, I dream in color, and I *love* to dream. In my favorite dreams, I am flying. Using only my own mind and will, I periodically take to the skies in my dream world. I love the freedom and the power that this brings. I love the weightlessness and ability to fly above most earthly trouble.

Since the beginning of time, dreams have been the subject of interest and study. They have been used as oracles and omens for seers, as indicators of our mental state for psychologists and other scientists, as social small talk with our friends and acquaintances, and as sources of many beautiful, powerful expressions in art, music, and literature.

My students talk about dreams as well. They dream vividly and their dreams usually involve lots of action that does not make sense to them or us when they share. Sometimes the dreams are funny and involve people in our class. Other times my students are scared beyond belief or puzzled by their dreams.

Talking about dreams is as natural as talking about what happened to you over the weekend. Mining our dreams for writing ideas is also a natural process and can be encouraged in our students.

The Quick Write Lesson

1. Sharing Mentor Texts

Have a conversation with students about the concept of dreaming. Help them realize that dreaming can have two meanings—our hopes for what we want to become and what we want to accomplish in the future, as well as the movies in our heads in which we engage at night. You may want to discuss daydreaming, as well.

Share the book *Dream: A Tale of Wonder, Wisdom and Wishes* by Susan V. Bosak (or another appropriate text) with your students. You and your students may just spend time enjoying the story with its wonderful illustrations, and you may also want to visit the related interactive website with them (www.legacyproject.org).

2. Writer's Notebook

Remind students of the discussion of dreams and the different meanings of that word—our hopes for what we want to become and what we want to accomplish in the future and the adventures seen as a movie in our head as we sleep. Invite students to share waking dreams, as well as sleeping dreams.

Ask them to list their dreams in their notebooks:

- List personal dreams for the future in their notebooks. They may want to create a chart in which to record different categories. You may want to discuss possible categories with them, such as family, education, career, hobbies, achievements, and so on.
- They may want to list dreams that have come true for them already and dreams on which they are still hoping.
- They may have inherited dreams or hopes and visions of the future from parents or other people and want to list those as well.

Night dreams tend to be disjointed and nonlinear. Webbing (or sketching) what students remember first about a dream may help them access details that have been forgotten or pushed to the back of their memory upon waking. They can put a simple title or phrase in the center to remind them of the dream and begin to expand the web by adding details. In my experience with webbing dreams, the more I write, the more I can remember, and sometimes the pieces begin to fit together in a cohesive narrative—but sometimes not. Those that don't fit together make better poems.

3. Quick Write Possibilities

Invite students to write about a dream they have about their future.

- Ask them to write a piece as if this dream has been fulfilled.
- What are they doing?
- Who are they in their dream?
- Who is with them?
- How are they feeling?

Or

Invite them to write about a dream they have had while sleeping. Because of the nonlinear nature of dreams, students might be encouraged to write poetry or to experiment with forms (see quick write "What Container Will Hold My Words?").

Remind your students that they should choose the genre that seems appropriate for their dream.

The Mentor Text

Dream: A Tale of Wonder, Wisdom and Wishes by Susan V. Bosak
Related website: www.legacyproject.org

Additional Resources

The following poems by Langston Hughes may also be used to talk about waking dreams. They're available at http://www.poemhunter.com/langston-hughes/.

- "Dream Deferred" (Harlem)
- "Dream Variations"
- "Dreams"

The following poems are my responses to this quick write.

Dreamscape

Dreaming knowledge
is ancient.
I remember the woman in the cave
with the pipe—blowing
powerful smoke on her daughters
washing their souls with feathers and bones
filling their dreams with collective memories
tribal history and traditional night fire stories.

The daughters breathe in
the smoke filling their mind
and hearts with the knowledge
and forgotten images of their people.
Every muscle remembers
every memory.
Now connected with their ancestors
calling up their
wisdom
yet still dreaming
new knowledge.

The Key

I dreamed I lost a key last night.
The key belonged to my mother.

What did the key open?
The place where I lost it
had long playground-slide conveyor belts.
Some way I dropped a lacy white scarf
to which the key was attached.
Why was I there?
What was the place?

I dreamed I lost a key last night.
What did the key open?

2 Art, Lenses, and Visions

Writing the World We See

Writers see the world differently. We notice detail, relationships, juxtapositions, and patterns. We converse with what we see and look beyond the obvious limits of our human sight. The quick writes in this section force close observation of our everyday world and time, including objects and people we encounter, as well as events and places we experience. Several quick writes in this section use objects, artwork, or photography as a stimulus for writing. They promote

- Descriptive writing
- Poetry
- Letters
- Personal essays
- Persuasive essays

Seeing Things and Having New Eyes

Grades 4–12

Description, Poetry, Personal Essays

Seeing Common Objects in New Ways

> • What do we see when we look and then look again?

Background for the Teacher

Writers see differently. We look with new eyes, noticing the big picture and the small, easily neglected details of everything we see. Often, with objects we encounter, we note their presence with curiosity and a keen intent to remember—sometimes to simply enjoy the image or to later render it in our work. We mentally register not only the obvious—color, size, and shape—but also the more subtle texture and complexity. We notice how the object is presented—the context—as well as comparisons and contrasts. Unbidden similes and metaphors begin to form. We begin to string words together in our writer's mind to give life to what we see. We consider actual uses and conjure new ones. We juggle words to describe and define the positions and relationships that others may fail to see, the juxtapositions and paradoxes that give us pause and set our minds to wondering.

One way to write about objects is to deliberately make surprising similes and metaphors. The attempt is to present the object in a new way. When the fourth and fifth graders in the Student Writing Project were asked for ordinary metaphors or similes about the sun, they initially made the obvious comparisons to golden or yellow balls. As we dug deeper and challenged each other, the sun became a "dab of butter in the sky" or a "glowing lamp lighting our day." At the time of this lesson we were preparing for the big fourth-fifth grade race, an annual tradition at our school. Recalling a fellow student's face after a particularly vigorous practice, one student described the evening sun as a "ball as red as Michael's face after training for the big race." We continued to generate unusual comparisons that helped us think about things in new ways.

The Quick Write Lesson

1. Sharing Mentor Texts

Share the poems "The Pointe Shoe" and "The Salt Shaker of 1,000 Colors" with your students. Or read several poems from *All the Small Poems and Fourteen More* by Valerie Worth.

- Ask them to notice how small, specific details are included.
- How does this add to the image in their minds of the object described?
- To what does the writer compare the objects?
- Notice any unusual details that surprise them or make them look at the object in a new way.

The Pointe Shoe

The pale satin is smooth
and shiny on the sides and back,
with matching pink ribbons
painstakingly sewn on,
stitch by stitch
by hand.

The satin whispers
of rows
of ballerinas,
arms crossed in front of
pink leotarded chests,
holding hands
moving on toe points across
a stage.

The toe—the box—however,
speaks a different picture—
that of bleeding toes—
boxed in by hard glue—
screaming for relief,
wondering why the cushion existed—
a fuzzy, lamb's wool cup
hidden inside
the deceitful pretty pink satin.

The Salt Shaker of 1,000 Colors

15 holes up on top with ivory circles.
Bumpy like the Blue Streak*
Rusted on the bottom,
What has it been through?
Is it still alive?
Inside is as smooth as a baby's bottom.
Has it been through a stampede
Of bowls and survived?
It is still strong.

---

*A popular roller coaster at a nearby amusement park

Source: © Copyright 2006 by Michael Lipster, Student Writing Project.

2. Quick Write Possibilities

Provide students with a variety of objects to consider and see in a new way. I keep a bag of objects to use with young students, adult groups, and everybody in between. Periodically, I add new items to this bag. (The current contents of my bag are listed as a poem in Resources.) Invite them to sit with their chosen object and see past the obvious. They should describe their object in as much detail as possible, including the smallest, most specific information. Also ask them to include at least one surprising simile or metaphor or other unusual but apt descriptor. You may want to practice making similes and metaphors if these concepts are new to your students.

Or

Students may also try writing a list poem. This involves working with multiple items at once, creating a poem by simply listing the items. Ask them to consider what is on or in their desks, in a drawer, or on a shelf or in their bedroom. (See the list at the end of this quick write of the contents in my bag of objects as an example.)

Read students' excerpts from Albert Goldbarth's *Library*, in which he lists books on his library shelves. The Poetry Daily website has a page devoted to this poem, which includes the full text and allows readers to enter their own additions to Goldbarth's poem (see http://www.poetry-daily.org/special_features/library.php).

Sometimes lists are embedded in other pieces of writing. Nick Lantz includes a list in his poem "Fork With Two Tines Pushed Together" (Grades 9–12; see http://www.poets.org/viewmedia.php/prmMID/22706).

The Mentor Texts

All the Small Poems and Fourteen More by Valerie Worth

These 99 short poems from the original first four volumes by Worth and 14 new poems each describe an object in unique and surprising ways. They are perfect models for writing about ordinary items.

Additional Resources

The following books all deal with one or more objects and encourage us to revise our concept of each object:

Seven Blind Mice by Ed Young

This illustrated fable shows how our perspective changes what we see and may encourage children to look at the objects about which they are writing from several points of view.

Flotsam: A Life in Debris by Denis Horgan

In these personal essays, Denis ponders events in his life allowing the objects on his desk and in his office to suggest the direction of his story.

My Bag of Objects Contains

A Tattered Bible with the Spine Missing
(A dried rose hides in the pages)
The Red Book (Quotations from Chairman Mao Tse-Tung)
McGuffey's Eclectic Primer (Revised Edition)
A blank CD and clear case
One frayed length of rope
One pink pointe shoe
An African thumb piano from Kenya
One gray work glove
A silver picture frame with no picture
A silver box with velvet purple lining
A wooden letter opener (my grandmother's)
A wire high heel shoe (decoration left
from a gift wrapping)
A truck made of Legos constructed at least
20 years earlier by one of my stepsons
A cameo in reverse—a black woman
on white background
A wooden cross made by Simok Indians in Argentina
A beaded African bracelet, either Maasai or Zulu
Four fortune cookies with the fortunes inside intact
A white china bowl trimmed in gold (my grandmother's)
A multicolored salt shaker (my grandmother's)
An old skeleton key to a door in my grandmother's house

Who Wore the Hat?

Grades 6–12 (adapts for 4–5)

Poetry

Questioning Object to Discover the Nature of Its Uses and Its Owner

- ### What do I see as I ask questions about an object?

Background for Teachers

When we look at objects, what do we see? Our first response to that question is probably color, size, and shape. As we continue to look, we also see texture and quality, intricacy or simplicity, solidity or frailty. We see the "what" of the object first. Once we have the initial image, we begin to compare this object to others, both present and absent. We consider the context in which it appears. And if we are thoroughly observing, we may even think about what it is *not.* These are simple, obvious observations.

Writers, however, automatically continue to look and ponder whatever they see even further. Writers will question things beyond the "what." Do I have this object in my house? Is it mine or someone else's? What connections does this object have for me? For others? What is the purpose of this object? How else can it be used? We dig into the emotions of the object. What do I remember, long for, or hide from as I see it?

Writers will converse with the object to learn its history, its essence. We may ask about its owner, as does Nancy Patz in *Who Was the Woman Who Wore the Hat?*

In this haunting book, the poet questions a lone woman's hat shown in a glass case in the Jewish Historical Museum in Amsterdam. Unlike other items displayed nearby, the case contained no label or information about the hat. The hat, alone, remained to speak for the woman who wore it. With questions that contain what Ralph Fletcher in *A Writer's Notebook* (2003) and *What a Writer Needs* (1993) calls "writing small or concrete details," meaning very specific and particular minute details, we begin to gain understanding of the woman who might have owned this hat.

The Quick Write Lesson

1. Sharing Mentor Texts

Read *Who Was the Woman Who Wore the Hat?* to your students. Examine and discuss how the author describes the hat through its association with its owner and her life. Ask them to notice how she uses only questions.

- What further descriptions of the hat do the presented images suggest?
- What else do you wonder about the woman who wore the hat?
- What questions would you add to those of the author?

The following two poems, written in the manner of Patz's book, may be shared with your students as additional models.

Whose Hands Wore the Gloves?

Whose hands wore the gloves?
Were they gnarled and sinewy
with veins that show
or plump and soft and pink?

Did those hands bathe well-loved babies at night
or beat a silent timid wife?

Whose hands wore the gloves?
Did the hands work with wood or steel or earth?
And when did the grease become permanently smudged
on the soft gray surface?

Was he gruff or sweet?
Did he treat his mother well?

Who wore the gloves?
Did he work for someone else
or in his own backyard?

Did he eagerly come home
to light and chatter?
Or did he face each night alone
Eating weariness with his supper?

Who wore the gloves?
Was he building up
or tearing down?

Is he alive
or is he dead?

Who wore the gloves?

The Rope

[Inspired by the movie *The Great Debaters*]
The rope is frayed
and grey and worn
just how much would it hold
or pull or bind
and for how long?

Was it at one time connected to a longer length of rope?

Did it hang someone
from a tree for being born
black and alive?

The rope is old now
and harmless
or is it?

It still conjures history
and memories
and tales told in the dark
of trees bearing strange fruit

and men intent on stunting
the growth
of my family tree.

The rope is frayed and grey and worn
but just how much
did it hold
or pull
or bind
and for how long?

2. Quick Write Possibilities

Provide a selection of various objects from which students may choose. (For the list of objects that I use, see "My Bag of Objects Contains" in the Additional Resources section of the previous quick write, "Seeing Things and Having New Eyes." If you have done this quick write, you may invite the writers to use the same object again for this current quick write.) Ask them to question the object—writing a series of questions that go beyond the visible. The questions can be about the object, addressed to an unseen addressee or addressed directly to the object itself. Encourage them to ask questions about purpose and history, memories and connections, emotions and relationships. Suggest that they ponder the paradoxes presented by the object. How does this object affect their own lives?

The Mentor Text

Who Was the Woman Who Wore the Hat? by Nancy Patz

Additional Resources

Shoes on the Highway: Using Visual and Audio Cues to Inspire Student Play-wrights by Maureen Brady Johnson (2005)

The appendix of *Shoes on the Highway* presents a series of photographic images of individual shoes in the street. These images are available for no cost online at http://books.heinemann.com/shoesonthehighway/default.aspx

Bring Life Into Learning: Create a Lasting Literacy by Donald H. Graves (1999)

Graves describes an approach to learning in which polarity, paradox, and particularity explain the wants and needs of people—literary characters, as well as historical and living characters. He suggests we question the characters to gain a better understanding of their motives and that we also question artifacts used by these people to discover more about the complex relationships of people and events.

Head Swivelers

Grades 4–12

Narrative, Personal Essay

Things We Have Said That Have Shocked Others

- What is appropriate to say or not say?

Background for the Teacher

Growing up, I was not allowed to say *butt* for that part of the body that we sit on. Everyone else I knew could—even their parents said it. As far as I could tell, it was not a bad word, but for some reason, I was not allowed to say it. I was not even allowed to say *behind*. It had to be *bottom*. We all have words that we could not say as children or words that still cause a raised eyebrow or head turn in certain circumstances.

As my students recently engaged in lively debate and penetrating third degree of our two candidates for class president, one candidate proclaimed a promise of video games for everyone and daily pencil leads for students' mechanical pencils. When pushed on this point and his unrealistic ability to keep these promises, he indicated he could indeed keep the lead promise "unless he was *pissed off* at someone." At this point 23 heads swiveled in unison in my direction to see my reaction. I rarely react visibly to shocking student statements, notes, or other behaviors. He, noting the looks of the students, immediately protested that he had "not cussed," at which point we acknowledged this was true but questioned whether his word choice was truly presidential. Ultimately, he lost the election and graciously congratulated his opponent. Was it his wild promises or his language that defeated him?

In my classroom right now, I have a boy who describes himself as homeless. "It's embarrassing," he said as another teacher and I were asking questions trying to determine why his sister had not been in school for five days. It seems the grown people in his home created such a ruckus one evening that they were all put out of their apartment, as he told the story. He was actually staying with relatives. He knew his story was a head swiveler.

What makes your head swivel? What have you said that has made heads swivel?

The Quick Write Lesson

1. Sharing Mentor Texts

Choose one of the books below to read to your students. Select your text based on your classroom curriculum, students' interest or needs, and age. All are picture books or poetry that deal with serious issues in compact, yet complex texts suitable for all ages. All will lead to complex and higher level discussions of contemporary issues. The discussion may generate head swivelers.

For the younger children needing lighter fare, I recommend *The Pain and the Great One* or *Into the Forest*.

Discussing the ideas in the books in terms of the books' characters will in turn open the door to talk about the same issues related to them personally.

2. Writer's Notebook

> It is important for students to realize that you are a legally mandated reporter of any incidents that indicate abuse or neglect of any kind or criminal activity. They need to know that if anything they write indicates such issues, you would be obligated to share it beyond the two of you.

For this activity, assure writers that these notes will not be seen by anyone but themselves, unless they choose to share. A technique I have used in the past with students is to fold and staple anything they do not want me to read when I collect their notebooks. This gives them a sense of security. Interestingly, even though it is offered, most students do not use this option. Most really want you to read everything.

Use these activities as you are comfortable, considering your writers, school, and community culture.

- List words you are not allowed to say in your home that "everybody" else can say.
- Why are you not allowed to say the words listed?
- List secrets that you are not supposed to talk about (family, school, friends, neighborhood).
- List ideas you have that you think no one else shares.

3. Quick Write Possibilities

Ask your students to think about the last time they said something aloud or thought something that they knew other people would not agree with, approve of, or even believe. Have them think about the following:

- What happened?
- Why were people shocked or surprised?
- Have your ideas changed as a result of this reaction?

Or
Write about who decides the appropriateness of conversations or ideas.

The Mentor Texts

Been to Yesterdays: Poems of a Life by Lee Bennett Hopkins
   Includes the poem "Clutching" in which a boy's mother uses the N-word.

Homelessness
December by Eve Bunting

Sibling Rivalry
The Pain and the Great One by Judy Blume

AIDS
Daddy and Me by Jeanne Moutoussamy-Ashe

Divorce and Separation
Amber Was Brave, Essie Was Smart by Vera B. Williams
Into the Forest by Anthony Brown

Race

Let's Talk About Race by Julius Lester

Family Secrets, Race

Mississippi Morning by Ruth Vander Zee

Death

Michael Rosen's Sad Book by Michael Rosen

Sweet, Sweet Memory by Jacqueline Woodson

Aging

The Hundred Penny Box by Sharon Bell Mathis

When I Am Old With You by Angela Johnson

Violence, Dangerous Neighborhoods

Life Doesn't Frighten Me by Maya Angelou

Something Beautiful by Sharon Dennis Wyeth

Horizons

Grades 4–12

Personal or Persuasive Essays or Letters

Limits and Horizons in Our Lives

- What are the limits of our experiences?
- What is at the edge of our life?

Background for the Teacher

On November 5, 2008, we woke up facing a new horizon. Barack Obama, an African American, had been elected president of the United States of America. This is beyond the experiences of Americans in this country. This is beyond what many considered historically, politically, and socially possible in this country. The very complexion of this recent campaign was extraordinarily distinct and changed the world as we know it from that point forward. In record numbers, young people and those disenfranchised, or simply uninterested, became informed and actively involved in determining the future of our country and the world. This was an exhilarating time. We wondered: What will change? What will be accomplished? What will we learn? What will we be called upon to do? We, as a nation, stood at the edge of a new horizon.

The horizon is the line where the land or sea appears to meet the sky. Whether standing with our feet firmly planted on land or moving gently in our vessel on ocean waves, we can see no farther than that horizon line, making it easy for us to understand how our forebears believed the earth was flat and that they might fall off the edge. In visual art, the horizon line is manipulated to make us feel the vantage point the artist desires. Moving the line in a drawing or painting can make us feel we are higher up looking down or below the horizon looking up.

Horizon comes from a Greek root that means limit and is also the word we use to describe the range or limit of a person's knowledge, experience, or interest. Thus, we talk about expanding our horizons when we have new experiences.

Metaphorically and poetically, the horizon encompasses the unseen possibilities, the new day that is dawning, the new experiences beyond that horizon line, all that is waiting to be seen, all that will be accomplished, and the new worlds waiting to be created.

I recently discovered a beautiful book called *Horizons* by Jane Yolen. Jason Stemple, her photographer son, sent her photos of horizons as he traveled and encountered them. She, in turn, was inspired to write of her own expanding horizons. The result was a wonderful collaboration. Upon finding the book, I was moved to go through my own store of photographs to see how many horizons I had seen and captured. There were more than I expected, each calling up memories, and suggesting experiential and knowledge-related edges of my own. Photography is a new interest of mine, and simply having successfully taken landscape images is expanding a horizon for me. It was affirming to be able to replace the standard Windows screensaver on my computer with a meaningful landscape of my own—a seascape of St. John taken from St. Thomas, U.S. Virgin Islands.

The Quick Write Lesson

1. Sharing Mentor Texts

Share several poems from Jane Yolen's *Horizons.* My favorites are "Sand, Sun, Stone," "Mirror," and "Horizon."

- Ask students to discuss how physical and metaphoric horizons are depicted in each poem.
- Ask them to think about how these poems might represent their own horizons.

Tell your students that meeting "new days" is often marked with writing. The horizon can be a personal event such as turning 10 (share Billy Collins's poem listed below) or having a child or beginning school or learning a new skill.

The horizon can also be a collective new day, changes for the world—such as selection of a new president (share Maya Angelou's poem listed below), the collapse of a cruel and unjust political regime, the death of a world leader, or a scientific innovation.

Or

You may want to share letters written to President Obama or another important figure as they faced new positions, responsibilities, or some other life change. (See sites below for letters written to President Obama by authors Alice Walker and Toni Morrison.)

2. Writer's Notebook

Invite your students to think about the limits or edge of their own experiences. Have them make a list in their notebook:

- What is beyond that edge?
- What do they expect to learn and do?
- Where do they expect to travel and what will they see?
- What new experiences are they looking forward to?

3. Quick Write Possibilities

Ask students to consider the horizons they have listed in their notebooks. You may want to have students share aloud the edges of experience and knowledge that they have listed. Have them select a particular area in which they are facing a new day or horizon.

- Where are they currently standing?
- What can they see from where they stand?
- What are they expecting beyond the horizon line?
- How will they get beyond the line?

They may choose to express their ideas in poetry as in the mentor texts that have been shared.

Or

They may write a letter to a person who is leading them to expand their horizons. Writers Alice Walker and Toni Morrison have both written letters to Barack Obama, celebrating the new day he represents and also giving advice. (See the sites below for copies.)

The Mentor Texts

Teaching With Fire: Poetry That Sustains the Courage to Teach edited by Sam M. Intrator and Megan Scribner

"On Turning Ten" by Billy Collins

"The Journey" by Mary Oliver

"On the Pulse of the Morning" by Maya Angelou
The inaugural poem read at the inauguration of Bill Clinton, 1993

Horizons: Poems as Far as the Eye Can See by Jane Yolen, photographs by Jason Stemple

Alice Walker's letter to Barack Obama (http://shiva2731.blogspot.com/2008/11/alice-walker-open-letter-to-barack.html)

Toni Morrison's letter to Barack Obama (http://www.observer.com/2008/toni-morrisons-letter-barack-obama)

Artful Reading and Writing

Grades 4–12

Descriptive or Reflective Essay

Using Paintings to Inspire Writing

- ● What does this painting mean?

Background for the Teacher

In *Pentimento,* Lillian Hellman describes how paint on old canvasses sometimes becomes transparent with age. When that happens, we are able to see through the newest layers of paint to the once hidden original lines and sketches, and sometimes even to complete former paintings. We wonder how many times the artist covered up images and replaced them with new ones. We wonder if he was covering work with which he was less than pleased, found new interests, or simply had not recently sold enough paintings to afford new canvasses.

For those of us who do not paint, the process of covering a canvas with daubs of color to make an image emerge is mysterious and magical. Even though we may not paint or draw or even understand the principles by which we might begin to do these activities, we can all view the work with pleasure (or displeasure or perplexity)—and this experience can be an inspiration for writing.

Our fifth-grade classes took a field trip to the Columbus Museum of Art last year. Prior to our trip, we received several additional resources to introduce our students to the process of observing and describing art, including a PowerPoint that taught us how to "read art" and a CD of 12 paintings on which we could practice our new skills. Immediately before our excursion, a docent from the gallery came to our classes and shared additional works with us and encouraged a variety of ways to look at them. No student was unsuccessful with this activity, and the excitement was uncontainable.

As we look at visual art, no matter who we are, we can *describe* what we see—the colors, the lines, the images, and the textures. We can notice what is depicted and in what manner. We can identify the mood of the work and how it makes us feel.

After noticing and describing, we are encouraged to *interpret* what we are seeing. What does it mean? We can speculate about what the artist was trying to portray and why. Why would a particular color be used? Why was this medium, this subject chosen? We can ask many questions and infer much as we look.

The final step is to *support our interpretation* with details or elements from the painting or work—proving what we think. My students immediately likened this part of the process to using evidence to prove an inference or conclusion when reading a text, which we were learning to do at the time. We continued to use this analogy and the term *artful reading* for the remainder of the year whenever we looked at visual images and art. We also made direct links to the writing process as we realized that the artist chose the elements of his work in the same way we carefully choose a particular word instead of another one as we write.

The Quick Write Lesson

1. Sharing Mentor Texts

Share with your students either the poem "Ringside" by Ron Koertge inspired by *Stag at Sharkey's*, the 1909 oil painting by George Bellow, or

"Early Sunday Morning" by Dan Masterson, inspired by an oil painting of the same title by Edward Hopper. These narrative poems are favorites of my students and can be found in *Heart to Heart* (listed under Additional Resources below), and the suggested paintings are available at http://www.artchive.com/artchive/B/bellows/sharkeys.jpg.html and http://www.artchive.com/artchive/h/hopper/earlysun.jpg.html.

Help your students to use the strategies described above to *artfully read* the paintings.

- Ask them to consider why the writer might have chosen a particular painting. Discuss their interpretations of the painting and the story behind it.
- Does it spark any memories or connections?
- Ask them what they might have written about the same painting.

Use any of the sites listed below in Additional Resources to locate other paintings and other visual works of art that you may prefer for your particular students.

2. Quick Write Possibilities

Choose a painting that is appropriate for your age-group. With both adults and children, I first use *La Debacle* by Theodore Robinson (available on the Columbus museum website listed below) because it lends itself easily to narrative like the model poems, but the sky is the limit on the choices of images or paintings and narrative is not required.

Ask the students to consider the painting in the ways suggested above. Ask them to write a story, poem, or reflection inspired by the painting. They should weave the details of the painting into their writing to construct a piece that stands alone, yet is obviously connected to the painting as well.

Here are two samples, written four months apart. Notice that each one is written from a different perspective and evokes a different mood. Yet each is in response to the same painting and quick write suggested above. You may want to encourage your students to write more than one piece about the same painting. This will provide invaluable practice in considering perspective and voice.

Artful Reading 1

She has waited here each day . . . hoping that
today would be the day. Each day she brings the book
that remains closed as she sits and watches, sits and waits.

She must remain here. The road remains empty—no footfalls,
no shadow of approaching, no finality to her wait.
How many days has she dressed in her frock
and limped slowly and painfully to this same
familiar seat at water's edge?
When will she turn her head and see me instead
of faithfully and foolishly waiting for him?
I can see her
He can not.

—Salem Teacher Writing Project, 2/7/08

Artful Reading 2

I sit here
everyday waiting
in my purple and pink frock
my straw bonnet perched (more uniform
than protection from the sun)
atop my tightly wound bun.

Each day I bring
the thick yellow
book, but
it sits on my lap.

I watch the water instead.
The few small fish jump
and the lapping waves
break my reflection.

No one comes.
No one passes.
Not today—
Not ever.

This road and
its untended flowers
is mine.

The bridge is mine
and these rocks.

I wait each day
for something

to be different
but . . .
take comfort
in the fact
that it is always
the same.

—CAWP Summer Institute, 6/17/08

Additional Resources

There are numerous books that pair art and writing. In the following books the poetry was inspired by the art.

Heart to Heart: New Poems Inspired by Twentieth Century American Art edited by Jan Greenberg

This book includes lithographs, sculpture, mixed media, and photographs ranging from pop art to familiar classic works.

Side by Side: New Poems Inspired by Art From Around the World edited by Jan Greenberg

This work by Greenberg continues the marvelous pairing in *Heart to Heart*, this time moving into the 21st century and including international work.

Words With Wings: A Treasury of African-American Poetry and Art selected by Belinda Rochelle

This beautiful collection pairs 20 poems by African American poets with 20 works of art by African American artists. The poems and pieces of art address the history, culture, and identity of African American people.

Columbus Museum of Art Resources

Artful Reading PowerPoint, by Barbara Zollinger Sweney, Melissa Keeley, and Kathleen Canalos

The paintings shared with my class prior to our field trip are available at http://www.columbusmuseum.org/monet_education/pdf/images.pdf.

For more information about the paintings mentioned above, go to http://www.columbusmuseum.org/monet_education/index.html. (Your own local gallery should also have educator additional resources.)

Online Resources for Visual Art

There are numerous sites where you may locate visual art to share with your students.

http://www.artcyclopedia.com/

Many paintings are available on this searchable site.

http://gardenofpraise.com/art.htm

This set of various safe paintings is appropriate for elementary students but useful for all ages. It is an excellent collection of art with a wide variety of work. Caution: The context of the art works is a religious home schooling site, so you may want to select the section you wish students to view.

Web Museum (http://www.ibiblio.org/wm/paint/auth/)

Books About Art

Your students may also enjoy these multilayered, multi-genre books which focus on art. These two were an instant hit with my students last year. Despite the fact that we may consider viewing art to be a sophisticated activity, they pored over the books each day as they waited for their buses. These provide additional sources for art that may inspire student writing.

Baby Einstein: The ABCs of Art by Julie Aigner-Clark

This ABC book features famous art and can be enjoyed by upper elementary grades despite the name.

Art Fraud Detective: Spot the Difference, Solve the Crime! by Anna Nilsen

Provides an opportunity to closely consider art details of famous pictures as students attempt to determine who has altered the paintings in the gallery. A magnifying glass is included for serious study of details.

Snapshots: Capture the Moment

Grades 4–12

Descriptive, Personal or Persuasive Essay, Poetry

Using Photographs to Inspire Writing

> • Can I take a picture of this moment with my writing?

Background for the Teacher

It is summer and my cousins and I stand in a sweaty bunch while my uncle takes our picture. There we are, front teeth missing, arms laced around each other, one cousin waving. Or it is Christmas of every year, any year, and we are framed, forever holding that sweater or necklace or tie that came from someone outside the frame. We are smiling, whether we like the gift or not, because the one taking the picture said, "Say cheese," or some such silly phrase designed to make us put on our best face for the camera.

Taking pictures is a way of daily life in our world, thanks to this century's digital conveniences (or nuisances, depending on your perspective). Our cameras have gotten smaller and our phones do double duty, visually recording our lives.

We use photography to capture and remember the moments, the events, and the people that matter. We use photography to share the same with others, to enjoy these captured memories in that particular moment and for years to come. With photographs we document our lives and our presence here in this world. And when we consider the photographs of others, our world is informed, enlarged, and mediated. We are lifted beyond ourselves and transported to other worlds and experiences. As we look at a photo, we flesh out the captured moment mentally and verbally, describing it, remembering its purpose, narrating its story, telling its context, interpreting the images, and noticing or recalling what is absent.

Photography is magic in that we can look at the same photos again and again with enjoyment each time but perhaps with a different focus and lens. *I didn't notice that she wasn't smiling last time I saw this one. . . . Why is he turned toward the left? What was he looking at? I can't remember.*

We can consider photographs from a variety of perspectives in order to foster storytelling and writing in various genres. I have used the following questions or ones similar for many years with my students anytime we analyzed not just photos, but illustrations in books, paintings, and other visual representations which depicted people:

- Who is in the photo or picture?
- What is happening in the photo?
- What happened right before the photo was taken?
- What happened right after the photo was taken?
- Why were these folks included? (or this object or this scene?)
- Who is not in the picture? Why?
- Who or what is just outside the frame of the picture?
- What was the photographer's (or artist's) thinking or purpose?
- What was the purpose or thinking of those in the picture?

As we consider these questions, we can begin to write from several different perspectives: the photographer, one of the people or objects in the photograph, one of those onlookers not included in the photograph, or someone who is completely absent at the actual taking of the photograph.

Working with photographs can be an excellent way to think about alternative perspectives, particularly when considering unfamiliar photos, those not having anything to do with our own family, friends, or local community—*Where are you in the photo? Who do you identify with and why?*

The Quick Write Lesson

1. Sharing Mentor Texts

Invite your students to talk about the many ways they use photography in their own lives and other possible uses of photography in which they may not currently be involved.

Share one of the selections below and consider how the author has used photography to make meaning. For those photos involving people, the questions above may be helpful. For those not involving people, speculative discussion can be fostered about people who may come to this place or have created objects or buildings that appear, or may have related in some way to other aspects of the environment. You may want to help students understand the concept that photos are edited, in that someone made a conscious decision to include or not include what shows up in the resulting frame. Linking this idea to writing may help some students grasp the idea of deliberate choices in writing to construct their own intended messages.

2. Quick Write Possibilities

Prior to this writing, students may be invited to bring in photographs. Invite students to write about a photo they have brought with them. Reminding them of the questions used to analyze and discuss the photos may be helpful. Encourage them to see the photo with new eyes—writing from a different perspective or writing about something unusual or something not noticed before in the images.

Or

Invite them to write about photos that are unfamiliar (see the sources below for files of images that can be used). You may want to tie in with a current unit of study in science or social studies or literature themes. Again, the above questions and suggested perspectives may be helpful to spark ideas for your students.

Additional Resources

Remember the Bridge: Poems of a People, by Carole Boston Wetherford

Includes photographs, as well as drawings depicting African American history.

Monumental Verses by J. Patrick Lewis

> Features famous monuments around the world.

A Cool Drink of Water by Barbara Kerle

> Depicts the sources and containers for water around the world.

Something Permanent, photographs by Walker Evans, poetry by Cynthia Rylant

> Features photographs of the Great Depression.

Carver: A Life in Poems by Marilyn Nelson

> Includes photographs throughout this biography in poems.

The Brothers' War: Civil War Voices in Verse by J. Patrick Lewis

> Features the work of Civil War photographers.

In Short: A Brief Collections of Creative Nonfiction by Judith Kitchen and Mary Paumier Jones, editors

> "My Mother in Two Photographs, Among Other Things" by Aleida Rodriguez, pp. 138–141

Additional Resources for Teachers

Reading Photographs to Write With Meaning and Purpose (Grades 4–12) by Leigh Van Horn

Write What You See: 99 Photos to Inspire Writing by Hank Kellner

> In addition to this book, Kellner's website (http://www.creativity-portal.com/prompts/kellner/) includes many photography-related features, including additional quick writes and photos.

Sources for Files of Photographs

Shoes on the Highway: Using Visual and Audio Cues to Inspire Student Playwrights by Maureen Brady Johnson

> Files of photos (a free download) for teachers to use as writing quick writes—two collections: one of shoes on the highway and the other of rocks in various locations (http://books.heinemann.com/shoesonthehighway/default.aspx)

> Newseum is a source for ever-changing collections of photographs. Two such sets include

> *The Pulitzer Prize Photographs: Capture the Moment*, edited by Gyma Rubin and Eric Newton

Both a book and an online collection (http://www.newseum.org/exhibits-and-theaters/permanent-exhibits/pulitzer/).

Images of Hate and Hope—Freedom Summer (http://www.newseum.org/mississippi/)

The Library of Congress Prints and Photographs Online Catalog—searchable (http://www.loc.gov/pictures/)

Smithsonian Photography Initiative (http://click.si.edu/)

Click! Photography Changes Everything, is a collection of original essays, stories, and images—contributed by experts from a spectrum of professional worlds and members of the project's online audience—that explores the many ways photography shapes our culture and our lives. A project of the former Smithsonian Photography Initiative, texts and content for *Click!* were commissioned and compiled between 2007 and 2010.

This was my response to an unfamiliar photograph used in a writing class.

The Photo

The yellow lights, two of them,
soften the air and
the aura in the room.
A thin curtain separates this space
from a second room.

They sit close at the table.
Five people, shoulder to shoulder,
one at the head, the speaker and
two on each side.
An open hexagon.
Room for one more.

They listen to the speaker
hunched forward,
one leaning into the speaker
one with head tilted away
considering the words.

The food and conversation
glued them
together.

The thin curtain blurs
complete seeing and

complete hearing of
the conversation
But—it is interesting
and important.

The intent looks reveal
concentration.
Hands move through the air
cutting ideas
into visible points.

Looking into the light
bathing the room
I wait for
an invitation.

Here is my response to a familiar photo taken by my father
of my sister and me when we were about 4 and 2.

The Photo

Here we sit
in church dresses
and Sunday hair
frozen forever
miniature imitations of ourselves
predictions of who we will become
in the uncomfortable crinolines
and prickly lace
of little girl loveliness.
Each face suffers only a hint of a smile.
We sat on an unseen piano bench.
My dad took this photo.
I remember this day.
My sister holds a hairbrush
—the only object that would keep
her still or quiet or looking
at the man with the camera.

Our different arm positions
bothers my eye and my heart.
Am I pulling away—refusing
to embrace
this plumper cuter version
of me?

Proverbially Speaking: Words to Live By

Grades 4–12

Proverbs, Essays, Information Reports

Examining Traditional Proverbs and Sayings

- What do the old folks say?
- What does traditional collected wisdom say?

Background for the Teacher

Whenever we kids—my sister or my cousins—would overstep our boundaries and dare to ask one of the grown-ups about a word, a name, a comment, or a situation we had overheard mentioned in grown-up conversation, my maternal grandmother would say, *"Lay-o for meddlers."* I heard this often in my life but still cannot be certain that I have written the words correctly. I don't know where it originated or what it literally means. Yet there is not now, nor was there ever, a question about what this phrase meant when it was spoken by my grandmother. It was her way of saying, "Mind your own business. This is not for children's ears."

We have all grown up with words and phrases and pieces of lore that guide our thinking and our living. Families and friends, countries and cultures regulate lives and pass on precious knowledge, history, and reminders of who we are through clever, sometimes cryptic words, phrases, and sayings. Those words become part of the fabric weaving in and out of our lives as needed to provide us with wisdom, encouragement, and explanations of life. They become our maps—showing us the way to success and the land mines to avoid according to those who have come before us. Knowing the words by which a culture, a community, or an individual lives tells us much about how they think and view the world, how they act and what they value, what we may expect of them, and what they might expect of us.

The words that guide us come variously from our famous leaders and thinkers, holy books, Benjamin Franklin and William Shakespeare, ancient wisdom . . . and our grandmothers. Some proverbs we all know. *A stitch in time saves nine. Pride goes before the fall. The early bird gets the worm. A rose by any other name* . . . Others, like *Lay-o for meddlers*, have meaning only for our family or some other small select group. Proverbs and sayings last because they are true—not prove-it-with-reference-books true, but gut-level true. They last because they pack hundreds of lifetimes of wisdom and experience into just a few words. They last because they make us think—remind us of what we know and awaken in us what we have forgotten. They last because we *get* them—they turn on our proverbial lightbulb, shining the light of clarity, revealing essence and gestalt.

Some long-forgotten proverbs reenter our current political culture and become rallying cries for reform and justice and compassion. *It takes a whole village to raise a child.* Hillary Rodham Clinton caused us to remember and reconsider this Nigerian Igbo proverb when she used it as the title of her 1996 book, *It Takes a Village: And Other Lessons Children Teach Us.* Some proverbs enter our popular culture and get us through our "everyday": *Better late than never.* And some we question and wonder when they apply and to whom: *Curiosity killed the cat.*

We all remember movie lines—our favorites that strike a chord within, as well as the ones so corny that we groan as with a bad pun. My favorite from the big screen is when Shug tells Celie in *The Color Purple*, "I think it pisses God off when you walk by the color purple in a field and don't notice it."

Another personal favorite that guides my life and shapes my actions is, *Don't be surprised when people do what they always do.* And of course, because I talk so much, I love the Kikiyu proverb, *Talking to one another is loving one another.*

My sister has two proverbs framed on her walls. The *ruin of a nation begins in the homes of its people*, a Ghanaian proverb, and *He who does not cultivate his field, will die of hunger*, a Guinean proverb. Each time I visit her home, I reconsider these ideas anew. Proverbs do not grow old and stale. They, like classic literature and scriptures, remain current and fresh, alive, and relevant.

Sometimes just the right word can lift our spirits, guide our entire lives, start us down a new, yet unclear path, and focus our work.

What words have sparked an epiphany, a revelation, a great insight for you? What words guide your life and inform your eyes and your heart on how to see the world? What words are taped to your refrigerator and framed on your walls?

The Quick Write Lesson

1. Sharing Mentor Texts

Share with your students one of the suggested picture books or another of your own choosing based on a proverb. Invite the students to discuss the particular proverb involved in the story, how the story illustrated that proverb, and how it impacted the characters. Invite them to think about how this proverb relates to their own lives.

Share a select list of proverbs with your writers based on their ages and interests. The websites listed in Additional Resources may be helpful with choosing appropriate selections. Invite them to discuss the meanings of those on your list and to share others that they know.

- Where do they hear proverbs?
- How do proverbs affect their lives?

If your students come from other countries, they may want to share native proverbs with which the group may not be familiar.

- Do their families have certain sayings that guide their lives?
- Do they as individuals live by a particular proverb or saying?

2. Writer's Notebook

Ask your students to collect proverbs over the next few days and to jot down two or three of their personal favorites. They may want to try their hand at creating their own by revising an actual proverb or creating original ones. Students will enjoy sharing these with the group.

3. Quick Write Possibilities

Invite students to write a piece based on a proverb.

They may want to write an essay or information report about the veracity, the impact, or the origin of a particular proverb.

Or

They may want to write a story in which a proverb plays an important role for the main character.

Additional Resources

The websites below are comprehensive resources for locating proverbs and sayings:

- http://www.great-quotes.com/
- http://www.quotesandsayings.com/proverbial.htm
- http://www.quotemountain.com/

It Takes a Village by Jane Cowen-Fletcher

Yemi is proud to Be watching her brother "all by herself." As the story unfolds, however, it becomes clear that so many more are also watching.

It Could Always Be Worse: A Yiddish Folktale by Margot Zemach

In this familiar tale, a wise rabbi gives strange advice to a man complaining of a noisy, overcrowded home. He shows the man that it could be much worse so that in the end he appreciates his home just as it is.

"Time Flies When You're Deconstructing Aphorisms"

This NPR story about Julian Baggini's book, *Should You Judge This Book by Its Cover? 100 Fresh Takes on Familiar Sayings and Quotations,* analyzing ways we use and misuse familiar sayings, can be read or heard at http://www.npr.org/templates/story/story.php?storyId=126807556.

Opportunity Costs

Grades 4–12

Poetry, Personal Essay

Effect of Decisions We Make

- If I do this, then what?

Background for the Teacher

We relish the idea of choices—we want to be able to decide—taking all issues into account, weighing the options, making our lists of benefits and downsides. The more choices there are, the happier we are, although the more choices there are makes our final decision all the more difficult. Not having a widely varied menu from which to select makes choosing easy and life simpler—but we are not always satisfied with easy.

While studying economics with my fifth graders, one of the concepts I had to introduce was *opportunity costs,* the notion that every business decision comes with a cost—the choices that were not made or given up at the very moment you chose. For example, when you chose to buy this piece of land for your next building instead of that one, the one not purchased is the opportunity cost. In student language, when given a choice of the movies or skating, and you choose skating, then the movies are your opportunity cost.

This idea of having lost a choice forever is intriguing to me. What are all the things I have not chosen in life? What is the sum total of all the choices and the opportunity costs I have ever made in life? Will I ever get those opportunities back again? I think about jobs I chose and those I turned down. I think about purchases made and those items left in the store. I think . . . and the list goes on as I survey my past decisions and wonder what they cost me and what if I had chosen differently. Would the opportunity costs be significantly different? How would this affect my life then and now?

The Quick Write Lesson

1. Sharing Mentor Texts

Review and discuss the concept of opportunity costs with your students and help them develop several examples illustrating the concept from their own lives or classrooms. Then share with them Robert Frost's well-known poem, "The Road Not Taken," read by Robert Frost, available at http://www.poets.org/viewmedia.php/prmMID/15717. You may also want to share "There but for the Grace" by Wislawa Symborska, in *Teaching With Fire* or available at http://tylerpoems.blogspot.com/. Both poems deal with the "what-ifs" of taking various paths and making particular choices.

- What are the choices that the poets face?
- How do they make their decisions?
- How does this connect to their own decisions for and against particular paths?

2. Writer's Notebook

Ask your writers to list as many important decisions as they can that they have made in life. Suggest leaving a space after each one, and in that space, begin to list the opportunity costs or the rejected choices. For example, adult writers may have opted to move to another state at one point, at the same time rejecting their current job or another local job opportunity. Continue listing choices and their costs until each one has a substantial list.

3. Quick Writing Possibilities

Ask each writer to choose a life-changing decision made in life. Suggest writing a poem in which they speculate about the road actually chosen and the other roads not taken. Consider all the what-ifs, the emotions of choosing, and the costs.

Additional Resources

Teaching With Fire: Poetry That Sustains the Courage to Teach, Sam M. Intrator and Megan Scribner, editors

The Things They Carried

Grades 6–12 (Adapts for 4–5)

Personal or Persuasive Essay

Essentials in Our Lives and the Lives of Others

- What things are essential for us personally? For soldiers?

Background for the Teacher

What is necessary to carry with us as we leave home, whether we go around the corner, to school, to work, or to a friend's house or venture far beyond our usual stomping ground? There are certainly things we deem essential, and there are things that we simply must have with us, not of necessity, but for habit, comfort, or sentimentality. One of the minor fears we face in life is having the contents of our pockets, bags, or backpacks revealed, not because we are carrying anything illegal or illicit, but because the items reveal much about our personal preferences and inner life. What will people think of the implications revealed by our personal items? We may feel that same dread as our luggage is about to be searched at customs. And surely there is no greater affront than knowing someone has gone through our personal things without our knowledge or permission.

Thinking about what we need in specific settings and situations is just good planning and preparation. I don't go to the grocery store without a list, my coupons, and my charge card. Attending a birthday party at someone's home means bringing a gift, a card, and perhaps even a dish of food or favorite beverage. Coming to writing class means bringing writing utensils and notebooks or computers and textbooks. The list of necessities for playing a sport or for traveling gets longer. Comedian George Carlin pokes gentle fun at us and our necessary things in his famous routine dealing with the "stuff" we keep and then carry around as we move or travel.

As they go into battle, soldiers also consider what they need, both in combat and at rest. Tim O'Brien gives us a glimpse of soldiers' gear in his famous short story, "The Things They Carried," set in Vietnam (see O'Brien, page 2, if you would like to read this detailed list to your students).

The usual things the soldiers carry can be divided into three main categories: standard equipment issued to every soldier based on assignment, location, and current legislation, personal items needed for hygiene and comfort, and also sentimental items and things carried for luck. So a toothbrush and a tattered letter may occupy the same space and both be considered essential by an individual soldier. Later passages of O'Brien's story list items of a more personally meaningful nature—the torn love letters, as well as chatty letters that were not written out of love, the pictures of loved ones, and amulets kept for luck or remembering a safer time.

In order to avoid fatigue, soldiers can obviously carry only a limited amount. Every item must have a valid reason for inclusion. There is a scene in the movie *Platoon* when the squad leader in Vietnam dumps unnecessary items from Charlie Sheen's rucksack.

In March 2011, hearings were held in which Defense Secretary Robert Gates and Joint Chiefs chairman Mike Mullen talked to lawmakers about the importance of funding appropriate and adequate state-of-the-art equipment for our soldiers. Several years earlier, in 2004, the Senate approved reimbursement of soldiers who purchased their own protective armor for combat. In 2006, however, the Pentagon banned the use of protective armor not issued by the military, citing the inability to guarantee the quality and safety of commercially purchased armor. This is a continuing debate within military and legislative circles.

The Quick Write Lesson

1. Sharing Mentor Texts—Grades 6–12

Invite your writers to discuss issues that concern soldiers and how they are equipped. This conversation may include reflection upon which items would be most essential for combat and survival and which sentimental items would also be important. Share with them an excerpt (pp. 1–6) or all of Tim O'Brien's short story "The Things They Carried."

You may also want to share selected sections of *Soldier* by Simon Adams, which gives detailed descriptions and illustrations of various kinds of dress, equipment, and weaponry used by our modern soldiers in the United States, and also items used in the past and in other nations and empires.

If you are currently studying a specific war, you may also want to share and compare dress and equipment of soldiers from that particular period.

There has been much discussion in the last several years about what the government will pay for, what soldiers are paying for, and what is allowed. You may also want to discuss the ongoing debate about funding for equipment for our soldiers. Small groups may want to discuss the following questions:

- What items are deemed necessary for our soldiers today?
- Should soldiers be allowed to buy additional equipment?
- Should soldiers have to buy their own additional equipment?
- Is there any item that soldiers should not carry or not be allowed to carry into battle?

Sharing Mentor Texts—Grades 4–6

Invite your writers to discuss issues that concern soldiers and how they are equipped. This conversation may include reflection upon which items would be most essential for combat and survival and which sentimental items would also be important. You may want to point out how important letters are to a soldier far from home, if your students do not mention this. Share excerpts or the entire book *Letters to a Soldier* by David Falvey and Julie Hutt's fourth-grade class. Each two-page spread includes a letter from a student to Falvey and his response. After reading, invite students to further discuss the importance of letters to soldiers and to the people who have written to them, citing information from both Falvey's responses and the students' letters, as well.

2. Writer's Notebook

In their writer's notebooks, invite students to think about the things they feel are necessities in their own lives.

Invite them to list the contents of their pockets, purses, or backpacks. Beside each item they may want to note its significance. Is there a pattern within the items that implies something about them personally?

3. Quick Write Possibilities

Reminding your writers of the writing work and discussions above, present them with several possible writing options:

Invite them to write about an item they carry with them. This may include a description of the item, its personal significance, and an explanation of its necessity. In the context of other items carried, how does this item fit?

Or

Invite them to write about things that soldiers carry. This writing may address the following issues and questions:

- What items are deemed necessary for our soldiers today?
- Should soldiers be allowed to buy additional equipment?
- Should soldiers have to buy their own additional equipment?
- Is there any item that soldiers should not carry into battle?

Elementary students may want to deal solely with letters and why they are important if they have read *Letters to a Soldier.*

The Mentor Texts

The Things They Carried by Tim O'Brien

This collection of related stories, considered a novel by many, is about a platoon of American soldiers in the Vietnam War.

Soldier (DK Eyewitness Books) by Simon Adams

This is a comprehensive compendium of information about soldiers throughout the ages, from medieval knights to modern troops. It includes descriptions and illustrations, including such topics as military dress, weaponry, and vehicles as well as training and missions.

Letters to a Soldier by David Falvey and Julie Hutt's Fourth Grade Class

Mrs. Julie Hutt's fourth-grade class in Roslyn, New York, wrote to a soldier in Iraq to thank him for his service and to find out what it's like to be a U.S. soldier. In the introduction, Falvey explains how important these letters were to him because they allowed him "to forget the serious nature of my life in Baghdad." The children's letters and artwork with the soldier's responses are included.

Additional Resources

Can Soldiers Buy Extra Gear? by Daniel Engber (http://www.slate.com/ articles/news_and_politics/explainer/2006/01/can_soldiers_buy_ extra_gear.html)

This regular column, Explainer, addresses questions related to news and current events. The particular article was posted on January 3, 2006, and deals with reimbursement for military equipment purchased by soldiers.

The History We Know

Grades 4–12

Expository or Personal Essay

Misconceptions About History

- What misconceptions do we have about events in history?

Background for the Teacher

As a young person, I learned from history books that Columbus "discovered" America and that George Washington cut down a cherry tree and refused to lie to his father about his guilt. Generations following me learned that Rosa Parks wouldn't give up her seat on a Montgomery bus because she was simply "tired." Yesterday, and still today, our history books are fraught with misconceptions, historical untruths, and myths, as well as missing voices and perspectives. Sometimes the omissions are due to simplification for younger readers or space limitations. Other misconceptions are caused by the connotations of word choices. And still others are due to presenting a particular slice of history in isolation, without the background or foreground. And sadly, some errors are due to the deliberate mis-telling in the interest of or to the detriment of a particular group.

The words we use to tell the story of events, situations, and circumstances, communities, people, and nations determine how we think about the events and people involved. If an enslaved people is described as unintelligent, childlike, and happy, singing as they work, then it is easier in the minds of both slave owners and witnesses to excuse the atrocity of slavery.

If Columbus discovered America, it must mean that the people living there were lost before he arrived and needed the help of outsiders to be a complete and thriving society—and at the same time, ignores the fact that Columbus himself was the one lost.

If Rosa Parks was simply tired, this ignores her agency in the situation, and the forethought of her entire community, as they prepared for the subsequent boycott and legal battle that followed this bus incident. And what about the people who refused to give up their seats before her and were arrested, such as 15-year-old Claudette Colvin? We don't hear some stories in history unless we dig deeper and use multiple sources.

My students were surprised to learn from Howard Zinn's *Young People's History of the United States* (Vols. 1 and 2) that Native Americans had been made slaves before Africans, that the Declaration of Independence did not declare independence for everyone in the colonies, and that the Emancipation Proclamation did not emancipate all slaves in the United States. They were appalled to learn that people they were told in their social studies book were the first ones here were removed forcibly from their homeland and marched many miles away to small reservations during the event that became known as the Trail of Tears. They returned to our history book with new curiosity about what other stories were missing and what other facts and events had an underside or alternative rendering.

The Quick Write Lesson

1. Sharing Mentor Texts

Discuss how certain events in history come to be written or told in specific ways. To illustrate, you may want to use a particular event at your school or in your community and discuss who might write about it and how.

- Who might be the most logical person to report?
- Where might the reports be shared or published?
- Who might be left out of the narrative?
- Who is a person who may not even be asked about the event?

Use the related text sets below to discuss one event in history. Selections below deal with Columbus's landing in the Americas or Rosa Parks and the Montgomery Bus Incident as well as Claudette Colvin.

As an alternative, you may select an event from history that you are currently studying. Read several brief accounts of the event. In either case, you will want to discuss which information given by the author helps you understand the situation. Discuss the words that the author uses to describe the event.

- How do they determine how we think about the story?
- Whose perspective is represented?
- What else do you want to know?
- What has the author omitted?

Discuss where other information can be obtained about this event.

2. Writer's Notebook

Invite your writers to list events in history or science that they had always understood in a particular way and found out later that what they believed was incomplete, or partially or completely wrong. Next to each item on the list indicate the correct information and sources of both if possible.

You may want to allow time for students to discuss their lists in pairs or small groups. They may be interested in the similarities and differences in their individual lists.

3. Quick Write Possibilities

Invite your students to think about a recent event that you have been studying in social studies or history. It may come from the lists they have created above. Ask them to think about what surprised them about this event. They may compare what they have always thought with the actual events as recorded in their textbook and/or in other sources. They may also include how they came to know differently about this event and the effect the differences had on their own thinking and lives.

You may want to provide the Quad Entry Journal for Nonfiction (see Figure 2.1), which suggests ways to think and write about the perspectives of an author and the world in relationship to your own, to spark other writing related to this topic.

The Mentor Texts

Rosa Parks

Rosa Parks: My Story by Rosa Parks and Jim Haskins

If a Bus Could Talk: The Story of Rosa Parks by Faith Ringgold

Rosa by Nikki Giovanni and Bryan Collier

Figure 2.1 Whose Story? Whose World? What Lens?

Quad Entry Journal for Nonfiction	
What does the author know, believe, and feel?	*What does the author assume I know and believe and feel?*
Write a summary of the text (or an episode) from a perspective different than the author's or write from the perspective of a person related to the information but not included in the text. Write a dialogue between yourself and a person, place, or object in the text.	Write a poem/personal essay starting with *I believe* or *This I believe.*
What does this text as a whole say about the world?	*What is my own perspective?*
Write about the social justice issues addressed (or not addressed) in this text.	Write a letter to the author explaining your point of view. Include similarities and differences between your perspective and the author's.

Claudette Colvin

Claudette Colvin: Twice Toward Justice by Phillip Hoose

Claudette Colvin: The First to Keep Her Seat. *We Were There, Too! Young People in U.S. History* (pp. 214–217) by Phillip Hoose

Christopher Columbus

Encounter by Jane Yolen

Follow the Dream: The Story of Christopher Columbus by Peter Sis

Additional Resources

For Teachers

She Would Not Be Moved: How We Tell the Story of Rosa Parks and the Montgomery Bus Boycott by Herbert R. Kohl and Cynthia Stokes Brown

"The Politics of Children's Literature: What's Wrong With the Rosa Parks Myth?" by Herbert Kohl, *Rethinking Popular Culture and Media*, Elizabeth Marshall and Ozlem Sensoy, editors (a PDF copy is available at http://www.wou.edu/~ulvelad/courses/ED632Spring11/Assets/RosaParks.pdf)

General U.S. History

We Were There, Too! Young People in U.S. History by Phillip Hoose

A People's History of the United States: 1492–Present by Howard Zinn

A Young People's History of the United States: Columbus to the Spanish-American War (Vol. 1) by Howard Zinn, Rebecca Stefoff (adapter).

A Young People's History of the United States: Class Struggle to the War on Terror (Vol. 2) by Howard Zinn, Rebecca Stefoff (adapter).

Lies My Teacher Told Me: Everything Your American History Textbook Got Wrong by James W. Loewen

The Remains of the Day

Grades 4–12

Satire, Scientific Report or Article

Our Common Objects as Viewed by Archaeologists

- What will our common objects mean to archaeologists in the future?

Background for the Teacher

One hundred years from now when our descendants pick up our dead cell phones, broken hair dryers, or microwave ovens, will they be able to deduce what these items are and how we used them?

Archaeologists do just that with artifacts—tools and ornaments and art of another time—the remains of a former day. They study the artifacts and attempt to describe the culture and determine the what and why and how of an object. Sometimes they are correct in their speculations, but other times they are completely wrong. The misconceptions about the significance of artifacts and their functions can be humorous and have given rise to several well-known satires or parodies of archaeological, anthropological, and sociological reports. Written in mock scientific language, these parodies prove hilarious in their seriously erroneous analyses.

I was introduced to one of the first of such parodies in a sociology class. I was horrified at the customs detailed in "Body Rituals Among the Nacirema," only to discover that this famous satire by Horace Minor dealt with bath habits in which I myself participated. ("Nacirema" is "American" spelled backwards; once that is known, everything becomes clear in the article.) The scientific descriptions and details transformed daily American hygiene habits into elaborate and exotic—at the very least—and horrible sounding torture, at its worst. Sociologists, anthropologists, and others teaching about culture have been assigning this article and asking students to create and write about additional rituals and other discoveries about the Nacirema since the introduction of Minor's article in the June 1956 issue of *American Anthropologist*. A quick search on the Internet of "Nacirema" reveals many additional clever versions, written as such assignments, and also some subsequent "official" versions that have been published. Neil B. Thompson revisited the Nacirema after the fall of their civilization and published "The Mysterious Fall of the Nacirema in Natural History" in 1972. Later, in 1992, Gerry Philipsen examined the speech patterns of the Nacirema.

The Quick Write Lesson

1. Sharing Mentor Texts

Share "Body Rituals Among the Nacirema" with your group. Discussion about this article may include the way we view other cultures and their customs with an eye of superiority—thinking they are not like us. Your group may also discuss how the scientific writing structure, language, and vocabulary influence, either positively or negatively, what we think about the group of people.

To have the greatest effect in terms of truly considering how this article affects thinking, you will not want to reveal the true identity of the Nacirema until after the discussion, so that your writers will have the full impact of being influenced by perceived distance and scientific objectivity from a group of people that is actually themselves.

Once they know the secret, discussion of how the author achieved his desired effect would be helpful as students think about how to write their own satires of a normal, customary activity in their culture.

As either alternative or additional texts, you may share *Motel of Mysteries* by David Macaulay or *How Humans Make Friends* by Loreen Leedy. Both of these books are parodies, as well, in the above tradition.

2. Writer's Notebook

Ask writers to make a map or sketch of their bedroom, another room in their home, their classroom, or another room in your school. They should sketch in as much detail as possible and then begin to label items in the way an anthropologist or archaeologist might label them as they come upon them in the distant future.

You may want to remind them to be creative, but also to consider the authentic use of an item and how simply using alternative language to describe that very same use will present an alien perception of the item. For example, a hairbrush may be labeled Hair Catcher (especially if several hairs are stuck in the bristles), and likewise, a mirror might be labeled Instant Portrait Maker.

3. Quick Write Possibilities

Invite students to write a scientific report or article on their latest discovery of an item or their analysis of a particular cultural custom or activity based on one or more discovered items. Encourage them to include scientific structure, language, and vocabulary similar to the models. They may want to include information about the significance of their discovery. How will it influence other investigations, as well as modern life?

The Mentor Texts

"Body Rituals Among the Nacirema" by Horace Minor (https://www
.msu.edu/~jdowell/miner.html?pagewanted=all)

How Humans Make Friends by Loreen Leedy

Motel of Mysteries by David Macaulay

Additional Resources

Both of the following "shorts" included in *In Brief: Short Takes on the Personal*, edited by Judith Kitchen and Mary Paumier Jones, can be used to invite further reflection on artifacts and archaeology:

- *Artifacts of Memory* by Josephine Jacobson, pp. 270–272
- *Artifacts* by Brenda Miller, pp. 244–248

The Face of Reality

Grades 4–12

Persuasive Essay, Editorial Columns or Letters to the Editor

Reality TV Programs

> - What happens when cameras follow people around in their everyday lives?

Background for the Teacher

We are nosy. We like to see what other people say and do. Thus, reality TV has become a phenomenal success. Like the "stories" or soap operas that our grandmothers followed, these shows feed our hunger for knowing about other lives. It is fascinating to eavesdrop on private conversations and to peek in on interactions and relationships that usually remain behind closed doors and pulled curtains. During the screenwriters' strike, which began in November 2007 and lasted through February 2008, reality shows hit an all-time high, as they did not rely on traditional scripts. While the shows are not scripted in the usual sense, the producers have full control over the editing, which may or may not reflect accurately the totality of all film available. During the 100-day strike, a multitude of new reality shows hit the airwaves with varying degrees of popularity and success.

Reality shows run the gamut from showing the lives of tattoo artists, top models, and other celebrities to game shows involving road trips, dating, outdoor adventures, weight loss, substance-abuse rehab, or dancing. Some take us into worlds that we would not in real life enter, such as operating rooms, police beats, and truckers rolling across frozen lakes. Some of the most popular are game shows, such as *Big Brother* and *Survivor*, which have houseguests live together in a house, on a remote island, or some other location. Both premiering in 2008, these two shows ushered in our current reality show craze.

As a kid in the 1950s, I watched *Candid Camera*—and was always amazed at what people did when they didn't know a camera was there. Now I am equally amazed, and sometimes appalled, at what people do when they are positively aware that the camera and millions of people are watching. With these new shows, we have seen the rise to celebrity of heretofore unknown folks. They make the rounds on the talk shows, blog, write books, begin new businesses, and sometimes rise to genuine stardom from reality-show beginnings.

Children have gotten into the reality game, as well. *Kid Nation* was a reality show that premiered in 2007, featuring 40 kids, ages 8 to 15, who lived on a privately owned ranch. The premise of this show was that the kids would attempt to create a functioning society, including establishing a government. There are still websites devoted to this program. The whole concept reminded me of *Lord of the Flies*. As I remember, there were several controversies related to this show, including the fact that the participants missed school for the duration of the show, and one child was burned while cooking. I remember reading in the paper at the time that parents felt lines were fed to the children and scenes sometimes reshot to create particular effects, yet the kids were not treated as traditional actors or paid standard actors' fees.

Leonard Pitts Jr., columnist for the *Miami Herald*, along with others, questions the role that the TV reality spotlight played in the suicide death of Russell Armstrong, husband to reality star Taylor Russell of *Real Housewives of Beverly Hills*. According to Pitts, "people around him blame it on the pressures of seeing his wife file for divorce as his finances crumbled. . . ." This all transpired in public view, not only on the TV screen, but in the blogs and related media connected with the show and its cast of characters. Is TV to blame or would this have happened anyway? Do we have the right to know about every little detail of the reality stars' lives? Why exactly do they put themselves in this position?

And how is this affecting our students? A recent research study by the Girls Scouts has documented the detrimental effects of reality TV shows on girls.

The Quick Write Lesson

1. Sharing Mentor Texts

Select an editorial or column from those below or from a recent magazine, newspaper, or online site about reality shows in general or a particular reality show that is of interest to your students in particular. Discuss how the columnist presents his or her views—what facts are provided, how the opinion is supported, the effectiveness of examples chosen, and questions readers still have concerning the writer's presentation or the issue in general. You may want to read more than one article to compare views, style, and techniques.

You may also want to share the findings of the recent Girl Scout study (see link below) and discuss both the negative and positive findings of this study. Invite your students to share how their own views connect and relate to the findings.

2. Quick Write Possibilities

Invite your writers to compose an editorial or persuasive piece about reality shows. Ask them to explain their opinion, supported with facts, evidence, examples, and other information. Also include why this all matters—why it is important and to whom.

Or

Invite your students to respond to the findings of the Girl Scout study, indicating how the findings affect them, whether they have questions about any of the findings, and further research they may want to see conducted.

Mentor Texts

Real to Me: Girls and Reality TV (Girl Scout Research Institute Study-2011) (http://www.girlscouts.org/research/pdf/real_to_me_factsheet.pdf)

"Reality Shows Have Real Consequences," by Leonard Pitts Jr., Columbus Dispatch, August 22, 2011 (http://www.dispatch.com/content/ stories/editorials/2011/08/22/reality-shows-have-real-consequences .html)

"Local Columnist Joe Banner on Reality TV and the Arab Spring" by Joe Banner, *Winston Salem Journal*, August 31, 2011 (http://www2.journalnow .com/news/2011/aug/31/wsopin02-joe-banner-guest-columnist-reality- tv-at—ar-1345181/)

"Reality TV Shows Have Poisonous Effect on Kids" "by Esther J. Cepeda, *Chicago Sun-Times*, October 24, 2011 (http://www.600words .com/2011/10/reality-tv-shows-have-poisonous-effect-on-kids.html)

Information about Kid Nation available at http://en.wikipedia.org/wiki/ Kid_Nation

Reality TV International Debate Education Association (http://www.idebate .org/debatabase/topic_details.php?topicID=823)

This site includes comprehensive data, both pro and con, on reality TV shows, with a host of helpful links if students want to do more detailed research on this topic.

Pros and Cons of Reality TV Shows, The First Post. The Week. (2008, October 28) (http://www.theweek.co.uk/tv/35579/pros-and-cons-reality-tv-shows)

Metaphors: Seeing the World in Other Words

Grades 4–12

Personal or Persuasive Essay

Metaphors

> • How do metaphors color the way we see the world?

Background for the Teacher

Everyone naturally uses metaphors as we try to make sense of our world and articulate our understandings of our journey in this world. We use metaphoric language as symbols of larger concepts, beliefs, or issues, to define and describe ideas and situations, to argue our passionately held points, and as tools of learning and discovery.

Metaphors can help us imagine something more abstract and complex in familiar and concrete ways. When we were studying the Revolutionary War in social studies, our History Alive series provided an apt metaphor to help my students understand the complex relationship between the colonies and their founding country. There was no student who did not quickly grasp the comparison to a parent-child relationship as they considered the protection and provision provided by Great Britain, the process of rule-setting, the rebellion of the colonies, the ensuing punishments and squabbling among the sibling colonies, and final independence. They were able to return to that metaphor and extend it to include each new piece of information and event, with both familiarity and understanding, as we discussed the complex concepts and relationships related to the revolutionary period. Metaphor often goes both ways—my students also gained new understanding of the parent-child relationship, as well, as they used this extended metaphor for learning about a historical period.

America itself has sometimes been described metaphorically as a *melting pot*, connoting the way that folks came to this country with the goal of assimilating and also knowing this was expected of them by those already here. More recently, however, educators and other social scientists describing this process of immigration and integration in America have been prone to use the descriptively more accurate term of *salad*. Each metaphor shapes our thinking in particular ways. If we are indeed a melting pot, our differences are no longer visible, yet they contribute to the final dish in some unidentified way. If instead we are a salad, then we recognize and appreciate each difference, as it remains visible, while still contributing to and enhancing the final dish in a visible and positive way. If each of these two metaphors is extended, what else does it say about our nation and its people? What actions might we take based on the particular metaphor that we accept as reality?

Metaphors rest on direct or implicit comparisons by equating one thing to another, based on perceived similarities. Metaphors we use intentionally, and sometimes unconsciously, shed light on our thinking. For this reason, spies want to use our metaphors to determine our world views and, perhaps, ultimately to shape both our thinking and our actions. The Metaphor Program is currently being researched and developed by the Intelligence Advanced Research Projects Activity (IARPA), a small research intelligence agency of the U.S. government. They want to understand how speakers of English and other languages, including Farsi, Russian, and Spanish, understand the world by analyzing use of metaphors in their ordinary conversation.

The thought is that by understanding the metaphors, we may understand the beliefs and thoughts of particular cultures, based on their preferred or predominant metaphoric images. Research studies by Paul Thibodeau and Lera Boroditsky (2011) have shown that metaphors can influence how we think about topics and what related actions we subsequently suggest.

For more on the Metaphor Program and research studies by Thibodeau and Boroditsky and about metaphors, see the suggested articles listed below in Additional Resources

The Quick Write Lesson

1. Sharing Mentor Texts

Talk about common metaphors with your students. There are sets of metaphors built around just one word, such as these "wolf" phrases (a wolf in sheep's clothing, crying wolf, wolfing down food), or they can describe an entire situation or concept. (The whole world is a stage. Life is one big party. Silence is golden.) Invite students to share common metaphors. Discuss with them how these metaphors help us think about the similarities being compared.

Share one or two of the books suggested below with your writers to consider metaphors for school, the world, or poetry and writing. After sharing an excerpt or the entire book, invite students to analyze metaphors they encountered in the texts.

- What elements are being compared?

Discuss whether these are apt comparisons.

- What are the similarities?
- Where does the metaphor fail or begin to break down?
- What other metaphors are related to the same topic or concept?

Or

High school students may be interested in reading an article in *The Atlantic* on the Metaphor Program and discussing potential advantages and disadvantages of such an endeavor.

- How could this program help our society?
- What are potential dangers to our world?

2. Writer's Notebook

Select one word and list all the metaphors that are built around that one word.

- How are they similar?
- How are they different?
- What is being compared?

Example: Eggs—*don't put all your eggs in one basket, walking on eggshells*

Example: Boat—*miss the boat, rock the boat, sink the boat*

What are common metaphors for the world, school, or writing? List words that are associated with these concepts.

3. Quick Write Possibilities

Invite students to choose and define a metaphor for the world, school, writing, or a topic related to your current areas of study. They may revisit their earlier list from their writer's notebook for ideas. In their essay they should explain their metaphor and why they feel it is an appropriate one. One possible and obvious way to begin their essay is to simply state their metaphor in simple terms, such as "The whole world is a stage," and then expound on their idea.

Or

Invite students to write a persuasive piece about the Metaphor Program. How do they think it will benefit our world and help to understand cultures? What are potential dangers and reasons they think the project should not proceed?

The Mentor Texts

"Why Are Spy Researchers Building a 'Metaphor Program'"? by Alexis Madrigal, *The Atlantic.com*, May 2011 (http://www.theatlantic.com/technology/archive/2011/05/why-are-spy-researchers-building-a-metaphor-program/239402/#slide1)

Metaphors We Think With: The Role of Metaphor in Reasoning by Paul Thibodeau and Lera Boroditsky, *PLoS ONE* (http://www.plosone.org/article/info%3Adoi%2F10.1371%2Fjournal.pone.0016782)

World/Life

Nothing Ever Happens on 90th Street by Roni Schotter

If the World Were a Village by David J. Smith

School

Once Upon an Ordinary Day by Colin McNaughton

Hooray for Diffendoofer Day by Dr. Seuss with Jack Prelutsky and Lane Smith

Poetry/Writing

A River of Words: The Story of William Carlos Williams by Jen Bryant

Nothing Ever Happens on 90th Street by Roni Schotter

Additional Resources

For Teachers

Metaphorical Way of Knowing by Sharon L. Pugh, Jean Wolph Hicks, and Marcia Davis

Metaphors and Analogies: Power Tools for Teaching Any Subject by Rick Wormeli

3

Passion, Power, and Purpose

Writing to Change the World

What do we want to say out loud to the world? How do we get people to listen? The quick writes in this section examine ways to raise our voices in our world to effect change, to identify injustice, to heal. These quick writes challenge us to address the world with our words and consider the transformative effect of our words on the world. They lead to

- Personal and persuasive essays
- Poetry
- Speeches
- Other public-focused writing

Rites and Righteous Celebrations: Celebrating Events in Our Lives With Special Words

Grades 4–12

Speech, Poetry

Remembering and Celebrating Special Events

- What words do we use to honor and remember special days and events?

Background for the Teacher

When Cho Seung-Hui killed 32 of his classmates and teachers at Virginia Tech on April 16, 2007, and then shot himself, I immediately became obsessed with understanding who this man was and how writing related to this tragedy. Why? Because two years earlier he had been a student in the writing class of my favorite poet, Nikki Giovanni. At that time she and her students recognized an indefinable, yet disturbing and eerie quality in his writing. Nikki had Seung-Hui removed from her class after frightened students complained about him and attendance finally dropped from 70 to seven. She refused to obey the pressure to make public the poetry he had written in her class. A quick search on the Internet, however, easily produced not the controversial poems, but copies of his nightmare plays full of violence and death and obscenities.

Ultimately, though, it was not the horrible imaginings and the graphic machinations of this sick young man that impressed me, but the healing and peace brought by the short poem-speech in which Nikki Giovanni addressed the gathered Virginia Tech mourners and survivors on April 18. Neither she nor the convocation audience predicted the way her poetry would become the healing agent for this mourning, confused community. By the next day, her words were plastered everywhere—hanging on walls on homemade posters, imprinted on T-shirts worn by sobbing students, blaring from whole-page memorial spreads in newspapers, and pervading the Internet, where, in addition to transcripts of the text, audio versions were readily available as well. The television showed the convocation address multiple times in its entirety.

Her poem was only 258 words and took only one minute and 40 seconds to present. Yet those few words demonstrated the power to heal, memorialize, celebrate, and touch not only the Virginia Tech community but the watching world as well. Her simple refrains, *We are Virginia Tech!* and *We will prevail!* became both balm and rallying cry simultaneously.

How do we choose words for significant occasions? What is required to invite or incite, to unite, to remind or to mark the day?

For marchers on Washington in 1963, it was Martin Luther King preaching, *I have a dream.*

For those witnessing the inauguration of William Jefferson Clinton in 1993, it was Maya Angelou challenging us, *Here on the pulse of this new day.*

For those attending a women's rights convention in Akron, Ohio, in 1851, it was Sojourner Truth asking, *Ain't I a woman?*

For those in Gettysburg listening to Lincoln, it was, *Four score and seven years ago. . . .*

Kennedy captured us by urging, *Ask not what your country can do for you, but what you can do for your country.*

For the Osage in the winter of 1811–1812, it was Tecumseh urging, *Brothers—We must be united, we must smoke the same pipe. . . .*

For listeners to Barack Obama's nomination acceptance speech, it was, *The time is now.*

And then there are also words repeated so often in our lives at celebratory rites that we know them by heart, and they signal both the universal event and our response.

At weddings, the drama begins as the celebrant intones, *Dearly beloved, we are gathered here today. . . .*

It is the rhythm and sometimes rhyme; it is the repeated refrain that calls us to rise to the occasion, to collectively remember, and to stand in unity with the speaker—on our feet and in our hearts. It is the power of the words, the metaphoric images that infuse our minds with the spirit of the day and the collective strength of being there together as one. As humans in society, one way we create community is by honoring our special days—good and bad, expected and unexpected—with words we especially construct for the occasion. We gather to celebrate with words the routine celebrations of life's natural changes and the extraordinarily special days.

The Quick Write Lesson

1. Sharing Mentor Texts

Share models of speeches, addresses, and commissioned poetry from significant events. You may want to start with those mentioned above. You will find a large selection of speeches at the following sites:

- http://www.famousquotes.me.uk/speeches/index.htm
- http://www.americanrhetoric.com/

Nikki Giovanni's "We Are Virginia Tech" speech can be found at http://www.vt.edu/remember/archive/giovanni_transcript.html.

We want our students to begin to understand the power of strong and stirring words. With your students, identify what makes each model speech powerful and memorable.

- Which lines stand out?
- Is it the word choice, the sentence structures that makes the speech powerful?
- Is it the refrain or a particularly vivid image or metaphor that captures our attention?
- What makes us, years later, remember a particular line?

2. Writer's Notebook

Invite your students to list possible events on chart paper or in their notebooks. Beside each event, they may also want to list the purpose of the indicated speech and the emotion they are dealing with either for themselves or for the audience, as well as the desired or resulting emotion. Students may want to take time to share either in the larger group or in small groups and add to their lists from this sharing.

3. Quick Write Possibilities

Ask the students to identify an important event in history or a recent event in the news. Then invite them to write a speech or poem appropriate for their chosen event. Remind them to use in their own writing the features identified as making the models powerful and memorable.

Or

Students may instead want to identify an important personal event and write words to speak on that day in honor of this event. Younger children may be asked to write words to say on their birthdays or the birthday of a relative. They may choose instead another important family event such as Mother's Day or a family reunion. A recent school event, an awards assembly, or being chosen good citizen could be selected, as well as receiving their first communion or the first day they read a book by themselves.

Additional Writing Possibilities

- Locate books of primary sources that include speeches of historical events as you study particular segments of history. Students can analyze them and write new speeches in today's language.
- Commission students to present speeches they have written on special occasions.
- Create your own classroom celebrations to honor with special poems, speeches, and stories.

Additional Resources

Celebrations: Rituals of Peace and Prayer by Maya Angelou

Included in this collection of Angelou's work are poems commissioned or written for specific occasions: "On the Pulse of Morning," read at President Clinton's 1993 inauguration; "Amazing Peace," presented at the 2005 lighting of the National Christmas Tree at the White House; "A Brave and Startling Truth," which marked the 50th anniversary of the United Nations; "Mother," which honors the woman who gives us life and raises us. Also included are poems written for other celebrations, public and private: a bar mitzvah wish to her nephew, a birthday greeting to Oprah Winfrey, and a memorial tribute to the late Luther Vandross and Barry White. A CD with the poet reading these works is included with the book.

I Have a Dream by Martin Luther King Jr.

This beautiful picture book presents Dr. Martin Luther King Jr.'s speech in its entirety, with a foreword by the late Coretta Scott King and paintings by 15 Coretta Scott King Award and Honor Book Artists.

I'm in Charge of Celebrations by Byrd Baylor and Peter Parnall

The young woman in this picture book creates and celebrates ordinary yet remarkable events in the desert, such as Coyote Day, The Time of Falling Stars Day, and Dust Devil Day.

Sweet, Sweet Memory by Jacqueline Woodson and Floyd Cooper

A little girl is urged to speak about her grandfather on the day of his funeral, as others are sharing stories and memories. It is his own words that she is finally able to share: *Everything and everyone goes on and on.* These words are repeated throughout the book as everyone remembers Grandpa's approach to life.

My Big Words

Grades 4–12

Letter to the Editor, Editorial Column, Persuasive Essay, Poetry

Power of Well-Chosen Words

- How can well-chosen words effect change?

Background for the Teacher

Wanting to say something and not having just the right words is the most frustrating feeling. It's like trying to do home repairs without the necessary or appropriate tools. How could we repair a leaky pipe under our bathroom sink without a wrench or even being able to name that particular tool?

Words are useful for naming, explaining, and claiming what is ours.

Words that denigrate, devalue, or tear down an individual or collective group because of race, gender, nationality, sexual orientation, physical ability, or other characteristics can have effects reaching far beyond the moment the words were uttered. The N word shouted or whispered in just the right tone in a crowd led to the lynching of thousands. Other words have led to horrendous cases of gay bashing and other hate crimes.

Words can be devastatingly hurtful.

Much can be accomplished with the right word at the right time. A friend or pastor can comfort those enduring difficult situations or assuage grief for those in mourning with well-chosen words. Poets can spark a revolution with a metaphor. One voice, one word can move a multitude to action. A child speaks a careless word on the playground, and tears ensue. A husband offhandedly remarks on his wife's spreading shape, and silence for days is the result. Likewise, one affirming word, and a spirit is lifted. Love can turn on a smile, and a complimentary word can foster new life.

Words can heal and calm as speeches given following 9/11 by Mario Cuomo and others demonstrate. The words spoken by Nikki Giovanni after the Virginia Tech shooting proved to be a balm for all involved. (See the previous quick write, "Rites and Righteous Celebrations: Celebrating Events in Our Lives With Special Words.")

Words are the tools writers use to express themselves, to raise their voices in political and social situations, as well as to comfort and heal. Writers seek to harness the power of words.

Sometimes we know the words we want to say, but we are not sure how and where to utilize them to accomplish our purposes. *Who should I tell? How should I write this message?* Reading the words of others in similar situations can help us begin to envision our own words telling our hearts and minds to whomever needs to hear. Are we writing an editorial on the latest school board action or the governor's new budget or his proposed reforms for education? We can read editorials in the local newspaper to gain ideas on how to start—a structure or framework on which to lay our own words. Do we want to write a letter to the president about his health care initiatives or foreign policies? What has already been written to him? How do we address public officials? Looking at the correspondence available online or from other sources will be crucial to getting started with your own correspondence.

Words offer us a way to act as change agents in our world. Making conscious decisions about which words to use and how to use them can change our home, our neighborhood, our school, and our world.

The Quick Write Lesson

1. Sharing Mentor Texts

Share *The Boy Who Collected Words* by Roni Schotter with your students. Encourage them to begin to collect new, interesting, wonderful words in a section in their notebooks. I keep a list entitled WORDS in my computer to which I add any words, along with their definitions, that I like and want to keep for later use in my writing.

Choose one of the resources listed below to share. Each one shares how words are important in a famous person's life. Invite students to discuss how words were used in the person's life to bring about change.

For upper high school or adult groups you may also want to show and discuss the short film *What I Want My Words to Do to You*.

2. Writer's Notebook

Invite students to list or web ways they use words in daily life including purposes and outcomes. They may also make notes about the various types of writing they use, as well as listing people, places, circumstances, or situations in which they wish to see change. What changes? Sharing these with the group and listing on a chart or overhead may spark additional ideas for your writers.

3. Quick Write Possibilities

Invite students to write about what they want their words to do. Their writing may take the form of a poem or personal essay and include ideas from the writer's notebook activity—and include responses to the following questions:

- To whom are they speaking?
- What change do they wish to see?

They may want to include specific words they might say.

- What are the results of their words?

Or

They may want to choose a specific real situation in which they want to see a change and write to the appropriate person or entity regarding this issue. Their writing may take the form of a letter to the editor, editorial column, persuasive essay, or speech.

Mentor Texts

The Boy Who Collected Words by Roni Schotter

What I Want My Words to Do to You (Video)

This writing workshop with 15 women imprisoned for murder includes a final public performance with celebrities such as Mary Alice, Rosie Perez, and Glenn Close. For a three-minute movie trailer or preview along with access to several other clips from the film, go to http://www.youtube.com/watch?v=szBDN-Hp4PU. For a description, study guide, lesson plans, and purchase information related to this film, go to http://www.pbs.org/pov/whatiwant/.

Additional Resources

Abe's Honest Words: The Life of Abraham Lincoln by Doreen Rappaport

Martin's Big Words: The Life of Dr. Martin Luther King Jr. by Doreen Rappaport

I Have a Dream by Martin Luther King Jr. (an illustrated edition of the speech with a foreword by Coretta Scott King)

Well-known illustrators have collaborated to create this work of art.

The Color of My Words by Lynn Joseph

In the Dominican Republic, a young girl is called upon to write powerful words to speak for her village in the face of developments/rebellion.

"Letter to the World" by Emily Dickinson (poem)

Online Speeches and Letters Related to Social Justice and Civil Right Issues (http://www.sojust.net/speeches.html and http://www.sojust.net/letters.html)

The poem below was my response after watching the film *What I Want My Words to Do to You.*

My Words

I want my words
to span the distance
between
and be heard

or recognize the closeness
and unite us more.

I want my words
to lay bare the hidden
reasons for failure
and the subtle causes
of discontent.

I want my words
to awaken
new thoughts
new ideas
to move beyond
the has been
to open a door
to the can be.

I want my words
to rest
on solid rock
knowledge and wisdom
unseen richness and vision
reaching out to the one
who waits
for just a word.

I want my words
to chafe and arouse
to soothe and assuage
to lift and separate
good from evil
right from wrong
is from is not
can't from can.

I want my words
spoken softly
or screamed out loud
to return to me
carrying answers
having spoken and done
what only honest
words can do.

Encounters

Grades 4–12

Narrative, Poetry

New People or Groups Coming Together

> • What happens when different people or groups come together?

Background for the Teacher

We sometimes encounter people we know in unexpected places. My students are always both shocked and delighted to run into me outside of school. Upon meeting me in JCPenney in the local mall, one former student exclaimed, "*You* shop here too?" with wide-eyed surprise. This meeting outside class allowed him to realize that I led a normal life when not in school. Upon encountering me at the Ohioana Book Festival, another student realized, "Wow, you really love books all the time—not just at school!"

We often encounter people we don't know. What happens when two people or groups or nations or cultures come together? As individuals, we can come together and discover that we have interests and intentions in common. We may even have mutual friends or acquaintances. On the other hand, we may find the other person unlikable, disagreeable, or annoying, or for some other reason, we may not be able to connect with her in a positive way.

My students in fifth grade learn about Columbus's voyage to the New World. This encounter between two very different cultures resulted in what is called the Columbian Exchange, the process by which goods, ideas, cultures, and diseases moved between the East and West. Until relatively recent years, this encounter has been told predominantly from the European perspective using words like "discovery" and "manifest destiny" and "savages." Only in recent years have we begun to make history alive in the elementary and middle grades, through an inquiry approach and use of primary sources, attempting to gain understanding of all perspectives in historical events and situations. Until recently we did not even acknowledge that there might be perspectives different from those included in the textbook, media, and mainstream story.

As a teacher, not just in social studies, but in every text and lesson, I strive to foster critical literacy and thinking, to present and encourage discovery of more than one point of view, and to help students actively consider the impact of events and ideas. One effective way I have relied upon is through related literature—allowing books to tell as many sides of the stories as possible and then digging through the narratives and fleshing out the stories that still remain untold.

The Quick Write Lesson

1. Sharing Mentor Texts

We recently engaged in this type of "seeing all sides" activity as we read about Christopher Columbus in our social studies unit on early explorers. To follow up on the more traditional story from the textbook, we read together *Follow the Dream: The Story of Christopher Columbus* by Peter Sis. Despite the fact that this book tells the traditional story from Columbus's point of view, the students were shocked to learn the additional fact that his crew wanted to turn back and that Columbus kept two logs, so the men would not realize how far they had traveled. So even in versions of the "known story" there is more to know and investigate. We then turned to *Encounter* by Jane Yolen for a different view. Her book tells of Columbus's landing through the eyes a young native boy. When we finished reading, one of the discussion points was the idea that many characters were pictured but did not speak in the story. Also there were characters that would have had to have been a part of the story, yet were not even shown. For example, in *Encounter*, as the little boy is telling the story, his mother and father are never pictured, nor do they speak, although you know they must be there in the events. To foster discussion and reflection, I asked,

- Who is telling the story?
- Who spoke and acted in the story?
- Who is not talking, and who is not even seen?

An additional critical question is

- What impact does this event have? On whom?

You may want to share this book or similar texts with your students, asking similar questions in order to begin to closely examine all possible perspectives.

2. Quick Write Possibilities

After reading *Encounter* or another book to your students in which there are several points of view and many characters with whom they can identify, invite them to identify one character to consider more closely. It may be a character that was actually in the text or a character inferred by the events. You may find it helpful to allow your writers time to brainstorm and share characters from which to choose. Then invite them to write as that person—a narrative or poem or other piece of their choice. They may want to write about the events of the days told in the book, events prior to or following the events, or simply thoughts and opinions their character may have had related to the events.

One student chose the "zemis" (which is the little boy's personal stone god) as his character. I chose to be the father of the little boy who is telling the story and is carried off by Columbus's men as they set sail for home. "Encounter" is below and can be used as a mentor text.

The Mentor Texts

Encounter by Jane Yolen

Follow the Dream: The Story of Christopher Columbus by Peter Sis

Additional Resources

Yo! Yes! by Chris Raschka

A simple picture book with only two words on each page, which carry the meaning of this chance encounter between two young boys who don't know each other. This book is fun to read and play with the intonations.

Encounter

I am a Taino man—
important in my tribe.
I am wise and good,
honored by my people.
I always know what to do
And do what is right.
Yesterday they came—
those pale white men.
They grinned,
Showing their teeth.
We welcomed them
and feasted them
and smoked with them.

That is the way we do
when strangers come,
but these strangers . . .
are not from the earth.
Their eyes are cold
light and dead,
not warm and brown
and alive.

My son kept crying,
"Don't welcome them!"

We didn't listen because he is a child.

This morning before sunrise,
those strangers took four
of our strongest men . . .
and my young son.
And left.
My number one son
and my number three son—
my baby—gone.

We should have listened.
All we have left . . .
beads on a string and small bells.
Today I will pray
to my *zemis*
to guard my sons . . .
until they return.

Secrets

Grades 4–12

Personal Essay, Narrative

Secrets in Our Lives and the Lives of Others

- What are our secrets?
- How do they affect others?

Background for the Teacher

We have all been told information in confidence with the instructions not to tell anyone, only to discover that everyone already knows the information anyway. These kinds of secrets are usually gossip that people delight in sharing, whispering the delicious, titillating details amid giggles and wide-eyed mock shock and comments like, "No she didn't!"

Some secrets, however, are important to keep. In *January's Sparrow* by Patricia Polacco, a family is on the run, traveling on the Underground Railroad. The conductors and others who help them, as well as the family members themselves, must each be trusted to keep their secret. The lives and safety of each member of the family depend on this ability to maintain secrecy. It becomes second nature for them to avoid openness and honesty related to their travels and their background.

Keeping secrets is sometimes the greatest gift we can give another person. In my school there is a counseling group run by an outside social agency for children whose parent(s) may be alcoholic or in other situations that create painful homes. One boy who participates in the group shared with his classmates that it was a good place to talk, "because you could share your feelings and thoughts and they didn't tell." For him this sanctuary of peace and secrecy was important. He felt safe there to share what may not be voiced in any other venue. My best friend is that place for me, as is my prayer group.

Sometimes secrets are dangerous for the simple fact that they are almost always eventually revealed—leaving a wake of pain, mistrust, betrayal, and confusion. Family secrets are like that. The kind where lots of people know, but not the person directly affected—children who have never been told they are adopted or that somebody other than the person they call Daddy or Mommy is actually their parent. Or the kind of secret where an important human trait or a life fact or event has been hidden, such as race or terminal illness or a marital affair or an abortion.

We keep secrets because we cannot reveal our insecurities, our shortcomings, or our sinister deeds. We don't want to be embarrassed or laughed at. We keep our secrets to protect and be protected. We keep secrets to be liked. *Who would like us if they knew . . . ?* We keep secrets to be important. Information is power and control. We keep secrets to re-create the world in our own imagined vision.

Gifting another with secrecy can also be a pleasant and fun thing as we prepare a surprise party or trip or some other special gift for a friend, family member, or coworker. We keep those sorts of secrets with delightful anticipation of the time of revelation and the wonderful feelings our secret gift will bring.

And who can forget the secret childhood joy of having a secret place just your own, an attic corner or hidden "underplace"? Who can forget the collective delight in having a secret clubhouse or tree house, a secret place to meet with friends and plot against those not friends, siblings, or grown-ups, or simply to hang out without interruption and prying eyes?

Secrets are not just personal. The corporate world is bursting with top-secret information. Businesses are made or broken by secrets—including trade secrets that would ruin the tycoons if revealed. The recipe for Coca-Cola or KFC or a Big Mac's special sauce—we may have speculated about them or seen the coveted "real recipe" on the Internet.

Secrets are at the center of many good novels and movies. We love knowing what the characters in the story do not. We loved being surprised when the characters knew and we did not. We love secrets. We also hate them. It's the fodder for fights on the playground and arguments in the home. *Why didn't you tell me . . . ?*

As you read aloud books that involve secrets, there is always a collective "aaaahhh" as an unsuspected secret is revealed. We enjoy that moment of suspense and relief, that moment when all the puzzles come together. My husband and I saw *The Book of Eli* this past week. Together we "aaah-hhed" in satisfaction as the ultimate secret was revealed. We traced back in our heads and aloud to each other, examining the clues and prefiguring moments that registered with slight dissonance as we watched, but that we could not account for until we knew the secret.

Secrets can burden us beyond our deepest strength, and they can also give us the greatest pleasure. They can make us money or break us, destroy our reputations or motivate us to our greatest achievement. What is your greatest secret?

The Quick Write Lesson

1. Sharing Mentor Texts

Select one of the books below, or another story involving significant secrets, to share with your students. They may also want to consider how the secret is discovered and the ramifications of the discovery.

- Does this situation connect to their own lives?
- What would they have done in this situation?

2. Writer's Notebook

Invite students to list secrets. They can be funny or serious. They can be personal or group secrets. (One caution: If the secret involves someone else in the class or group, I always require that that person be consulted and permission obtained before including them in a piece of writing. I ask students to adhere to this policy for any pieces of writing involving others.

I apply this rule even for notebook activities and quick writes. It just keeps the peace—and avoids unnecessary humiliation, embarrassment, and anger.)

3. Quick Write Possibilities

Invite students to consider a secret about themselves or someone they know.

- Ask them to write a fictional story in which this secret plays an important role in the plot.
- How and why is the secret kept?
- Is this an appropriate decision?
- Does the secret get discovered? If so, how?

Or
Write a true narrative about a secret that is important in their own lives.

The Mentor Texts

Life-Changing Secrets

January's Sparrow by Patricia Polacco

Mississippi Morning by Ruth Vander Zee
   The main character discovers his own father is a Ku Klux Klansman.

Secret Places

Both books below include secret places in which children are able to either be alone or meet friends.

The Secret Garden by Frances Hodgson Burnett

Ziggy and the Black Dinosaurs by Sharon M. Draper

The Work of Our Hands

Grades 4–12

Essays, Poems

Our Hands Reveal Who We Are

- What do our hands show the world about who we are?

Background for the Teacher

We hold in our hands everything—literally. We use our hands constantly to accomplish the work we do, to take care of ourselves, and to help others. We all remember fondly those hands that fed us, cared for us, comforted us, and held our hands. Likewise, we remember those hands that were not so kind. Bill Withers sang about all the actions, both loving and sometimes disciplinary, of his grandmother in "Grandma's Hands." We talk about "hands on" work, meaning direct involvement in a project. New technological devices are touted as "hands-free," indicating they allow us to busy our hands in other ways, rather than holding the device while using it. Our hands, with their opposable thumbs, whether fat and new or gnarled and old, allow us to participate in life in a way most other creatures cannot. We take special care of our hands with hand soap and hand creams. We have entire businesses devoted to their beautification and care.

Hands are also a traditional subject for artists. A quick search on the Internet reveals numerous art books and collections containing sketches of hands in every possible pose and position. And then there is the most famous painting of hands, Michelangelo's famous ceiling painting in the Sistine Chapel, *The Creation of Adam,* which, at its center, shows the hand of God and the hand of Adam.

Our hands tell our story. We are young—our hands are small. We work hard—we may have calloused hands and dirt under our fingernails. Or we don't work hard—our hands are soft and flawlessly manicured. Our stress and nerves may have bitten our nails to the quick. Short nails may indicate a pianist or violinist. One art teacher I know always had smudges of color on her hands even when she was not at work. Our marital status is usually visible as a ring or lack of one on our hands. Our hands tell the world about us.

- What do you notice about your own hands?
- What story do they tell about you?
- What work are they destined to do?

The Quick Write Lesson

1. Sharing Mentor Texts

Invite your students to discuss why hands are important. Invite them to share how they use their own hands and consider whose hands are important to them.

Share *Dave the Potter: Artist, Poet, Slave* by Laban Carrick Hill with your writers. Ask them to notice the various ways that Dave uses his hands to create his pots of clay. The back matter tells about small poems that Dave etched on his pots. Discuss why he may have included these inscriptions. As they list the actions of his hands, they may also want to include adjectives that describe his hands and adverbs that describe how his hands are working.

For additional ideas about work that hands do, you may also want to share several selections from *Steady Hands: Poems About Work* by Tracie Vaughn Zimmer.

If you have read both texts to your students, you may want to invite students to discuss the differences in these two "containers"—both with contents about hands.

Sharing More Mentor Texts

You may want to share one or both of the short creative nonfiction pieces from *In Short:* "Hands" by Ted Kooser and/or "One Human Hand" by Li-Young Lee. Both of these essays focus on a close examination of a father's hands. Ralph Fletcher has included a similar short piece about hands entitled "My Fathers' Hands" in his collection, *Mentor Author, Mentor Texts.*

- How did these essayists see the hands of their fathers?
- What does each of these essays say about our connections to hands and the stories they tell?

2. Quick Write Possibilities

Invite your writers to write an essay in which hands are the focus. Students may want to write about the work that hands do or about a specific pair of hands that is important in some way to them. Encourage them to include both description and a particular point of view about the hands they have chosen to write about.

Resources

In Short: A Collection of Brief Creative Nonfiction edited by Judith Kitchen and Mary Paumier Jones:

"Hands" by Ted Kooser (pp. 128–130)

"One Human Hand" by Li-Young Lee (pp. 293–294)

Mentor Author, Mentor Texts: Short Texts, Craft Notes and Practical Classroom Uses by Ralph Fletcher:

"My Father's Hands" (p. 29)

Dave the Potter: Artist Poet Slave by Laban Carrick Hill

Steady Hands: Poems About Work by Tracie Vaughn Zimmer

Additional Resources

These Hands by Margaret H. Mason

Hands: Growing Up to Be an Artist by Lois Ehlert

I Call My Hand Gentle by Amanda Haan and Marina Sagona

"Prayer for My Unborn Niece or Nephew" by Ross Gay

This single poem, which also contemplates hands, is available at http://www.poets.org/viewmedia.php/prmMID/22600.

The poem below, written in response to this quick write, may also be shared as a mentor text.

Hands

I look at my hands
Hands that are not mine
They are there
at the end the arm
that I know to be mine.
But *these* hands—etched with tiny thin lines
dry and purple-veined
are foreign to my eyes.

The only features
I recognize are the uneven nails
bitten to the quick
with torn scrappy cuticles
the work of thinking
and worry
and sometimes idleness
and those rings that
remind me
of love
and love of the unique.

When did these elderly hands
replace my own

and force me to acknowledge
face to face
hand to hand
my own mortality?

Numbering Our Village

Grades 4–12

Expository or Persuasive Essays

People in Our World

> • Who are the people in our world?

Background for the Teacher

More than ever, we are connected as a global community. Modern media and technology, including the Internet, television, online news journals, streamed videos, podcasts, and webcasts, as well as more traditional media, keep us continuously connected to and aware of happenings, conditions, and attitudes in near and far parts of the world. We can monitor politics and government, economy and ecology, education and health, and other trends in the lives of our global neighbors. With Facetime on our cell phones or Skype on our computers, we can conveniently communicate and meet face-to-face with folks on the other side of the world. We are able to share and impact each other worldwide to an extent and at a pace never imagined before.

Early in each school year in my classroom, we began to consider this concept of global connectedness and interdependence by reading *If the World Were a Village: A Book About the World's People* by David J. Smith. This book reduces the nearly 7 billion people in the world to just 100 in order to more easily talk about our lives and who we are in the world, all in terms of this smaller village. This village is defined and described in statistics that sometimes confirm our thinking about the world and oftentimes startle us.

After allowing my students to choose the sections about which they were curious to be read aloud, I invite them to make notes as they listen, focusing on the following:

- What facts did they already suspect or know?
- What facts surprised them?
- What do the statistics mean or imply?
- What statistics were not included about which they wondered?

Typically, each year they are surprised by the number of people who are hungry in the world and those who are unable to read and also by the fact that a few people use most of the world's resources. They usually know or suspect that Christians and Muslims make up the largest religious groups. They usually guess, just by considering the dominating size of China on the map, that a large number of people in the world live in Asia. (You will want to have a world map handy as you consider the statistics—in order to consider at the very least, the location of places being discussed, but also, more critically speaking, to consider how geography, proximity to other nations, and other factors may influence the statistics.)

The information in this book leads to many discussions, and we pull the book out again and again throughout the year. One of the most important questions for us always becomes

- Why do you think this is true?

For example, the section on Ages ends with this statement:

- "While the number of children in the global village is shrinking, the number of elderly is growing."

We had a lively discussion on this, with students suggesting many possibilities—parents are having fewer children; some are dying of disease, famine, on violence; the elderly are living longer; medical care is better; and so forth.

To continue the conversation about global connections initiated by this book, we considered the diversity of nationalities, languages, and religions that made up our own classroom community. We also considered our families, foods we like to eat, and the homes in which we live. The students each completed forms collecting this information. Several students then collected, tabulated, and summarized the data on charts that we posted outside our room, announcing who was in our "village" (see Figures 3.1–3.9).

Figure 3.1

Figure 3.2

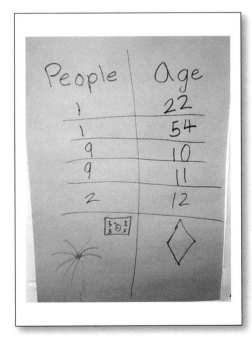

Figure 3.3

Figure 3.4

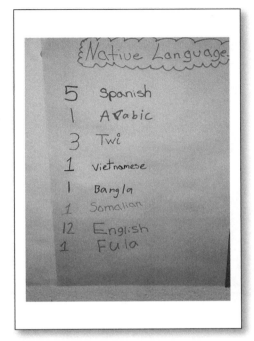

Figure 3.5

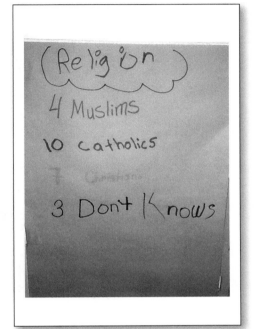

Figure 3.6

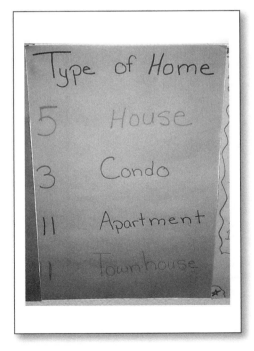

Figure 3.7

Figure 3.8

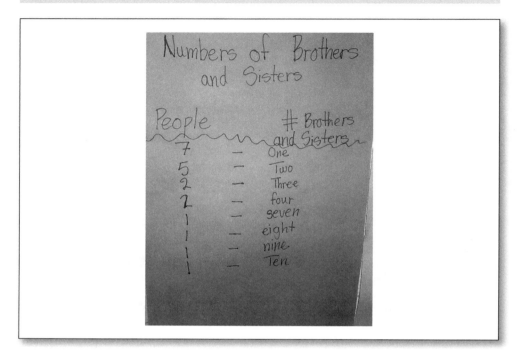

Figure 3.9

In 2007, classroom village statistics in part were as follows:

Native Countries

Somalia—1

Bangladesh—1

Guinea—1

Ghana—3

Mexico—4

Palestine—1

Vietnam—1

Canada—1

United States—11

Religion

Muslims—4

Catholics—10

Christians—7

Don't Knows—3

Once all the data was collected, tabulated, and displayed, our conversations continued—this time around our own statistics. My students were always interested in how our classroom matched or didn't match the world. Again we critically analyzed the information, asking why certain things were so.

The Quick Write Lesson

1. Sharing Mentor Texts

Share *If the World Were a Village* (or *If America Were a Village* or both). After explaining how this book works (7 billion to 100), allow the students to discuss topics that might be expected to be in the book, and then invite them to indicate sections that they most would like to know about.

While reading, you may want your listeners to take notes as indicated above:

- What facts did they already suspect or know?
- What facts surprised them?
- What do the statistics mean or imply?
- What statistics were not included about which they wondered?

Or

You may want them to take notes related to a current area of study. They may wish to share their notes in small groups or with the larger group, noting similarities, differences, questions, surprises, and perhaps even some disbelief.

2. Writer's Notebook

Invite students to list statistical information about themselves: nationality, language, religion, age, number in family, type of home, and so on. Your students can discuss information they wish to know about each other in order to generate a list of statistical information each should include. They may want to share this information with each other and tabulate group results as we did above.

3. Quick Write Possibilities

Read the next to last paragraph on page 29 of *Village*, "Past, Present and Future" (*If the World Were a Village*): "Around the year 2150, there will be 250 people in the village. This is an important number because many experts think that 250 is the maximum number of people the village can sustain. And even then, there may be widespread shortages of food, shelter and other resources."

Or

Choose another quote from the book to support your current studies in either science or social studies.

Invite students to respond to this quote in one of the following ways:

- Write a personal essay explaining how this quote directly affects you.
- Write an essay on how we as a global community should respond to this information.
- Write an essay analyzing either the classroom statistics collected or a set of statistics from the book.

The Mentor Text

If the World Were a Village: A Book About the World's People (2nd edition) by
   David J. Smith

This remarkable book takes the 6.9 billion people of the earth and imagines this whole world of people as a village of just 100 people; then it gives the relevant statistics based on this 100. If the first edition is still available in your area, it is interesting to compare the changes. David J. Smith's companion website to *If the World Were a Village* can be found at http://www.mapping.com/village.shtml. This site includes more global population and geography information and is updated regularly.

Additional Resources

If America Were a Village: A Book About the People of the United States by David J. Smith

This Child Every Child: A Book About the World's Children by David J. Smith

Similar to the books above, this book contains statistics and stories that compare the lives of children around the world.

One World, One Day by Barbara Kerley

This book takes us on a journey around the world in one day through breathtaking photography to compare the daily essential activities in our lives from sunup to sundown.

Children Just Like Me: A Unique Celebration of Children Around the World by Anabel Kindersley, Barnabas Kindersley, and UNICEF

Watering Our World

Grades 4–12

Persuasive Essays

Water Availability and Usage

- How does the availability and usage of water impact the world?

Background for the Teacher

Did you drink a glass of water today? Did it come from a faucet in your home? I can bet is was clean and free of contaminants. I can also imagine that you drank as much as you wanted, taking for granted that there would be more water when you returned for more. There would also be enough water to bathe in later and to cook your meals.

One billion people in our world do not have access to clean drinking water, and as many as 5 million children die yearly due to preventable water-related diseases such as dysentery or diarrhea. Water is life—as essential as air for all living creatures. Water is life—or death—in developing countries. In those countries, people spend many hours daily locating water and carrying it back to their homes. Generally, this work is done by girls and women. This continuous search for water is the primary reason girls in many countries are unable to attend school. The average girl walks 3.5 miles a day over unpaved roads, sometimes making several trips. Most of these girls have no shoes. This daily water duty prevents them from helping their families to grow food and also from later getting jobs to buy food, let alone an education that might lead to an end to generational poverty.

Based on a true story, Linda Sue Park's novel *A Long Walk to Water* tells the story of Nya, one such girl in the Sudan whose life revolves around water. She must walk twice daily to a pond two hours away for water; eight hours of her day is spent obtaining water for her family. Side by side with her story is also told the journey of Salva Dut, who as a result of war, becomes one of the lost boys and survives to eventually return home and build a well for his village and others—freeing Nya to go to school.

In real life, Salva became one of the first of the lost boys to settle in the United States. In addition, he has gone on to start a company, Water for Sudan, dedicated to providing water and wells for Sudan. Several of the resources below share his remarkable story.

Providing water for an area without easy accessibility is not just a concern in the Sudan but a global issue. At the United Nations Millennium Summit in 2000, world leaders agreed to set measurable goals for combating hunger, disease, illiteracy, environmental degradation, and discrimination against women. Eight specific areas are targeted to be achieved by the year 2015 through these Millennium Development Goals. The seventh goal, which is to ensure environmental stability, deals in part with safe drinking water being accessible to all people.

- How can we assure that everyone has adequate, clean drinking water?

The Quick Write Lesson

1. Sharing Mentor Texts

Share an excerpt from *A Long Walk to Water* with your students. You may want to use the opening sections (which tell Nya's story) of Chapters 1, 2, and 3 (pp. 1, 2, 14). Together these portions give an image of the difficulties of gathering water. Encourage your writers to imagine what life would be like if they spent most of their day locating and carrying water to their homes. One bucket of water weighs about 22 pounds.

- How many buckets would be enough to carry out their normal daily activities such as bathing, cooking, and drinking?
- What about luxury activities such as watering flowers or swimming in a backyard pool?

You may also want to share two sections of *One Well: The Story of Water on Earth* by Rochelle Strauss: "Access to the Well" (pp. 20–21) and "Demands on the Well" (pp. 22–23). These two selections deal with the amount of water available in our world and its inequitable distribution, as well as usage of water around the world. Students may be surprised to learn that in North America we use on average 55 buckets of water per person daily, as opposed to Haiti or Ethiopia, in which usage is about one bucket per person per day.

Two main laws affect how we use water in our nation. The Safe Drinking Water Act (SDWA) passed in 1974 by Congress allows the EPA to set standards for our nation's water quality and oversee the state and local agencies that implement these standards. Later, in 1986 and again in 1996, this law was amended to include many actions to protect our water and its sources, including our rivers, lakes, reservoirs, and so on. The Clean Water Act passed in 1972 is a set of amendments to the federal laws to prevent pollution of our water.

Students may want to investigate the water policies, guidelines, and laws in their own communities, cities, or states.

- How do these help or hinder the global water situation?

2. Quick Write Possibilities

Invite your students to consider the inequitable distribution and usage of water in the world. What solutions do they propose to provide safe, clean water for everyone?

Write a persuasive essay or white paper about the issue of clean water for all, including information related to the issues, causes, and potential solutions.

The Mentor Texts

A Long Walk to Water: Based on a True Story by Linda Sue Park

One Well: The Story of Water on the Earth by Rochelle Strauss

Additional Resources

PBS Need to Know article and video featuring Salva Dut. *A "Lost Boy" of Sudan Returns to Rebuild His Homeland*

This article and the related video tell the story of Dut's life in war-torn Sudan, his eventual journey to the United States, and his return home, which led to the development of Water for Sudan, a nonprofit organization, which now drills wells for Sudanese villages (http://www.pbs.org/wnet/need-to-know/video/video-a-lost-boy-of-sudan-returns-to-rebuild-his-homeland/6249/).

Water for Sudan—the homepage of Salva Dut's nonprofit organization (http://www.waterforsudan.org)

The video on the front page explains the importance of water and how Water for Sudan works to build wells for villages, as well as the impact of these wells once built.

Millennium Development Goals—United Nations Development Program (http://www.undp.org/mdg/goa17.shtml)

Additional Books About Water for Elementary Students

A Drop of Water: A Book of Science and Wonder by Walter Wick

Scientific information and experiments related to water. Beautiful full-page photographs with many close-ups.

A Cool Drink of Water by Barbara Kerley

This book, illustrated with color photographs, shows how people all over the world obtain water.

A Drop Around the World by Barbara McKinney

This book illustrates the water cycle by following one drop of water around the world.

A Drop of Water by Gordon Morrison

This book also treats the water cycle as we follow a child outside after a rain.

A River Ran Wild: An Environmental History by Lynne Cherry

This book shows the pollution and restoration of the Nashua River in Massachusetts.

The Bill of Rights

Grades 4–12

Petitions, Editorials or Letters to the Editor, Personal or Persuasive Essay

Knowing Our Constitutional Rights

> • How can we apply our constitutional rights to effect change?

Background for the Teacher

We were studying the Constitution, specifically the Bill of Rights, when the announcement came over the public address system that the fourth and fifth grades would no longer have recess in the afternoon so that time could be applied to study and preparation for the state test. *Groans! That's not fair! They got it last year! I don't believe this!* Both fifth-grade classes were upset, to put it in mildest terms. *Hey, Mrs. Holland, is this like in the Constitution where we can protest and it's legal?* We pulled out our history books and turned to the back where we each had a complete copy of the Constitution and all of its amendments. We had a lively discussion as the students pored over their books to locate the applicable parts and they quickly identified the First Amendment:

> Amendment 1: Congress shall make no law respecting an establishment of religion, or prohibiting the free exercise thereof; or abridging the freedom of speech, or of the press; or the right of the people peaceably to assemble, and to petition the Government for a redress of grievances. (http://www.usconstitution.net/const.html#Am1)

How could I not be thrilled at the application of our current lessons? Earlier in the year we had held a full-fledged campaign, with debates, speeches, and elections of class officers as well as a class council. It was the year of the historic 2008 elections—how could we not be politically involved! This issue they identified as a legislative matter for our class and quickly asked the council to meet. The council decided that a letter of protest should be written, addressed to our principal, outlining their concerns, and requesting a meeting, along with a petition signed by each class member indicating support. The president and vice president of the class were designated to deliver it. They reported that their meeting had been positive—the principal had agreed to think about it.

The principal did indeed change her mind. (As I remember, she had changed it before the meeting with the students, as a result of reconsideration on her own part or perhaps teachers persuading her, but I didn't have the heart to tell my students—the participation in this process held too important a lesson.) The wild cheering when it was announced that the policy would change and they would indeed have afternoon recess could be heard throughout our hallway—and I silently cheered over the practical application of classroom learning.

The Quick Write Lesson

1. Sharing Mentor Texts

With your students, identify a current issue in your classroom, school, or community, and then research the Constitution, Bill of Rights, and other amendments to determine your rights in this particular issue or case. Discuss with your students specific actions they might take based on their findings. They may want to further discuss this in small groups.

Or

Select one or more of the books about the Bill of Rights or U.S. Constitution suggested below to share with your students. You may just enjoy reading the explanatory and background information, or you may want to connect information read to specific classroom, school, or community issues.

Or

A petition is one effective way to initiate change. Change.org is a website that enables anyone to implement a grassroots campaign on any legal or social issue. Share with your students several of the online petitions. Issues are listed at the bottom of the page. You may want to start with those under the education category, or you may wish to allow your students to select a category of interest with which to begin. Each includes an accompanying letter as well as updates on where the related legal actions stand.

With Grades 4 and 5, you may also want to read *Click, Clack, Moo: Cows That Type* to your students and then discuss how the animals effectively initiated changes they wished to make at their farm. Discuss with them areas in their classroom, school, or community in which they would also like to see change. What action can they take to initiate these changes?

2. Writer's Notebook

Invite your students to create a list of current classroom, school, local, national, or global issues in which they desire a change. Beside each item they may want to write a brief statement indicating the specific change they would like to see. Ask them to circle or star the three issues that are most important to them.

3. Quick Write Possibilities

Invite your students to identify an issue in which they desire to see a change. They will want to refer to the lists in their notebooks. Related to this particular issue, ask them to write both a letter detailing the concerns and desired changes, along with a petition supporting their position. They may also indicate who they think would be the appropriate person/place to deliver the letter and petition. They may also want to indicate who they think might support them as well as who might not and why.

The Mentor Texts

Click, Clack, Moo: Cows That Type by Doreen Cronin

This clever book details how negotiations were handled between the unhappy cows and other farm animals and the farmer.

Change.org (http://www.change.org/)
(http://www.change.org/start-a-petition)

This nonpartisan site enables anyone to begin a grassroots campaign and create an online petition. Many issues and petitions are listed already on the site, or you can create your own.

U.S. Constitution Online (http://www.usconstitution.net/const.html)

The site includes the entire Constitution, along with all amendments, in an easy-to-use format with individual links to each section.

Additional Resources

A Kids' Guide to America's Bill of Rights: Curfews, Censorship, and the 100-Pound Giant by Kathleen Krull

History and explanations of the Bill of Rights, along with examples and applications.

We the People: The Story of Our Constitution by Lynne Cheney

This book details the context and development of our Constitution.

We the People: The Constitution of the United States of America by Peter Spier

The Constitution is presented in simplified language and includes related historical facts.

We the Kids: The Preamble to the Constitution of the United States by David Catrow

The preamble is presented in simplified language with examples and illustrations that clarify the text.

Contingency Plans

Grades 4–12

Contingency Plans

Planning for the Unexpected

> • What do we do if the unexpected happens?

Background for the Teacher

We all do it. We make backup plans, plans for the "just in case" situations that end up different than we desire or intend. We call them Plan B. Or if you are like me, you may also have a Plan C and D as well.

Contingency plans may never be used, but they give us peace of mind, and in the event of the unplanned or worse, they allow difficult situations to go smoothly, unforeseen catastrophes to be dealt with, and life's not-so-little surprises to be handled with grace. Contingency plans address the "what if" and "suppose this" of whatever we are doing.

History's great events and the behind-the-scenes plans that led to these events most likely had alternate plans, in case things did not go off without a hitch. Paul Revere had one—*one if by land, two if by sea.*

I grew up during the 1950s, during the Cold War. In elementary school, we routinely had bomb drills in which we quickly knelt under our desks—for girls, no graceful feat, as we weren't allowed to wear pants to school then. The government's contingency plan in the event of a nuclear bomb was bomb shelters or fallout shelters. I remember the yellow and black symbol, three yellow triangles on a black circle, that appeared on the school, churches, and other buildings in my neighborhood—those that had sturdy basements, those that would protect us from the radioactive ashes or fallout from a nuclear explosion.

We are warned by safety officials to have plans in the event of fire, flood, tornadoes, and other natural disasters. Employers have contingency plans for work stoppages or employee strikes. Likewise, employees, particularly in this age of troubled economy, have backup plans in the event that they lose their current jobs. Those suddenly fired and caught off-guard and without a contingency plan flounder as they struggle to right their lives. And we remember the digital consternation we all faced as Y2K approached with its threat to crash all of our computers. Contingency plans abounded as to how to reconfigure or repair our computers in the event they crashed as the calendar moved us into the year 2000.

Less extreme contingency plans involve planning rain dates for ball games or alternative locations for outdoor concerts in the park. As teachers, we certainly have contingency plans for those lessons and activities that may not go as smoothly in the classroom as they did in our heads.

Contingency plans are even the subject of literature. In May 2009, Steve Waters's play about climate change in the near future, in which a huge flood has destroyed parts of England and threatens to sink its east coast, opened in London. David K. Wheeler penned a collection of poems in which the title piece is "Contingency Plans."

The government preparing for every possible situation that can face its citizens is critical for the safety and survival of a country's inhabitants. One surprising way that our government is accomplishing this is by considering the imaginative ideas of science fiction writers. The U.S. Department of Homeland Security at its 2009 Science & Technology Stakeholders Conference included science fiction novelists on the panels. According to Rolf Dietrich, Homeland Security's deputy director of research, "the writers help managers think more broadly about projects, especially about potential reactions and unintended consequences." Who better to think about what could happen in the future, the technologies that are still to come, and how we will use them to manage our lives and save ourselves in the event of whatever may come?

How do you plan for those unexpected events and those sometimes predictable but undesirable events? What are the plans in your school in the event of a power outage? A fire? A tornado?

The Quick Write Lesson

1. Writer's Notebook

Invite your writers to list events or situations in which contingency plans would be desirable. These may include events at home or school. In addition, they may also want to list concerns on a larger scale, such as their city, state, or nation.

Allow time for students to share their lists and perhaps add a few items to their list that they have heard during the sharing.

2. Sharing Mentor Texts

You may want to gather copies of your school emergency plans—the contingency plans that have been made in the event of fire, tornado, or hurricane; power outage; lockdown; or other type of emergencies. These can usually be found in the teacher, parent, or student handbooks for your school. After discussing the various types of situations in which there may be a need for an emergency or contingency plan, you may want to share your school plans with the students. After closely examining each plan, they may begin to notice patterns shared among the plans. For example, most plans will identify the situation, indicate procedures, specify people who may be responsible for certain procedures or acts, and list equipment and supplies that may be needed, locations where people are to meet or gather, and so forth. The FEMA and eHOW websites below both contain additional plans for more general disasters and weather emergencies. You may want to expand your examination of contingency plans to include these, as well.

Or

Read one or more of the literature selections below. *Tops and Bottoms* would be appropriate for Grades 4 and 5, while *The King's Equal* is more suitable for both upper elementary and middle school. Invite students to discuss how contingency plans were utilized by the main characters. If you read more than one of these selections or other related texts, they may compare the types of contingency plans used, components of each, and how they succeeded in each case.

3. Quick Write Possibilities

Invite your students to write a contingency plan for a family, school, community, or national event. This event may be weather- or disaster-related or may deal with a more everyday situation such as a lost pet, a canceled event, or hurt feelings of a friend or family member. They may include the components that your group noticed in the mentor plans such as identifying the situation, listing procedures, specifying people for specific tasks, and listing equipment and supplies that may be needed. What will ensure that their plans succeed in dealing with the event for which they are planning?

The Mentor Texts

Tops and Bottoms adapted by Janet Stevens

This is a trickster tale derived from both European and American Southern folktales. As each new crop division is negotiated with Bear, Hare has a plan for getting the best of the harvest, no matter what has been grown.

The King's Equal by Katherine Paterson

The old king is dying, and ancient law dictates that his son be the next king, but knowing his son's less-than-desirable character and understanding the fears of his subjects, he pronounces a blessing that serves as a contingency plan, ensuring the best interests of his people.

Additional Resources

Government and Commercial Contingency Plans

FEMA/ready.gov (http://www.ready.gov/natural-disasters)

This site provides a variety of plans for many different natural disasters and weather conditions.

Preparing for Disasters, eHow (http://www.ehow.com/how_7909709_prepare-disaster-contingency-plan-school.html)

This site outlines steps for constructing contingency plans for schools. Links also provide a number of different types of preparedness plans.

Airline Safety and Contingency Plans (http://www.airlinetraveladvice.com/safety.shtml) (found under the heading On Board the Aircraft—scroll down to the last section)

Other

U.S. Mission for Sci-Fi Writers: "Imagine That" (Novelists Plot the Future of Homeland Security) (http://www.washingtonpost.com/wp-dyn/content/article/2009/05/21/AR2009052104379.html)

Scientists are asking sci-fi authors for help creating contingency plans.

Of Thee I Sing

Grades 4–12

Expository Essays

Recognizing Noteworthy People and Actions

> • Whom do we identify as worthy of praise?

Background for the Teacher

Before Camelot, before we knew him as President Kennedy, then junior senator John F. Kennedy walked the halls of the Senate and daily admired the portraits of courageous senators who had come before him and made difficult decisions, taken transformative stances, and fostered positive changes in our nation. He most admired courage as a virtue and ultimately wrote the now classic book *Profiles in Courage* to honor eight senators who for him exemplified this virtue. The short biographical sketches tell amazing stories of a variety of kinds of courage. In 1957 he won the Pulitzer Prize for Biography for his work. His honorees include John Quincy Adams for breaking away from the Federalist Party and Robert Taft for criticizing the Nuremburg Trials for trying Nazi war criminals with ex post facto laws.

Inspired by her father's book and in honor of him, Caroline Kennedy assembled 14 writers to write 14 inspiring latter-day stories of courageous people and their deeds in the face of great self-sacrifice, including the loss of their careers for some, as a result. She includes Gerald Ford for his controversial pardoning of Richard Nixon and John McCain for his political crusade against campaign financing. Her compilation, *Profiles in Courage for Our Time,* continues the tradition of honoring political stances and deeds of courage.

The Kennedy family reinstated the Profiles in Courage Award in 1989, and each year in May, it is awarded to a public official at the local, state, or federal level who exemplifies that quality of political courage in the face of constituent and collegial pressure originally recognized, lifted up, and admired in Kennedy's *Profiles in Courage.* The award includes $25,000 and a silver lantern.

President Barack Obama has also chosen to write about 13 Americans he admires for their contributions to our nation and the ideals they represent. He invites us to honor the beauty that Georgia O'Keeffe illuminated in her art, the advances in science fostered by Albert Einstein, the courage of Jackie Robinson, and the generosity and compassion of Jane Addams as she worked to improve the lives of the poor. His book is written as a letter to his daughters and reminds us of the potential of each of us for greatness.

In addition to these books written by famous folks about folks that many of us know or have heard about, there are many books written by lesser-known authors about people of whom we have never heard. There are even such books about students ranging from elementary age to high school—including students who have saved friends from drowning, fires, or other dangerous situations; youth who have stood up to gang members, murderers, sex abusers, and other criminals; and students who have fought to change the gun laws, clean up their environments, or spearhead building parks in their neighborhood.

Who do we believe embodies the virtues we deem most important for our family, for our community, and for our world today? Who do we think shows us the best part of what it means to be a human being, an American, a global citizen? Whom do we see making the hard decisions, helping those who cannot help themselves, and making our world a better place? Who are the eight or 13 or 14 that you would identify? When you think of greatness, whose face comes to mind? Whose name rings out, rising above the crowd?

The Quick Write Lesson

1. Writer's Notebook

John F. Kennedy and his daughter, Caroline, both identified the virtue courage, along with people who exemplify that virtue, as critical to our nation. Barack Obama listed a variety of virtues and talents, along with people demonstrating them, as exemplars for us to admire and emulate.

Invite your students to identify several virtues they admire and five to 15 people who exemplify those virtues. These people may be famous, or they may be family or friends. They may want to make a brief statement beside each about why they have identified each particular person.

2. Sharing Mentor Texts

Select a book from the listed resources below to share with your students. You may want to select one, two, or several profiles to share with them. You may, instead, want to share several of the texts and select excerpts from each. Discuss with your students how people included in each text were selected, what virtues or talents they are intended to exemplify, and whether or not your students agree with the selection.

- Are there any patterns they notice among all of the texts shared, among people selected by a particular author, or among types of courage, integrity, and creativity represented?
- Who do they feel is missing from the collections?
- Are there noticeable categories of people omitted?

You may also want to examine the style in which the profiles are written in each text.

- How are the people introduced?
- Are quotes included to allow their words to speak for themselves?
- Are other people quoted talking about them?
- Are we reading about multiple events and situations or is just one particular event highlighted?

- Is technical language used related to the person's career or field?
- What else do they notice about how each subject is presented?

3. Quick Write Possibilities

Invite your students to consider the person or people they feel demonstrate the qualities they deem most important in our world. They may want to review the list they wrote earlier, or they may have revised their thinking after having shared the mentor texts.

Ask them to write about their person, explaining the criteria, justifying their choice, and clarifying why this person stands out from others with similar credentials. They may also want to include how this person is known or has personally touched or inspired them. They may want to write in the form of a nomination such as that required for the Profiles in Courage Award.

The Mentor Texts

Of Thee I Sing: A Letter to My Daughters by Barack Obama

Profiles in Courage by John F. Kennedy

Profiles in Courage for Our Time by Caroline Kennedy

Books Profiling Young People Making a Difference

It's Our World, Too! Young People Who Are Making a Difference: How They Do It—How You Can, Too! by Phillip M. Hoose

Kids With Courage: True Stories About Young People Making a Difference by Barbara A. Lewis

Profiles in Courage Award—John F. Kennedy Presidential Library and Museum (http://www.jfklibrary.org/Events-and-Awards/Profile-in-Courage-Award.aspx)

This site provides information about this prestigious award, including past winners, nomination forms, criteria and eligibility, and a profiles in courage essay contest that may be of interest to your students.

Profiles in Courage Award Recipients (http://www.jfklibrary.net/Events-and-Awards/Profile-in-Courage-Award/Award-Recipients.aspx)

This page includes a list of award recipients from its inception to the present day. Clicking on each name will provide further biographical information about each honoree.

Profiles in Courage Essay Contest (http://www.jfklibrary.org/Events-and-Awards/Profile-in-Courage-Award/Profile-in-Courage-Essay-Contest.aspx)

This page includes details for the Profiles in Courage Essay Contest. The first-place winner in this contest in awarded $10,000 and a trip to the Profiles in Courage Award ceremony. The nominating teacher is awarded a $500 public service grant and a trip to the ceremony as well. There are also sample winning essays available at this site. These may be shared along with other mentor texts used above.

We Are America

Grades 4–12

Personal and Persuasive Essays

Defining Americans

- ## What does it mean to be an American?

Background for the Teacher

Words create us and documents have made us. In America there are several documents that define us—several that say who we are here in America. These documents outline our collective rights and rules, our national principles and purposes, and our highest hopes and dreams. Throughout our history as a nation, we have also repeatedly been defined and redefined by the words of strong and courageous men and women—words on paper preserved for posterity and words spoken aloud to audiences—small and intimate or multitudes.

Words have led us to consider ourselves and how we interact with each other, both at home and abroad in the world with other nations. Words have sometimes spurred us to greatness, at others times shamed us into making sweeping changes, and often challenged the best part of our humanity to create a nation that continues to grow and create new possibilities. Some moments have given birth to special words that became our mantras, our mottos, our shining American visibilities. Other moments in our lives together have given us new documents—and new selves—to revere, to challenge, to make us strive for the best, and to continue to reach for an ideal national identity, in a sometimes less than ideal reality.

In troubling times and on momentous occasions, we return to these documents for direction, solace, and restoration. September 11, 2001, was one of those moments in which every American was forced to closely examine who she was and who we are as a nation. Each person in our country had to consider how he related as an individual to the collective. And, most important, we had to decide who were we going to be on September 12 and every day that followed.

This notion of who we are as a nation and as Americans is considered in a beautiful meditation by Walter Dean Myers and his son Christopher Myers following 9/11, after which an inspired Myers (Walter) felt impelled to reread all of our founding and governing documents, the documents he felt "formed the core ideas of what America is about—the Declaration of Independence, the Articles of Confederation, the Federalist Papers and the Constitution." With a mix of poetry and quotes from people in our history—famous and not so famous—and quotes from documents important to our collective identity, Myers examines the questions of who is American and what is America. In the back matter, each quote is examined in a bit more detail and sources are provided for further consideration, as well as art notes to supplement the painted images created by his son.

Sometimes being American means speaking a truth that others may not want to hear at the time. Many, such as Martin Luther King, Robert Kennedy, and Abraham Lincoln, have been killed for speaking a word that ultimately came to be accepted as truth by the majority of Americans. Following 9/11, Robert Shetterly, like Walter Dean Myers, was moved to consider the qualities of Americans and was inspired to paint portraits of 50 Americans who for him portrayed the strength and courage of his countrymen and countrywomen. He selected those who spoke truth to power. Under each painting, he includes brief quotes for each person represented and short biographies of each at the end of his resulting work, *Americans Who Tell the Truth.*

So what do those documents that Walter Dean Myers felt moved to reread tell us? How do they define and refine us as Americans? What do they tell us about who we are? Have you looked at them lately?

The Quick Write Lesson

1. Sharing Mentor Texts

Share with your students *We Are America* and/or *Americans Who Tell the Truth.* The texts selected for this writing invitation are not traditionally structured and may not be comfortably read in the usual way. You may want to introduce the books by explaining the ways in which each came to be written. Both contain introductory statements that explain the context in which they were conceived and created. You will also want to share how each book is structured and works, and how the containers for the respective ideas of both texts present the material.

You then may want to read preselected excerpts, or you may want to invite the students to indicate the parts they would most like to hear. Of course, time permitting, you may want to read the entire texts either in one sitting or over a period of days.

Discussion may focus on the unique containers and presentations of each text, the selected quotes, the visual images, and their respective relationship to the whole text.

- How do these books portray Americans and America?
- Who is American?
- What is America?

In addition, you may want to share portions of our founding documents that relate to recent studies in your class or simply have these documents available for students to reread.

2. Quick Write Possibilities

Invite your writers to consider, as did both Walter Dean Myers and Robert Shetterly, the notion of who we are as Americans and who we are collectively as America.

Invite them to write an essay about who is an American and what makes one so. This may include information from a variety of sources—our founding and governing documents, personal experiences, and observations. They may support or challenge information found in the documents and include personal opinion, as well as information from other sources.

Or

Invite your writers to select one of the quotes recorded in either *We Are America* or *Americans Who Tell the Truth* and write an essay about how that particular quote exemplifies what it means to be American, and collectively, America. Again they may include information, support, and examples from founding and governing documents, personal experiences and observations, and other sources. They may also want to write about why they think the author included the particular quote in his collection.

Or

They may want to select their own quote from one of the founding documents or a person they deem important to America in some ways and respond in any of the above suggested ways to the quote they have selected, including why they have chosen that particular quote.

The Mentor Texts

We Are American: A Tribute From the Heart by Walter Dean Myers and Christopher Myers

Americans Who Tell the Truth by Robert Shetterly

Additional Resources

American Founding Documents (http://www.foundingfathers.info/documents/)

This site includes the most important founding and governing documents of our nation, including the Declaration of Independence, the Constitution of the United States, the Bills of Rights, amendments to the Constitution (11–27), and the Federalist Papers.

A Guide to Naturalization (http://www.uscis.gov/files/article/M-476.pdf)

This guide, published by the U.S. government details the process of becoming a citizen of the United States. This guide was used as a text for my fifth graders for several years as we studied naturalization.

My response to this question can also be used as a text to share.

Who Are We in America?

Who are we
in the land of discovery
The place of opportunity
when the last piece of soil
is claimed
and maimed
and fenced
or blacktopped?

Who are we when the last ship has landed
and the first person is finally freed?

Who are we waiting for
when the speeches are done
and votes are counted?
Who is the one
who can make us one?

Who are we when
the floods rage
and the winds ravage

or rain fails and the sun scorches
our food and our heart-land?

Who are we when evil
stalks the poor, the hungry
the uneducated and the unwell?
Who are we when the angel of justice
must fight with the spectre of hegemony
and the ogre of greed
sucks up our air
and our water
and our oil
and our life?

When the last song is sung
and the first drum major for freedom
is followed
where will it lead us
and to what kind of America
and who will we be?

4 Containers, Craft, and Conventions

Writing in Different Genres

Y ou've written your words on paper and they are lying there dead. You think, "How come they don't shout as I intended? Is my writing really a story, or should it be a poem, instead?" The quick writes in this section promote experimenting with a variety of containers or genres for constructing our meaning, as well as considering craft and conventions as an integral part of the writing.

If That's a Poem: Introducing Mentor Texts

Grades 4–12

Poetry

Using Mentor Texts to Help Us Write

- How can we use someone else's writing to support us as we write?

Background for the Teacher

Writers must be readers. We learn to write by reading other writers. I write poetry, and, therefore, I read lots and lots of poetry. (I also read it because it nourishes and delights me.) I usually have a book of poetry in my purse and always have one or two in my car. I buy hardback books of poems because I want to be able to savor them again and again.

The poets I read teach me to be a better writer, even though I don't personally know them, have not attended writing workshops with most of them, or heard most of them speak. I have learned to break lines in more interesting ways from Nikki Giovanni, and it is always her voice, her rhythm that reads poetry in my head. She has also taught me to carefully consider the punctuation or lack thereof in my poems. I learned to question and worry the ordinary from Billy Collins. He has taught me that I can write about my ordinary day, or everybody's ordinary yesterday, with a recognizable familiarity, yet fostering a new perspective. I have learned from Samuel Hazo that I can take my readers to unfamiliar places and make them comfortable there by revealing and celebrating with specificity the surprising commonality of each moment. In the poetry of my mentors, I see what I am *trying* to do executed to perfection. I imitate and become better. I try what they are doing with words, structures, and topics, and then I have new containers for my ideas.

Katie Wood Ray (1999) urges us to "read like writers" to recognize and identify exactly what a particular writer is doing, and even name it, so we can talk about it and use it ourselves. Ray likens the process to that of a seamstress in the women's department store. The seamstress will turn a dress inside out to look at the hidden, underneath construction of the garment—the cut, the seams, and stitches. She may discover a new way to achieve a particular hang or fold. She can then return home and imitate what she has discovered, incorporating these new ideas into her own fashion creations.

In *Love That Dog* by Sharon Creech, Jack learns to read like a writer from his teacher, Mrs. Stretchberry. Initially, Jack does not understand "The Red Wheelbarrow," a poem his teacher reads, but later he uses the structure of William Carlos Williams's short poem to contain his own sad "so much depends upon" story. He discovers the cut and seams that will make his story "hang" just the right way.

We, too, can find the structures or frames to write the sentence, the paragraph, the story, or the poem that we want to write by reading other writers. The poem below was written to express frustration with my own attempt to write something totally different—a "Where I Am From" poem using George Ella Lyon's poem by the same title as a mentor text. I worked and reworked my draft numerous times, heeded feedback from peers to shorten, reworked again, added more details, took out details, feeling more displeased after each successive draft. I finally borrowed a container from Langston Hughes—"Harlem (Dream Deferred)"—to express my growing frustration.

Asking Langston About Where I Am From

What happens to a poem not written?
Does it lurk like an infection in the brain?

Or swirl like dirty bathwater
And then drain?

Does it languish like resentment—
Or bubble and churn
Like an unwatched pot
About to burn?

Maybe it just releases us
From its power.

Or dies—
An unwatered flower.

Notice that I am able to use the almost exact same container as Langston Hughes to reflect on my poetic dilemma. His frame becomes my frame for content, phrasing and line breaks, versification, and punctuation. He taught me how to write about my frustration using analogies I might never have attempted without his structure to suggest a direction and to support me.

The Quick Write Lesson

Sharing Mentor Texts

Read *Love That Dog* to your students. If you are not going to read the entire book, you may want to read pages 3 and 4, along with "The Red Wheelbarrow," which is in the back of the book.

Invite your students to discuss the meaning and structure of the poem and how Jack used this format to tell about his dog. Can they think of another structure that may have been equally appropriate to tell Jack's story?

Throughout the rest of this story, Jack experiments with many other poems read to him by Mrs. Stretchberry to inspire his writing. All of the poems are included in the back of the book and can also be shared with your students, along with other poems written by Jack.

Quick Write Possibilities

Choose a small poem to read to your students. Use an overhead or LCD projector or prepared chart to analyze the poem, line by line, phrase by phrase, discussing exactly what the writer has done.

Help your students select the essential parts that form a frame or structure to be borrowed for their own work. Have them try writing their own poems. Ways that writers acknowledge they have borrowed from another writer's container are often written below the title and include such phrases as *With thanks to . . .* or *With apologies to . . .* or *With the help of . . .*

My favorite texts for initial attempts with this quick write are listed in Additional Resources. Elementary students are particularly successful with the poems "Good Hope" and "Where I Am From." Older students and adults will be able to use a range of works.

"Good Hope" by Benjamin Zephaniah can be found in the anthology *Come to the Great World: Poems From Around the Globe,* selected by Wendy Cooling, also located online at http://beltincischool.blogspot.com/2010/12/poem-good-hope.html.

As students analyze this poem, they will discover the following frame:

I believe
I believe
I believe
If I didn't believe
I know
There is hope
Believe me

Source: Cooling, 2010.

One feature that makes this a perfect first poem for this quick write is that the possible framework suggested above is actually printed in bold print in the book, allowing writers to *see,* as well as hear, what parts to keep for their own structure as they examine this poem.

An additional poem found in this anthology that works well is the poem "It Makes Me Furious" by Teresa de Jesus, which deals with hunger and homelessness. Each stanza ends with the title line, *It makes me furious,* which provides a more open framework for students to express their own serious issues.

Once students understand the concept of borrowing structures, they can use it for longer texts as well, borrowing entire book structures to enliven projects, reports, and personal writing. Could a project best be presented as an ABC book, a counting book, a fairy tale, a diary, a log, or a cookbook? Once your students have understood this idea and begin to read as writers, they will discover many new ways to approach their writing and many new containers in which to present their writing.

Mentor Text

Love That Dog by Sharon Creech

Additional Resources

Come to the Great World: Poems From Around the Globe selected by Wendy
  Cooling

"Good Hope" by Benjamin Zephaniah

"It Makes Me Furious" by Teresa de Jesus

The following poems by Langston Hughes work well with this quick
write and are available at http://www.poemhunter.com/langston-
hughes/.

"Dream Deferred (Harlem)"

"Dream Variations"

"Dreams"

The following poems by William Carlos Williams also work well
(http://www.poetryfoundation.org/archive/poet.html?id=81496):

"The Red Wheelbarrow"

"Between Walls"

"Winter Trees"

Poem (As the Cat) (http://www.poemhunter.com/william-carlos-
  williams/poems/page-3/)

All of the above poems are also contained in the following comprehensive volume:

The Collected Poems of William Carlos Williams, Vol. 1: 1909–1939 by William
  Carlos Williams, A. Walton Litz, Christopher MacGowan

Where I Am From by George Ella Lyon (http://www.georgeellalyon.com/
  where.html)

Momma, Where Are You From? by Marie Brady

This picture book illustrated by Chris Soentpiet follows for several
pages the same pattern as George Ella Lyon's poem "Where I Am
From."

What Container Will Hold My Words?

Grades 4–12

Revising a Previous Piece

Choosing a Genre

> • What writing form or genre is best for my writing?

Background for the Teacher

You have written your words and put your heart and guts on the paper. The meaning is there, but it lies dead on the page and does not rise to life. This is not how you envisioned this piece, and the responses are less than enthusiastic from your writing group. Perhaps you chose the wrong container for your message. Just as the beauty of flowers is enhanced by the perfect vase, so the appropriate container or genre will both reveal and enhance the deepest meanings in your writing. The right container will empower your message and allow your words to soar.

One of my favorite books is *A Wreath for Emmett Till* by Marilyn Nelson. My writing friends will tell you that I ease this book into lessons and quick writes whenever I can because it is such a complexly perfect book. So much has been written about the unholy, unbelievable, unbearable story of the lynching of 14-year-old Emmett Till for allegedly whistling at a white woman. According to Nelson, the heroic crown of sonnets, the strict form she chose to re-present this intense story, protected her from the painful, paralyzing effect of the subject matter, enabling her to write a beautiful poem to honor his memory (see additional information about crowns in Additional Resources).

Another book that tells a similar story of that painful "separate but equal" time in America's history, *This Is the Dream* by Diane Z. Shore and Jessica Alexander, uses an entirely different format. The pattern in this book, while not actually cumulative, Is reminiscent of *This Is the House That Jack Built* as it moves forward with a repeated series of *This is the . . . that . . .* and stands in stark contrast to the strict and complicated format of *The Wreath for Emmett Till*. Placed side by side, these two books will foster much discussion about genre dictated by message and message enhanced by genre. Which leads the way?

In our afterschool writing project one year, as I sat with one of my students for a final conference and formatting of his piece for the anthology, we both felt like his World War III story rambled on, and although there was lots of action, it just didn't seem to move forward and make the reader care about the action. As we played with the format, I showed him how it might look if we broke the lines so that it looked more like free verse. He lit up after I showed two or three sample lines. He immediately began to tell me where to break the next line, deleting words as he went. The result, of course, was a poem that moved much faster and commanded more interest. Justin's grin, when we were finished, indicated our success in finding the right container for his futuristic military adventure.

The Quick Write Lesson

Sharing Mentor Texts

Share several of the books from the list below, asking students to consider the genre and format of the book—including illustrations, fonts, and any unusual features, as well as the message.

- Why might the author have chosen the particular genre?
- What other books do they know that are similar?
- Discuss whether the format works effectively for the message or whether they can envision another container that might enhance the message more effectively.
- Discuss the deliberate choices made by the author and illustrator, if applicable.

Writer's Notebook

Have your students list as many genres as possible. Review briefly what constitutes each one and name a book or work written in that genre.

Have students reread pieces they have completed or almost completed. Ask them to select one or two with which they are dissatisfied. They may want to make notes about what they were attempting to do in the piece, what succeeded, and where they are disappointed with the results.

Quick Write Possibilities

Invite the students to select one of the pieces of writing chosen above for this quick write. Tell them they will be rewriting the piece three different ways in a short amount of time. The only stipulation is that each time you say stop or your timer rings, they must immediately change genres. Once you begin, allow three or four minutes for each writing period. (Elementary students may need longer. You may want to give them 10 minutes for each writing time and only require two pieces.)

Students may share once they have completed this activity, evaluating for each other which genres matched the intended messages most successfully.

Resources

A Wreath for Emmett Till by Marilyn Nelson

A crown of sonnets is a set of 14 sonnets in which each succeeding sonnet begins with the last line of the preceding one. In a heroic crown of sonnets a 15th sonnet is added to the end and is comprised of the first lines of each of the preceding 14. In addition, Nelson has also woven many symbolic references to flowers, earlier poems, the Bible, and much more into her heroic crown.

Woolvs in the Sitee by Margaret Wild

This work depicts a future with unnamed, hidden horrors that plague the inhabitants. The altered spellings, as well as eerie illustrations, serve to enhance this future uncivilized feel.

Imagine That! by Janet Wilson

Aunt Violet is celebrating her 100th birthday. As she reminisces about her life in narrative form, time lines running down the side of each page share general, historical, cultural, and popular information about each decade of her life.

We Are All in the Dumps With Jack and Guy: Two Nursery Rhymes With Pictures by Maurice Sendak

Created in 1993 before the rise of the graphic novel to its now popular status, this work by Maurice Sendak imbues two old nursery rhymes with new meaning through his illustrations depicting poverty and hunger and one boy's solution.

Moses: When Harriet Tubman Led Her People to Freedom by Carole Boston Weatherford

Harriet Tubman's relationship and reliance on God to aid in her life's work is considered, with God's words in large capital letters and Harriet's thoughts in italics. The narrative itself is written in a "regular" font. This book is excellent for discussing decisions made about the way the words look and how that relates to the story.

The Lost Thing by Shaun Tan

A little mechanical creature is out of place in the "current Shaun Tan world." Last year my kids absolutely loved this book and had a pretty deep conversation about what the story meant in terms of human relationships/interactions and our world.

The Viewer by Gary Crew

This intense narrative recapitulates world history in a viewer, found in an old, mysterious box, with the boy eventually entering the world in the box.

And I Heard Them Say

Grades 4–12

Dialogue

Conversations in Our Writing

- How can we use conversations in our writing?

Background for the Teacher

Writers listen to other people's conversations. We eavesdrop in restaurants and on planes. We lean closer in the airport or at the football game to see the expression that accompanied the words that we are snatching from the air. Writers are nosy and curious and always eager for words, even stolen ones. We hear the world differently.

Every event, every conversation, and every encounter is potential writing. The words overheard at Starbucks early in the morning may later be spoken by the rushing young woman in your novel who is late to her first corporate meeting. The harsh words spit at the crying toddler in Macy's may be placed into the mouth of the weary mother in your poem "Ode to Motherhood." The argument with your friend may become a model as you write about a personal narrative in front of your fifth-grade class. (*Mrs. Holland, did that really happen?*)

Adding believable dialogue to stories will heighten the realism and credibility of your characters. It will show much about your characters without long and sometimes boring descriptions and will, in addition, move the action forward. Capturing the authentic voices of the speakers will put your readers in the midst of the scene as participants rather than allowing them to remain simply sideline observers.

The Quick Write Lesson

Sharing Mentor Texts

Read the poem "Memory" from the novel *Locomotion* by Jacqueline Woodson to your students. Ask them to pay close attention to the conversation in this poem. What does the dialogue reveal about Lonnie, the main character in this novel-in-poems?

Another book that can be used effectively for this quick write is the picture book *Saturday and Teacakes* by Lester Laminack, in which we get to peek at the relationship between a little boy and his beloved Mammaw. Again, pay attention to the dialogue in the book, and notice how it reveals the characters through their words to each other and their related actions. Discuss with your students how the writer indicates the talking. Laminack uses commas to set off the talking from the speaker, but no quotation marks—instead quotes are italicized. Look at other books to see how their authors indicate talking as well.

Writer's Notebook

The following activities and mini-lessons may be helpful before using the quick write.

In the poem "America Talks," Peter F. Neumeyer celebrates the constant talking and voices that we hear and the variety of what gets said. This poem was written in response to the painting *Barber Shop* by Jacob Lawrence and would be excellent to introduce the concept of listening and recording conversations.

About a week prior to using this quick write, ask your students to listen to conversations around them—at school, at home, during football practice, in stores—everywhere they go.

Students may make notes about these conversations in their notebooks to use for this quick write. Help them understand that writers collect conversations to use in later writing. Sometimes the collected conversations are used exactly as heard. Other times they simply provide ideas about what characters might say in particular situations, events, places, and relationships. I am still trying to figure out a way to include the following line overheard in a mall in a piece of writing—"Fifteen-year-old me bought this."

You may also want to teach students about how to write dialogue including use of quotation marks and commas, ways of indicating the speaker, lists of words to use instead of *said*, and ideas for using play format as an alternative way to record talking.

Quick Write Possibilities

Write a dialogue based on a conversation heard this week. Try to use mostly conversation, but indicate what the speaker is doing as he is speaking as a way to help your reader envision the context of the conversation. This is similar to blocking in a play. For example:

Looking hopefully down the road, the boy murmured, "The bus will be along shortly."

"I don't care how long we have to wait," replied his friend, shrugging and continuing to shuffle small rocks with his feet.

Share the following conversation. Notice how the story in this brief encounter is moved forward by the conversation and how the dialogue reveals information about the personality of each character and the relationship between them. While the entire conversation is fictional, the idea occurred when I overheard a man in a restaurant say, "Well, they did it again." I never heard the rest of the conversation but began to wonder where that conversation went.

Dialogue

He came in and plopped on the sagging green couch.

"Well, they did it again," he sighed.

"What—What did they do?" she asked, hoping it would not be a long answer.

"Well, you know how I always tell you folks at work are out to get me?"

"Mmmmm," she nods.

"Well, you know how I always stay one step ahead of them 'cause I'm clever that way?"

"Mmmmm," she nods. She had heard all of this hundreds, maybe thousands of times.

"And remember when they stole my idea and presented it to the boss? I was getting ready to be up with the big boys that time."

"Mmm," she murmured, hoping he would run out of steam soon.

"You know it was *my* day—that day. You know they ruined my life."

"Mmm," she murmured again like an incantation that she prayed would end this familiar rant.

"Well, today it's over!"

She sat up. This part was new.

"Oh?" she said with a slight lift of her head.

"Yeah—it's over!" He seemed to gain confidence and stature.

"Yeah—it was all over at 10:00 this morning!"

"Oh?" she said, now a knot forming in her lower stomach.

"They ruined my life and YOURS!"

"Mine?" Now she was frantic inside.

They danced this dance every day. Everyone was unfair. They all were out to get him. Sometimes twice a day . . . and it wasn't just work. It was everything. People on the train, in the grocery store, neighbors passing, kids playing on their way to school. His enemies were everywhere.

But never had he involved her in his tirades as anything but listener. *Never victim along with him.*

"Mmmm?" she looked up carefully.

"Yeah, all over today," he smiled.

The Mentor Texts

"Memory" from *Locomotion* by Jacqueline Woodson

"America Talks" by Peter F. Neumeyer from *Heart to Heart: New Poems Inspired by Twentieth Century Art* by Jan Greenburg

Picture Book

Saturday and Teacakes by Lester Laminack

Additional Resources

Yo! Yes! by Chris Raschka

Because there is only sparse conversation as two boys meet for the first time, this book allows students to focus on the expression and tone of voice and understand how important this is in creating conversations.

Flossie and the Fox by Patricia C. McKissack

This book will delight all ages. This clever Red Riding Hood–type story is a perfect model of how dialogue reveals the personality of the speaker.

We Had Picnic This Sunday Past by Jacqueline Woodson

This book lets us peek in on a family picnic and listen to all the talk. The words spoken are indicated by bold print.

The Story of My Story

Grades 4–12

Reflective Essay, Multigenre Project

The Origins of a Piece of Writing

- How did this particular piece come to be written?

Background for the Teacher

One of the reasons I love to hear authors speak about their work is to hear the story of their stories—what inspired them to write the books or stories or poems that they wrote.

Who inspired the characters and what real place became the setting? Do they draw on their own lives as do Patricia Polacco and Cynthia Rylant? Or do they create a fantastic imagined world entirely in their own minds as does J. K. Rowling? I want to hear the story of their struggle or ease in constructing an experience or concept into a piece that can be shared with others.

I also want to know how they came to be writers in the first place. I want to know who they read. And I want to hear if the voice on the page is the same voice that speaks aloud. Recently I had the pleasure of hearing Junot Diaz (*The Brief Wondrous Life of Oscar Wao, Drown*) speak and was delighted to hear the same irreverent genius that exudes from his books—the same speech that shocks, entrances, and educates simultaneously.

My students love to hear about how books came to be, as well. They often ask what I know about an author as we begin a book, and they soak in the tidbits that I can share either from reading about the author or hearing the author speak. *You mean you actually met . . .* they say in amazement. Knowing I was going to hear Jeff Kinney at the National Council of Teachers of English (NCTE) convention in 2009, when I returned, my students couldn't wait to hear what he said about his books (*Diary of a Wimpy Kid* series). I had taken good notes and simply shared them with the students. They were surprised to find out that he had not intended to be a writer but had been through several jobs. Hearing his story validated the pieces of papers hidden in their desks covered with small drawings and accompanying words—their own graphic novels.

That moment when you know you have to write something is unmistakable and magic. Langston Hughes was inspired to write one of his most famous poems, "The Negro Speaks of Rivers," on a train ride crossing the mighty Mississippi River. This story is detailed beautifully in *Langston's Train Ride*.

William Carlos Williams was introduced to poetry in high school. He loved the words and rhythms and rhymes and began to write his own poetry. He soon found the traditional frameworks from his schoolbooks frustrating and wanted to break free to let the words take shape on the page in their own way. *A River of Words: The Story of William Carlos Williams* creatively tells his story and includes several of his poems as well.

Sometimes, we discover a particular habit or incident in a writer's life that has significance for us and makes that writer come alive. It's like meeting that writer again and rereading all of her work with new eyes. Such a story is told in *My Uncle Emily* in the voice of her young nephew. He recounts how her gift of a poem for his class resulted in many questions, insults and a fight, a lie, and finally a truth "told slant."

Like these well-known writers, we, too, are inspired in a variety of ways to write. How do we think of ideas for our stories and poems and essays? How does our writing come to be? What makes us want to take up pen or press computer keys? Sometimes something happens that we just have to tell—we just have to write.

The Quick Write Lesson

Sharing Mentor Texts

Share a book or story about a writer with your students. It can be about how a particular piece of writing came to be, about that person's life and how writing entered into it, or about a particular incident or relationship. You may also want to share works by that particular author. Invite your students to make connections between the person and the writing.

- Does knowing about the writer help them understand the work better or on another level?
- Do they begin to see why a writer selected a particular topic or style or genre?

Writer's Notebook

Invite students to look through their notebooks or folders of writing to remind themselves of all they have written. Ask them to jot down five to 10 pieces, and beside those titles to make notes about the genre and why they wrote that piece. (*I was having a bad day. I just got my bike. I didn't want to move. I had just broken up with my boyfriend. I had just gotten a new job. It was my birthday.*) Students may want to share the titles, types of pieces, and contexts in which they were written. You may want to help them categorize the reasons and contexts by recording what they share on a chart. They will find a variety of reasons and contexts for what they have written.

Quick Write Possibilities

Ask your students to revisit their list of writings, genres, and reasons. Invite them to select one piece of writing of which to tell the story. Once they have selected a piece, they may want to play with genres to determine which will best tell their story. If you have used one of the suggestions in the Resources, you may want to remind them that the author's writing was integrated into the story. Can they do that? Is it appropriate to do for their story or essay? They may want to try to create a multi-genre piece to tell about their writing, its context, and its origin.

Resources

Langston's Train Ride by Robert Burleigh, illustrated by Leonard Jenkins

A River of Words: The Story of William Carlos Williams by Jen Bryant, illustrated by Melissa Sweet

My Uncle Emily by Jane Yolen, illustrated by Nancy Carpenter

Cumulative Poems

Grades 4–12

Sentences, Poetry

Improving Our Sentences

- How can we improve our sentences?

Background for the Teacher

Fifth-grade students are in transition. They know a lot about reading and writing but are not necessarily using and applying all that they can talk about. They are writing mostly declarative sentences, as well as an occasional question, but have learned to appreciate a variety of vocabulary and sentence structures in the texts that they are reading. They are also writing longer structures and clauses—but despite the length, these are, more often than not, only fragments rather than complete and correct sentences. This description may sound familiar no matter what the grade level of your students. Last year I set out to support my students' growth in this area.

Whenever we read aloud, we always do what Vicki Spandel calls *sentence stalking*—we are on the lookout for wonderful sentences that sound amazing to our ears and provide fantastically detailed images in our minds. When we find them, we deconstruct them to examine what the writer has done to accomplish the effect.

- Did the author use vivid verbs?
- Or specific adjectives?
- Or did the structure itself lead us to nominate this particular sentence as golden?
- Did the writer employ a chiastic structure?
- Or did she use a cumulative structure?

So often we teachers think we must limit learning from other authors to longer texts. A mentor text, however, can be a sentence, as well as a picture book, an article or essay, a poem, or a longer work such as a novel or informational text. It can be *any* text that we study or imitate as a model for our own writing. My students and I have discovered that imitating at the sentence level can dramatically improve our writing and give both texture and power to our words.

To support students at this level beyond the "we noticed—now what?" stage, I decided to learn all I could about sentence structures. What are the options for structuring sentences? Which one would be most empowering and generative for my students? Each year I attend the annual National Council of Teachers of English and National Writing Project (NWP) conventions with a particular goal in mind to further both my learning and that of my students. So 2008 was no different. I attended every session that dealt even remotely with sentence structures.

My own reading and online investigation, along with my gut, directed me to the cumulative sentence. I ultimately discovered several sources indicating this was the most powerful structure if I could only teach one.

Terry D. Phelps, in "A Life Sentence for Student Writing: The Cumulative Sentence" in the 1987 issue of *Journal of Teaching Writing*, indicated that research on this structure with students found it to be as powerful as sentence combining—which has remained an effective technique my entire 35-year career of public school teaching. Linda Christensen (1996) and Jeff Anderson (2005), as well as the presenters at my chosen sessions at NCTE/NWP and many others also confirm the power of the cumulative sentence structure.

The Quick Write Lesson

Sharing Mentor Texts

Now armed with way too much information, I began in earnest to try to provide this magic tool that would transform my fifth-grade students into Hemingways and Rylants and Morrisons. One winter day, we began by reading one of my favorite picture books about winter and snow, *Oh Snow* by Monica Mayper. In this marvelous snow poem, a little boy goes out into the newly fallen snow to see his changed world and enjoy the day.

When we finished reading, we listed all of the activities that the little boy enjoyed. Then, starting with the base sentence *The little boy played in the snow,* we began to add additional activities from our list to create a loose, long, comfortable, and conversational sentence—a cumulative sentence. (*A cumulative sentence is a base or independent clause with a string of words and phrases added to give further details or zoom in on the subject.*)

The little boy played in the snow, rolling down the hill, making snow angels, stomping his feet where no other boys had walked, and watching more snow fall.

Once we had created our sentences, we then talked about how poetry looks with its shorter lines and phrases. We broke our sentence into lines to create a poem.

Like magic the students discovered they had created impressive poetry.

The little boy
played in the snow,
rolling down the hill,
making snow angels,
stomping his feet
where no other boys
had walked,
and watching
more snow fall.

There were additional phrases on our chart that students opted not to use:

Riding down the hill
Pretending he is a tree
Seeing chickadees peck

This additional sentence/poem was created by the class the same day:

The snow fell covering the field . . . and spring,
sparkling white, making not a sound, hushing the world.

The snow fell
covering the field
. . . and spring
sparkling white
making not a sound
hushing the world.

Later that same year, in the spring, as we noticed the purple flowers in front of our school, we wrote sentences/poems about the signs of spring with the same delight and successful results. Try it—you will find it both fun and addicting. And as you hunt for wonderful sentences in your reading, you will find this kind of sentence everywhere, and your students will delight in knowing this special secret.

Quick Write Possibilities

As you invite students to write cumulative sentences and then cumulative poetry, you can spark their ideas in several ways. You may want to begin by sharing a picture book containing lots of action or description that can later be constructed into longer, loose sentences by adding phrases. You may want to hunt for cumulative sentences in your read-alouds or guided readings with the group, or you may simply suggest topics and allow them to let their words take wing. More sample sentences are included with the Additional Resources.

Invite students to write cumulative sentences and then share the sentences and resulting poetry, just as you would longer pieces.

Additional Resources

Sample Cumulative Sentences

He waded into the water, holding his trunks, closing his eyes against the salty spray, shivering as the water touched his bony knees, laughing at the unlikeliness of this whole scene.

The woman held her head down, not responding, wiping her eyes, making small gurgling noises, waiting for us to leave her alone, waiting to retreat back to her room, imagining what was in the package that awaited her, and praying she would not fall asleep before she ripped the paper off the red gift.

He plucked the rose from among all the roses growing in the garden, the roses with the soft red petals, stems covered with thorns, promising pain, yet offering immeasurable beauty, and handed it to his mother.

The monster parted the water, arising from his watery den, shining in the sun, showing his fangs, looking for his first landlocked meal.

The resources listed below aided me as I learned about cumulative sentences.

Critical Passages: Teaching the Transitions to College Composition by Kristin Dombek and Scott Herndon

Mechanically Inclined: Building Grammar, Usage, and Style Into Writers' Workshop by Jeff Anderson

Story Grammar for Elementary: A Sentence-Composing Approach by Don and Jenny Killgallon

Sentence Composing for Elementary School by Don and Jenny Killgallon

Notes Toward a New Rhetoric: 9 Essays for Teachers (3rd edition) by Francis Christensen and Bonniejean Christensen

This website gives both a definition and samples of the cumulative sentence (http://www.powa.org/revise/designing-effective-sentences?showall=&start=4).

Where the Action Is

Grades 4–12

Poems, Narratives

Using Verbs

> ● How can we use verbs to add excitement to our writing?

Background for the Teacher

We read several sports stories in my classroom. Their literature anthologies began the year with sports stories, stories of courageous women in baseball—women who were first in their fields and competed equally with men (such as Jackie Mitchell, who struck out Babe Ruth and Lou Gehrig), stories of sports failures and fears (such as the boy who was afraid to climb the rope in gym), and stories of fast-paced action, as well as poems that put us in the stands and summer backyards. During this period, I also read aloud several sports-related books that left the students breathless and on the edge of their seats. Why? What was the attraction in these books for both boys and girls?

Sports means excitement, movement, and a pace often driven by competition and winning. As we reread each book, we soon discovered that each one moved us forward with action. We were right there with the athlete, throwing the ball, rushing to the basket, swinging our bats, scoring the points, wind in our faces and cheers in our ears. As we analyzed what the writers had done to make our hearts beat faster, we discovered lots of verbs, in addition to many sensory details. We began to list these. We discussed how these words affected the story and our responses. It didn't matter whether we liked or participated in the particular sports that we had read about. We all liked some sport—either to watch or in which to participate. We all could begin to imagine our own special sport described in these exciting, breathless terms.

Ice skating was always one of my favorite activities in which to engage as a kid and still remains my favorite sport to watch on TV. As we continued to deconstruct the texts, I was already one step ahead—writing a skating poem in my head. And then, quite naturally, we all wrote our own sports poems.

The Quick Write Lesson

Sharing Mentor Texts

Select one of the sports-oriented books listed below to read to your students. After enjoying the poem several times, invite students to begin to identify how the writer moved the story forward, making it fast-paced and exciting. You and your students will want to identify specific words indicating actions and sensory words and phrases that bring the poem and the action alive.

Because *Jabberwocky* is Christopher Myers's colorful interpretation of the famous Lewis Carroll poem, it may not be the best to start with since identifying familiar words will be difficult. It can, however, bring an added dimension to the discussion of how the *sounds* of words bring excitement and move the action forward.

You may also want to read excerpts from recent sports columns or recaps of games, searching for similar active verbs and sensory details.

Writer's Notebook

After reading or hearing one or more of the sports poems and stories, ask your students to identify the sport about which they want to write. Have them sketch (not lovely artwork, but quick line drawings) to remind themselves of the movements, feelings, and sounds of that sport—to capture something their words cannot.

They then can begin to list actions connected with that sport. With the help of my students, I created the list for ice-skating included below:

Whirling
Gliding
Sliding
Spinning
Twirling
Spraying
Leaping
Falling

Next, ask your students to list sensory details connected with their chosen sport (see Figure 4.1).

Quick Write Possibilities

Invite students to write a poem about a sport. Remind them of how the action and excitement were created in the stories or poems that they

Figure 4.1 Chart of Sensory Details Connected to Ice Skating

Sights	Sounds	Feelings/Touch	Smells	Tastes
○ ice grooves ○ spray of crystals ○ colorful scarves	○ whirring ○ slashing	○ wind in face ○ weightlessness ○ flying ○ numb feet and hands ○ stinging cheeks	○ winter air ○ firewood ○ hot chocolate	○ dry mouth ○ hot cider ○ hot chocolate

have read in class—through active verbs and sensory details connected with the sport. They may also want to create a drawing to represent their chosen sport.

Mentor Texts

Hoops by Robert Burleigh and Stephen T. Johnson

Jabberwocky by Lewis Carroll and Christopher Myers

Casey at the Bat: A Ballad of the Republic Sung in the Year 1888 by Ernest L. Thayer and Christopher Bing

My ice-skating poem written in response to this quick write can provide an additional model.

At the Pond

Winter wind
brushing my face
stinging just a little
scarf flapping
legs pumping numb feet forward
accompanied by slashing
of blades
creating lacy designs
spraying
a wake of diamond crystals.
Whirling and twirling
flying—
weightlessly
over the ice.

Less Is Better

Grades 4–12

Short Forms Such as Haiku, Flash Fiction, Six-Word Memoirs

Writing Using Short Forms

- How can we condense our ideas?

Background for the Teacher

As teachers of writing, we often encourage our students to expand what they have written, to add more details, in order to help readers have a better image of what is happening or being described. We explore and explode individual moments in narratives to enable readers to see what we see. We identify, specify, and clarify to make our writing clearer. But sometimes we want to do the exact opposite: we want to distill our thoughts until we have just the gist—just a crucial kernel. Sometimes less is better.

I have facilitated many different kinds of workshops, retreats, and other group situations—for the church, for my school, and for my school district, as well as for the Columbus Area Writing Project. A favorite, effective way I have discovered to capture a collective sense of time spent together is the *Two Words* strategy of Linda Hoyt (2009). It is a safe, nonthreatening way to summarize and reflect for all ages. Each participant is invited to speak aloud two words that, for her, embody the experience. Heard all together, these words form a collective closure—a synthesis of the group work, process, and time together. This is much more powerful than having each member give long, sometimes rambling recounts of how the day has affected them. Instead, it creates a poetic connection that hangs in the air and confirms and affirms each member of the group.

There are several traditional written forms that require a similar reduction to the essential—rendering the core. The Japanese give us haiku, senryu, tanka, samurai death poetry, and one lovely form I have recently discovered, the haibun.

An English adaptation of the haiku is the lune, and a related Korean form is sijo.

In addition, we have several more modern forms that have been used with students for years. These include cinquain, Take Five, and diamante.

Newer "less is better" forms include 55 Fiction or Flash Fiction (limited to 55 words) and Six-Word Memoirs. And of course if you Twitter, there is Twitter poetry and fiction and a host of other 140-character possibilities. If you text, you have gotten used to reducing what you say to 160 characters.

The attraction to these forms is the same as my favorite ending for workshops mentioned above. It distills the ideas and renders the bare bones of our thoughts in stark images and naked truth.

Exploring these forms with your students provides them with alternative ways to express their ideas. I sometimes use one of these short forms at the end of units of study as another way to help students show what they know about a topic. The information is much more focused and centered than when they are asked to "write everything you know about X." (I do this on occasion as well, but that is another topic.)

Students love the limiting forms, treating their creations almost like puzzles that they must solve. The structures, while limiting the face of the products, not only free us to look at our topic in a more focused manner, but also force us to see in new ways, as we fit our ideas and words into the frameworks. (Also see quick write "What Container Will Hold My Words?")

Sharing Mentor Texts

Select a number of short texts to share with your students. You may want to focus on only one form, or you may want to share a variety of forms. Have students discuss the selections to determine the rules and begin to develop a framework for their own work. You may want to chart these and hang them up for references as the writers explore these shorter text types in their own writing. See Figure 4.2 for a reference chart of several short forms.

Figure 4.2 Short Forms

Haiku	3 lines, 17 syllables (5-7-5), related to nature
Senryu	Same as haiku only related to human foibles—usually cynical or humorous
Tanka	5 lines, 31 syllables (5-7-5-7-7), any topic
Samurai death poetry	Same as tanka except the focus moves from life (5-7-5) to death (7-7)
Haibun	Combines short prose passages with haiku
Lune	3 lines, 2 versions:
Robert Kelly Lune	5-3-5 syllables
Jack Collom Lune	He forgot the original Kelly version and used 3-5-3 words per line
Sijo	3 lines or 6 lines each with a fixed number of syllables per line 3 lines: 14–16 syllables 6 lines: 6–8 syllables Usually a joke or surprise or twist at the end

Cinquain	5 lines, varied topics and forms
Take Five	5 lines Noun 3 adjectives 3 participles (ing or ed) Sentence or 4 related words Noun or synonym
Diamante	7 Lines Noun 3 adjectives 3 participles (ing or ed) Sentence or 4 related words that shift toward opposite of first noun 3 participles (describing the noun at end) 2 adjectives (describing the noun at end) Opposite noun

Quick Write Possibilities

Invite students to select a topic in which they are interested. Ask them to select one of the short forms you have studied together to try out in their own writing. They can refer to the charts you have created for support as they create a piece following a particular framework. They may want to experiment with several structures to determine which best fits their content or to simply play with the variety of structures available.

The Mentor Texts

All of the suggestions listed below offer short texts or poems that can serve as models for your students and you as you explore limited and structured texts.

Not Quite What I Was Planning: Six-Word Memoirs by Writers Famous and Obscure From Smith Magazine, edited by Rachel Fershleiser and Larry Smith (http://www.smithmag.net)

Christmas Lights by Obediah Michael Smith (short poems)

Haiku: This Other World by Richard Wright

The World's Shortest Stories. Compiled and edited by Steve Moss

Also called *Fifty Five Fiction* because each story is 55 words long.

Braided Creek: A Conversation in Poetry by Jim Harrison and Ted Kooser

A correspondence in short poems (postcards) between two poet friends after Ted Kooser was diagnosed with cancer.

The Collected Poems of William Carlos Williams, Vol. 1: 1909–1939 by William Carlos Williams, A. Walton Litz, Christopher MacGowan

For Elementary Students

While appropriate poems can be found to share with younger students in all of the above texts, some contained may not be appropriate. The books below are specifically for children and will be appropriate for Grades 4 and 5.

Tap Dancing on the Roof: Sijo Poems by Linda Sue Park

All the Small Poems and Fourteen More by Valerie Worth

Short poems that describe everyday common objects in unique ways.

Additional Resources

Several short poem frameworks and samples are available at http://www.k12.hi.us/~shasincl/poem_frames.html#diamante1 (scroll down to the middle).

Quick Summary of Linda Hoyt's Two Word Strategy

http://www.worknotes.com/LA/Shreveport/DebbieRickards/OMITwo-WordStrategy.pdf

Comic Lives

Grades 4–12

Comics, Cartoons

Creating Comics and Cartoons

- How can we express our ideas in cartoon or comic form?

Background for the Teacher

I grew up during the heyday of comics. Comics and cartoons permeated my life from as early as I can remember. Saturday morning, as I lay on the living room carpet, eating my cereal, cartoons played on TV—good ones with animals fraught with human foibles, like Bugs Bunny, who forever outsmarted Elmer Fudd and Porky Pig, who ended each show— *That's all folks.* Ones like Mighty Mouse, who saved the day each episode with special powers. Early success in reading meant I could read the newspaper funnies to myself. My friends and I treasured those few comic books that we owned. We read and reread the adventures of Archie and the Gang. We learned about Army life from Sad Sack and Beetle Bailey. We rooted for Batman, Superman, and the Flash to quell the danger and zap the villains. We relished the sounds—BAM! KERBOOM! And we just laughed and enjoyed those animated animals like Tom and Jerry, Mickey Mouse and his lady friend, Minnie, and Popeye and Olive Oyl.

It was cartoons that introduced me to jazz and classical music. The soundtracks to cartoons were full symphonic orchestrations. I can still see Mickey and Minnie twirling wildly to Duke Ellington or Count Basie and Popeye and Olive cutting a rug.

As we grew older, so did the comics—we read *Peanuts* and felt wiser than Charlie Brown. We discovered political cartoons and satire. Comics took on a whole new life and helped us voice our opinions in humorous ways. They never grow old.

Comics may also offer a way to reach student writers who have not engaged with the more traditional school options for writing. My students were constantly drawing, and many had reams of tiny frames with serialized characters stuffed in their desks along with their social studies books and their writing folder. This writing they considered underground secret stuff to show to friends when they thought I wasn't looking.

Once we recognized this genre as legitimate in our class by including it as an option for reports and presentations, the creativity flowed, and some who were, in the past, remiss in turning in reports surprised us with both their talent and their clear understanding of the concepts they were illustrating.

Comics allow and promote a different kind of thinking, creativity, and excitement for writers.

The Quick Write Lesson

Sharing Mentor Texts

Invite your students to share the comics that they enjoy. These may be from the newspaper, comic books, or even graphic novels. Ask them to

Deeper Writing

examine and discuss the differences between this genre and others in which they typically write. What exactly makes a comic different from an illustrated story or picture book? They may notice the use of speech and thought bubbles, pictures to illustrate the action, frames or boxes to separate the events and interactions, and the way that our eyes move as we read comics, which is not the typical left-to-right, line-by-line reading, but more a "jumping around in the boxes." You may want to choose a graphic novel from the list below to share with the class to further note features and to consider also how the text flows in and around the pictures. You may also want to discuss the advantages and disadvantages of comics over other forms.

Quick Write Possibilities

Invite students to keep in mind the conversations from above and invite them to map out at least three frames to create a rough draft of a comic. They should include characters and an interaction, along with dialogue that has a beginning and an end. They may draw and write by hand or create the cartoon on an online program such as MakeBeliefsComix.com or use a software program like Comic Life.

Mentor Texts

Graphic Novels

Maus: A Survivor's Tale by Art Speigelman

MetaMaus by Art Speigelman

Persepolis: The Story of a Childhood by Marjane Satrapi

Pride of Baghdad by Brian K. Vaughan, art by Niko Henrichon

The Amazing Remarkable Monsieur Leotard by Eddie Campbell and Dan Best

Meanwhile by Jason Shiga

Bone, Vol. 1: Out From Boneville by Jeff Smith (series)

Foiled by Jane Yolen

Stories in Pictures

The Mysteries of Harris Burdick by Chris Van Allsburg

The Chronicles of Harris Burdick: 14 Amazing Authors Tell the Tales by Chris Van Allsburg

The Invention of Hugo Cabret by Brian Selznick

Wonderstruck by Brian Selznick

The Arrival by Shaun Tan

The Wall: Growing Up Behind the Iron Curtain by Peter Sis

Additional Resources

For Teachers

Teaching Visual Literacy: Using Comic Books, Graphic Novels, Anime, Cartoons, and More to Develop Comprehension and Thinking Skills by N. Frey and D. Fisher

Online comic strips (http://www.azcentral.com/ent/comics/)

Includes most well-known strips.

Reviews graphic novels for kids, teens, and young adults. http://www.noflyingnotights.com/

Comic Life is a program that allows you to create professional-looking comics drawing from the photographs and other pictures already stored in your computer.

Comic Life

- http://plasq.com/products/comiclife/win
- http://www.comiclife.com/

Create your own comics online (http://www.makebeliefscomix.com/Comix/)

For more sites where you can create your own comics, just enter "create comics, free online" in your favorite search engine. There are many others and they change regularly.

5 The Creation of a Quick Write

Developing Your Own

Once you and your students have used these quick writes and seen the powerful writing they generate, your students will be hooked and you will want to develop your own quick writes, tailored to your students' interests and their needs. This section will trace sources of ideas, the development of several quick writes, and ways to continue inviting deeper writing.

Where do you get your quick writes? How do you develop the quick writes? Where do you get your ideas? How do you choose books and other texts to go with the quick writes?

I am often asked the above questions after teachers experience one or more of my quick writes. There is a simple answer to those questions and then there is a more reflective, meta-answer.

The simple answer first—the quick writes arise, just as all writing arises, out of the stuff of my own life and thoughts, surroundings, people, places and things, current events, dreams and wonderings, and a continuing desire to push the limits on what can be created and written.

Once the initial idea dawns and has been extended to create a quick write, then what follows is what we know about writing—allowing writers time to think and write, providing models of good writing and writing possibilities, and allowing time for discussion and sharing of writing.

The longer answer considers how all of the above come together to create an effective writing possibility not only for myself, but for others, that leads to deeper writing—writing that is substantive, reflective, and meaningful.

Reflecting retroactively on the quick write development process, I realized that quick writes typically arose out of four main areas:

- Contexts
- Content
- Containers
- Lenses (which I call Container Linings)

CONTEXT

Where does writing come from? How do ideas arise? Where do we "find" writing?

All writing comes from somewhere—we don't write in a vacuum. It may be a conversation we overheard or in which we engaged that sparks an initial idea; it may be a picture or image, a piece of music or art, an experience or an event, a place, a person, a wondering, or a question. Something that we experience leads to an idea, a compelling force, a need to write.

For example, several years ago our writing project summer institute began, as always, with a retreat at Kenyon College. One stormy night my co-teacher Kevin Cordi (a renowned storyteller) told a terrifying story about the Blood Brothers. Shortly after the conclusion of his story, with each of us sufficiently scared out of our wits, all of the lights on the entire campus went out. What followed next was total confusion as we tried to figure out how to get back to our cabins near the woods in the pitch black.

The morning after this happened, I wrote a poem about this incident and then later again wrote about this incident in front of my class, modeling a personal narrative as they were beginning to write their own emotional stories. But I also began to reflect on the whole concept of "dark." Why *are* we afraid of the dark? In September 2011, a movie entitled *Don't Be Afraid of the Dark* played on this fear. What myths and symbols does the dark conjure? Then of course I thought about the opposite of dark—light, which led to thoughts about how we overcome darkness with light, both physically and metaphorically.

We often associate dark with the color black. As this idea rolled around in my mind, I thought of several books that I could possibly pair with these ideas. At the National Council of Teachers of English convention, I found *Pitch Black: A Graphic Novel* by Youme Landowne and Anthony Horton, which tells Anthony's story of homelessness, living in the dark tunnels under New York City.

In a totally different direction, both *Black Is Beautiful* by Ann McGovern and *Shades of Black: A Celebration of Our Children* by Sandra L. Pinkney and Myles C. Pinkney celebrate the variety of skin tones of African Americans.

An old favorite of mine, *Hailstones and Halibut Bones* by Mary O'Neill, includes poems about all colors.

What other colors do we associate with emotions? What other colors are symbolic for us? For example, in the West we associate white with virginity and wear white for weddings—I believe I have read that other countries use other colors. How does culture affect our interpretation of colors? Once I am interested in a concept, I usually research it in some way. So as I was writing this I became curious and did a quick check—what colors *do* brides wear in other countries? I wouldn't put it in a written quick write unless I can verify it, but I discovered this site with lists of cultural color meanings listed (http://www.empower-yourself-with-color-psychology.com/cultural-color.html).

A second site indicates that brides in China wear red, but it also links colors to advertisements and the psychological effects of colors (http://carolinkgd.wordpress.com/2012/01/05/psychology-of-color/).

This now adds another dimension to the writing possibilities, and we are beginning to see interests and ideas that could lead to more extended research as a follow-up to the quick write.

Through this process, I am now interested in a much more expanded concept of color than I was when I began. I have to decide where to draw the line (sometimes my tangents or wanderings among everything I find might lead to a second quick write). For example, here I could keep the original focus on dark linked to our fear as one quick write and only use books and resources that support that idea as mentor texts and then develop a second quick write dealing with the cultural and psychological meanings of colors.

Sometimes it is statistics or legal facts or news reports or some other background that I search for to support information in a quick write, such as in the quick writes "Watering Our World" or "The Things They Carried."

So out of the context of a night when the lights went out came two pieces of personal writing and a quick write about the dark and our fears, and perhaps one about black and colors in general. Below are sample quick write possibilities that could be presented to writers after sharing some of the mentor texts mentioned above.

Quick Write Possibilities

Invite your students to write about a time they were scared in the dark. Challenge them to use language that will help readers see the images they saw and feel the terror they felt. They may want to use a pattern or structure from one of the scary texts you have read together. They may write a personal narrative or essay or may want to tell a fictionalized story of fright.

Quick Write Possibilities II

Invite your students to write an essay about one color. Challenge them to include feelings, events, concepts, or other associations they have with that particular color. Remind them of the various ways that writers represented the color black in the mentor texts. They may want to model their writing after one of these or develop their own container for their "color" writing. See the suggested structure for creating and presenting a quick write in Figure 5.1.

CONTENT

What do I want to say? What is my message? What meaning do I want readers to construct?

Sometimes our meaning arises in a flash. We know exactly what we want to say. Other times we ponder and ruminate on what we mean. We may not even know yet.

I have been trying to write a piece about the conflicting feelings that engulfed me as my retirement approached. I had taken notes that entire last year and read several books that had a profound effect on helping me make meaning of this important life event. So far, I have written a poem and also a multi-genre/prose piece, but neither has captured the meaning I am struggling to make. I know the meaning I want to construct, and yet I don't really—not yet.

Conversely, sometimes the meaning is handed to us fully formed, the message as clear as a bell, and we can pour the meaning onto the paper in one sitting.

While rereading Elie Wiesel's *Night* and also leading a session for the writing project that focused on immigration, we read Luis Rodriquez's poem "Running to America" and an article that dealt with the trucks driven by a "coyote" in which Mexicans might cross the border. Within a matter of hours, I had read of two border crossings, both of which involved being crammed into awful, poorly ventilated, cramped spaces, facing fear and potential death. I immediately thought of the Middle Passage—the same conditions. What resulted the next morning was a poem written in almost one sitting. The first several lines of "Border Crossing Protocol" are below:

> Why must border crossings be cramped
> with people crushed and stuffed like smelts

in a sauce of sweat and urine and feces and fear?
Who decided that nakedness—with all precious
personal possessions stripped and stolen—was the
appropriate attire for such journeys?

The poem ends considering how each mother—no matter where she lives—wants the same things for her child.

Developing a quick write is no different—sometimes I read something and in a flash I know that this form can be a quick write. For example, I just recently finished reading *Lighthead* by Terrance Hayes. In this collection of poems, I encountered for the first time ever in my history of reading poetry a poem labeled as a *pecha kucha*. Immediately, I got excited. This was a form to which our summer institute participants had been introduced a couple of years ago by one of our members.

Pecha kucha, which literally means chit-chat, is a Japanese business presentation form designed to limit and loosely structure the presentation. Twenty slides are shown on a screen for 20 seconds while the presenter talks or annotates each one. This results in a presentation of six minutes and 40 seconds. This has become a popular presentation/entertainment form. After learning about this form, I attended one of the quarterly Pecha Kucha events in our city. The topics were widely varied.

Upon reading Hayes's poem, I immediately made the following notes on my Kindle:

Use *Lighthead* by Terrance Hayes

Write a poem or another piece in the container of an alternate medium, example pecha kucha—20 stanzas. Are they 20 seconds each when read aloud?

What other container could be used from what other media?

How does the container affect the process? the resulting writing?

So, I know exactly how I want to construct this quick write. I may not need anything other than Hayes's poems to begin. I will, however, look for other writings that have borrowed a container from other media. As I think, what comes to mind is a sonata with its classic form (introduction, exposition, development, recapitulation, coda). Would that make an effective written form? What about jazz improvisations or blues?

What about an abstract art piece or impressionistic piece—what would that look like in writing? Could I write a sculpture? The forms and media are endless. I get excited just thinking about the possibilities. The next step would be to search for more examples.

Fortune's Bones: The Manumission Requiem by Marilyn Nelson comes immediately to mind. It details the life of a slave named Fortune, his widow, and the doctor who rendered his bones after his death. Nelson pours the content, this painful story in the form of poetry, into a container the shape of a requiem.

CONTAINER

What container will hold my meaning? How can I present my meaning to my readers/audience?

Writing comes to us in containers that hold the meaning the writer wants to make. In our discussion above, we began to consider not only content but the containers to hold our writing—and how the containers might change or affect our meaning.

There is a quick write I use (see "What Container Will Hold My Words?") in which there is genre-switching at a rapid pace, using a previously written piece, as a form of revision and discovery. Writers often find during this quick write that their poem may actually be an essay, or their narrative may make a better poem. I suspect my dissatisfaction with my retirement piece that remains largely unwritten to my satisfaction is that I am using the wrong container.

When I speak of containers I mean genre, but I mean much more than genre. Container also mean the audience, where it will be published, how it is presented, and so on. For example, above I mentioned the poem "Border Crossing Protocol"—the genre is poetry; yet the finished container was a multimedia piece created with Movie Maker that included snippets of songs, images, meaningful transitions between those images, and narration (the poem "Border Crossing Protocol," as well as an additional poem that was necessitated by the images). I have shown the resulting movie itself as a stand-alone quick write for writing both to my students and to teachers.

Creating quick writes in which students are exposed to many containers as mentor texts is important as it enables them to envision a much wider array of possibilities to hold their own writing. For example, when I was writing the program booklet for our annual conference, I used program booklets from other conferences I had attended to consider possible formats and containers.

As you are working with writing ideas, consider all of the ways that resulting talking and thinking can be expressed. What genres are appropriate for the quick write suggestions and what final containers might result for the writing? As we pair books and other texts to our writing invitations, we want to intentionally present a variety of genres, forms, and structures to foster a multitude of possibilities.

CONTAINER LINING: OUR LENSES

How do we see what we are writing? What lenses do we wear as we write (or read)? What lenses will our readers/audience wear?

There is no reading and writing or anything else we do that is not filtered through the container lining. With both breadbaskets and pots for plants, there is often a lining which separates the contents of the container from the container itself. I have begun to think about this lining as the lenses we wear as we move through life—the lenses that individualize and color our reading and writing. We all have many lenses; some we wear always, and others we wear only on occasion. But there is always at least one lens through which we are filtering our experiences.

My lenses? I am African American, Christian (Episcopalian), teacher (former literacy coach, Title I teacher, classroom teacher, currently teacher in the Columbus Area Writing Project), Ohioan (born and raised), OSU alumna (two times—bachelor of science and master of arts), homeowner, wife, stepmother, and the list continues.

All of the above colors what I read in books and in the world—and also colors what I write. So "Border Crossing Protocol" was written through lenses that are particularly and specifically mine.

Figure 5.1 Suggested Structure for Creating a Writing Invitation or Quick Write

Topic—context/background story	How did this topic come about?
Mentor texts and discussion	What are ways to approach this topic/idea?
Writer's notebook	How can a writer think about this topic?
Quick write possibility	What are writers invited to write?
Sharing	What was written?
Debriefing of writing	How did the writing go?
	What was hard or easy?
	What was discovered?
	What might be done differently?

Effective quick writes provide writers with an opportunity to explore their own lenses, to look through alternative lenses, and to discover multiple perspectives. Considering the lenses that others wear, as well as our own, will enhance and deepen both our reading and writing experiences. Providing the other side(s) of stories and the unknown or hidden elements in issues and situations provides an avenue for discovery and leads to deeper writing.

As you read, write, and experience this world, I urge you to be in what Donald Graves called a state of *constant composition,* both in regard to your own writing and also in terms of quick write construction, always ready to discover an idea, receive an inspirational spark, and envision a new writing possibility.

References

Anderson, J. (2005). *Mechanically inclined: Building grammar, usage, and style into writers' workshop*. Portland, ME: Stenhouse.

Augustine, D. (1975). The existential sentence: Opulence is having the Vienna Boys' Choir sing "Happy Birthday" to me. In W. Sparke (Ed.), *Prisms: A self reader* (pp. 66–69). New York, NY: Harper's College Press.

Belenky, M. F., Clinchy, B. M., Goldberger, N. R., & Tarule, J. M. (1997). *Women's ways of knowing: The development of self, voice and the mind*. New York, NY: Basic Books.

Bently, P. (1994). *The book of dream symbols*. London, England: Pavilion Books.

Calkins, L. M. (1994). *The art of teaching writing* (New ed.). Portsmouth, NH: Heinemann.

Christensen, F., & Christensen, B. (2007). *Notes toward a new rhetoric: 9 essays for teachers* (3rd ed.). Port Charlotte, FL: Booklocker.com, Inc.

Christensen, L. (1996). The read around: Raising writers. In *Reading, writing, and rising up: Teaching about social justice and the power of the written word* (pp. 14–17). Milwaukee, WI: Rethinking Schools.

Clinton, H. R. (2006). *It takes a village* (10th anniversary ed.). New York, NY: Simon & Schuster.

Dombek, K., & Herndon, S. (2003). *Critical passages: Teaching the transitions to college composition*. New York, NY: Teachers College Press.

Feinson, R. (2004). *Secret universe of names: The dynamic interplay of names and destiny*. London, England: Overlook Duckworth.

Fletcher, R. (1992). *What a writer needs*. Portsmouth, NH: Heinemann.

Frey, N., & Fisher, D. (2008). *Teaching visual literacy: Using comic books, graphic novels, anime, cartoons, and more to develop comprehension and thinking skills*. Thousand Oaks, CA: Corwin Press.

Graves, D. H. (1999). *Bring life into learning: Create a lasting literacy*. Portsmouth, NH: Heinemann.

Graves, D. H. (2003). *Writing: Teachers & children at work* (20th anniversary ed.). Portsmouth, NH: Heinemann.

Hoyt, L. (2009). *Revisit, reflect, retell: Time tested strategies for teaching reading comprehension*. Portsmouth, NH: Heinemann.

Kellner, H. (2009). *Write what you see: 99 photos to inspire writing*. Fort Collins, CO: Cottonwood Press, Inc.

Killgallon, D., & Killgallon, J. (2000). *Sentence composing for elementary school: A worktext to build better sentences*. Portsmouth, NH: Heinemann.

Killgallon, D., & Killgallon, J. (2008). *Story grammar for elementary: A sentence-composing approach: A student worktext*. Portsmouth, NH: Heinemann.

Kohl, H. (2011). The politics of children's literature: What's wrong with the Rosa Parks Myth? In E. Marshall & O. Sensoy (Eds.), *Rethinking popular culture and media*. Milwaukee, WI: Rethinking School, Ltd.

Kohl, H. R., & Brown, C. S. (2007). *She would not be moved: How we tell the story of Rosa Parks and the Montgomery bus boycott*. New York, NY: The New Press.

National Governors Association (NGA) Center for Best Practices, & the Council of Chief State School Officers (CCSSO). (2010). *Common Core State Standards for English language arts & literacy in history/social studies, science, and technical subjects*. Washington, DC: Author. Retrieved from http://www.corestandards .org/assets/CCSSI_ELA%20Standards.pdf

National Writing Project & Nagin, C. (2006). *Because writing matters: Improving student writing in our schools* (Rev. ed.). San Francisco, CA: Jossey-Bass.

Nelson, G. L. (2004). *Writing and being: Taking back our lives through the power of language*. Philadelphia, PA: Innisfree Press.

Pugh, S. L., Hicks, J. W., & Davis, M. (1997). *Metaphorical ways of knowing: The imaginative nature of thought and expression*. Urbana, IL: National Council of Teachers of English.

Ray, K. W. (1999). *Wondrous words: Writers and writing in the elementary classroom*. New York, NY: National Council of Teachers of English.

Romano, T. (1995). *Writing with passion: Life stories, multiple genres*. Portsmouth, NH: Boynton/Cook.

Thibodeau, P., & Boroditsky, L. (2011). Metaphors we think with: The role of metaphor in reasoning. *PLoS ONE*. Retrieved from http://www.plosone.org/ article/info%3Adoi%2F10.1371%2Fjournal.pone.0016782

Van Horn, L. (2008). *Reading photographs to write with meaning and purpose*. International Reading Association, Inc.

Wormeli, R. (2009). *Metaphors and analogies: Power tools for teaching any subject*. Portland, ME: Stenhouse.

Literature Cited

PICTURE BOOKS

Aliki. (1998). *Marianthe's story: Painted words and spoken memories*. New York, NY: Greenwillow Books.

Baylor, Byrd. (1985). *Everybody needs a rock*. Fort Worth, TX: Aladdin.

Baylor, Byrd. (1995). *I'm in charge of celebrations*. Fort Worth, TX: Aladdin.

Blume, Judy. (2002). *The pain and the great one* (Rev. ed.). New York, NY: Athenum/Richard Jackson Books.

Bosak, Susan V. (2004). *Dream: A tale of wonder, wisdom and wishes*. New York, NY: Communication Project.

Bradby, Marie. (2000). *Momma, where are you from?* New York, NY: Orchard.

Brown, Anthony (2005). *Into the forest*. Somerville, MA: Candlewick Press.

Bunting, Eve. (1996). *Terrible things: An allegory of the Holocaust*. Philadelphia, PA: The Jewish Publication Society.

Bunting, Eve. (1998). *Going home*. Logan, IA: Perfection Learning.

Bunting, Eve. (2000). *December*. Boston, MA: Sandpiper.

Charlip, Remy. (1993). *Fortunately*. Fort Worth, TX: Aladdin.

Collier, Bryan. (2000). *Uptown*. New York, NY: Henry Holt.

Cowen-Fletcher, J. (1999). *It takes a village*. New York, NY: Scholastic.

Crew, Gary. (2011). *The viewer*. London, England: Hodder Childrens' Press.

Cronin, Doreen. (2000). *Click, clack, moo: Cows that type*. New York, NY: Simon and Schuster.

Dragonwagon, Crescent. (1993). *Home place*. Fort Worth, TX: Aladdin.

Fox, Mem. (1989). *Wilfrid Gordon McDonald Partridge*. Brooklyn, NY: Kane Miller Book Publishers.

Friedman, Ina R. (1987). *How my parents learned to eat*. New York, NY: Houghton Mifflin.

Hamilton, Virginia. (2004). *The people could fly: The picture book*. New York, NY: Knopf Books for Children.

Henkes, Kevin. (1991). *Chrysanthemum*. New York, NY: HarpersChildrens.

Johnson, Angela. (1993). *When I am old with you*. New York, NY: Orchard.

Johnson, Dinah. (2000). *Quinnie Blue*. New York, NY: Henry Holt.

Laminack, Lester L. (2004). *Saturday and teacakes*. Atlanta, GA: Peachtree Publication Ltd.

Leedy, Loreen. (1996). *How humans make friends*. New York, NY: Holiday House.

Lester, Julius. (1994). *The man who knew too much: A moral tale from the Baila of Zambia*. New York, NY: Clarion Books.

MacLachlan, Patricia. (1994). *All the places to love*. New York, NY: HarperCollins.

MacLachlan, Patricia. (1998). *What you know first*. New York, NY: HarperCollins.

Mason, Margaret H. (2010). *These hands*. New York, NY: Houghton Mifflin.

McGovern, Ann. (1969). *Black is beautiful*. New York, NY: Scholastic.

McKissack, Patricia C. (1992). *Flossie and the fox*. New York, NY: Scholastic.

McNaughton, Colin. (2005). *Once upon an ordinary day*. New York, NY: Farrar, Straus and Giroux.

Mobin-Uddin, Asma. (2005). *My name is Bilal*. Honesdale, PA: Boyds Mills Press.

Myers, Christopher. (2000). *Wings*. New York, NY: Scholastic.

Pinkney, Sandra L., & Pinkney, Myles C. (2000). *Shades of black: A celebration of our children*. New York, NY: Scholastic.

Raschka, Christopher. (2007). *Yo! Yes!* New York, NY: Scholastic.

Rosen, Michael. (2008). *Michael Rosen's sad book*. Somerville, MA: Candlewick.

Rylant, Cynthia. (1993). *When I was young in the mountain*. New York, NY: Puffin.

Rylant, Cynthia. (1996). *An angel for Solomon Singer*. New York, NY: Scholastic.

Rylant, Cynthia. (1998). *Appalachia: The voices of sleeping birds*. Logan, IA: Perfection Learning.

Rylant, Cynthia. (2001). *The relatives came*. New York, NY: Athenum.

Rylant, Cynthia. (2005). *Let's go home: The wonderful things about a house*. New York, NY: Simon and Schuster Books for Young Readers.

Say, Allen. (2008). *Grandfather's journey*. Boston, MA: Houghton Mifflin.

Schotter, Roni. (1999). *Nothing ever happens on 90th Street*. New York, NY: Scholastic.

Schotter, Roni. (2006). *The boy who collected words*. New York, NY: Schwartz and Wade.

Sendak, Maurice. (1993). *We are all in the dumps with Jack and Guy: Two nursery rhymes with pictures*. New York, NY: HarperCollins.

Seuss, Dr., Prelutsky, Jack, & Smith, Lane. (1998). *Hooray for Diffendoofer Day*. New York, NY: Knopf Books for Young Readers.

Sis, Peter. (2007). *The wall: Growing up behind the Iron Curtain*. New York, NY: Farrar, Straus and Giroux.

Stevens, Janet. (1996). *Tops and bottoms*. New York, NY: Scholastic.

Tan, Shaun. (2007). *The arrival*. New York, NY: Arthur A. Levine Books.

Tan, Shaun. (2010). *The lost thing*. Melbourne, Victoria, Australia: Lothian.

Van Allsburg, Chris. (1996). *The mysteries of Harris Burdick* (Portfolio ed.). New York, NY: Houghton Mifflin Books for Children.

Van Allsburg, Chris. (2009). *The Polar Express*. New York, NY: Houghton Mifflin.

Vander Zee, Ruth. (2004). *Mississippi morning*. Grand Rapids, MI: Eerdmans Books for Young Readers.

Viorst, Judith. (2009). *Alexander and the terrible, horrible, no good, very bad day*. New York, NY: Athenum.

Weatherford, Carole Boston. (2006). *Moses: When Harriet Tubman led her people to freedom*. New York, NY: Hyperion.

Wheatley, Nadia, & Rawlings, Donna. (1998). *My place*. Boston, MA: Addison Wesley Longman.

Wild, Margaret. (2007).*Woolvs in the sitee*. Honesdale, PA: Boyd Mills Press.

Wilson, Janet. (2000). *Imagine that!* Markham, Canada: Fitzhenry and Whiteside.

Woodson, Jacqueline. (2005). *Show way*. New York, NY: GP Putnam's Sons, Penguin Group.

Woodson, Jacqueline. (2007). *We had picnic this Sunday past*. New York, NY: Hyperion.

Woodson, Jacqueline, & Cooper, Floyd. (2007). *Sweet, sweet memory*. New York, NY: Hyperion.

Wyeth, Sharon Dennis. (1998). *Something beautiful*. New York, NY: Double Day Dell Publishing Group.

Yashima, Taro. (1976). *Crow boy*. New York, NY: Puffin.

Yolen, Jane. (1996). *Encounter*. Boston, MA: Sandpiper.

Young, Ed. (2002). *Seven blind mice*. New York, NY: Puffin.

Young, Ed. (2011). *The house that Baba built: An artist's childhood in China*. Boston, MA: Little Brown Books for Young Readers.

Zemach, Margot. (1980). *It could always be worse: A Yiddish folktale*. New York, NY: Farrar, Straus and Giroux.

FICTION AND NOVELS

Anderson, Laurie Halse. (2009). *Speak*. New York, NY: Penguin.

Birney, Betty G. (2005). *The seven wonders of Sassafras Spring*. New York, NY: Athenum.

Burnett, Frances H. (2008). *The secret garden*. New York, NY: Oxford University Press.

Cisneros, Sandra. (1991). *The house on Mango Street*. New York, NY: Vintage.

Curtis, Christopher Paul. (2002). *Bud, not Buddy*. New York, NY: Yearling Books.

Dickens, Charles. (2011). *A tale of two cities*. Retrieved from The Literacy Connection http://www.online-literature.com/dickens/twocities/1/ (Original published in 1859)

Draper, Sharon M. (2006). *Ziggy and the black dinosaurs*. Fort Worth, TX: Aladdin.

Giff, Patricia Reilly. (2004). *Pictures of Hollis Woods*. New York, NY: Dell Yearling.

Hamilton, Virginia. (1986). *The magical adventure of Pretty Pearl*. New York, NY: HarperCollins.

Hamilton, Virginia. (2009). *The people could fly: American black folktales*. New York, NY: Knopf Books for Young Readers.

Joseph, Lynn. (2001). *The color of my words*. New York, NY: HarperCollins.

Kinney, Jeff. (2007). *Diary of a wimpy kid*. New York, NY: Amulet.

Lester, Julius. (2005). *The old African*. New York, NY: Dial Books.

Le Guin, Ursula K. (2004). *Gifts*. Orlando, FL: Harcourt.

Le Guin, Ursula K. (2004). *A wizard of earthsea*. New York, NY: Bantam Books.

Lowry, Lois. (2009). *Messenger*. New York, NY: Bantam Books.

Macaulay, David. (1979). *Motel of mysteries*. New York, NY: Houghton Mifflin.

Mathis, Sharon Bell. (2006). *The hundred penny box*. New York, NY: Puffin.

Meyer, Stephenie. (2008). *Twilight*. New York, NY: Little Brown for Young Readers.

Mosley, Walter. (2006). *47*. New York, NY: Little Brown for Young Readers.

Moss, Steve. (Ed.). (1998). *World's shortest stories: Murder. Love. Horror. Suspense. All this and much more . . .* Philadelphia, PA: Running Press Books.

Park, Linda Sue. (2002). *When my name was Keoko: A novel of Korea in World War II*. New York, NY: Clarion Books.

Park, Linda Sue. (2011). *A long walk to water: Based on a true story*. Boston, MA: Clarion Books.

Paterson, Katherine. (1999). *The king's equal*. New York, NY: HarperCollins.

Polacco, Patricia. (2009). *January's sparrow*. New York, NY: Philomel.

O'Brien, Tim. (2009). *The things they carried*. New York, NY: First Mariner Books.

Osborne, Mary Pope. (1991). *American tall tales*. New York, NY: Knopf Books for Young Readers.

Selznick, Brian. (2007). *The invention of Hugo Cabret*. New York: NY: Scholastic.

Selznick, Brian. (2011). *Wonderstruck*. New York, NY: Scholastic.

Van Allsburg, Chris. (2011). *The chronicles of Harris Burdick: 14 amazing authors tell the tales*. Boston, MA: Houghton Mifflin Harcourt.

Walker, Alice. (1992). *The color purple*. New York, NY: Houghton Mifflin.

Wiesel, Elie. (2006). *Night*. New York, NY: Hill and Wang.

GRAPHIC NOVELS

Campbell, Eddie, & Best, Dan. (2008). *The amazing remarkable Monsieur Leotard*. New York, NY: First Second Books.

Landowne, Youme, & Horton, Anthony. (2008). *Pitch black*. El Paso, TX: Cinco Punto Press.

Satrapi, Marjane. (2004). *Persepolis: The story of a childhood*. New York, NY: Pantheon.

Shiga, Jason. (2010). *Meanwhile*. New York, NY: Amulet.

Smith, Jeff. (2005). *Bone* (Vol. 1): *Out from Boneville*. New York, NY: Scholastic.

Speigelman, Art. (1992). *Maus: A survivor's tale*. New York, NY: Pantheon.

Speigelman, Art. (2011). *MetaMaus: A look inside a modern classic*. New York, NY: Pantheon.

Vaughan, Brian K. (2006). *Pride of Baghdad*. New York, NY: DC Comics.

Yolen, Jane. (2010). *Foiled*. New York, NY: First Second Books.

NONFICTION AND INFORMATION BOOKS

Adams, Simon. (2009). *Soldier* (DK Eyewitness Books). New York, NY: DK Publishing.

Aigner-Clark, Julie. (2002). *Baby Einstein: The ABCs of art*. Burbank, CA: Baby Einstein.

Banner, Joe. (2011, August 31). Local columnist Joe Banner on reality TV and the Arab Spring. *Winston Salem Journal*. Retrieved from http://www2.journalnow.com/news/2011/aug/31/wsopin02-joe-banner-guest-columnist-reality-tv-at--ar-1345181/

Bryant, Jen. (2008). *A river of words: The story of William Carlos Williams*. Grand Rapids, MI: Eerdmans Books for Young Readers.

Burleigh, Robert. (2004). *Langston's train ride*. New York, NY: Orchard.

Catrow, David. (2005). *We the kids: The preamble to the Constitution of the United States*. New York, NY: Puffin.

Cepeda, E. J. (2011, October 24). Reality TV shows have poisonous effect on kids. *Chicago Sun-Times*. Retrieved from http://www.600words.com/2011/10/reality-tv-shows-have-poisonous-effect-on-kids.html

Cheney, Lynne. (2012). *We the people: The story of our Constitution*. New York, NY: Simon and Schuster.

Cherry, Lynn. (2002). *A river ran wild: An environmental history*. Boston, MA: Sandpiper.

Ehlert, Lois. (2004). *Hands: Growing up to be an artist*. Orlando, FL: Harcourt Children's Books.

Ehrlich, A. (Ed.). (2001). *When I was your age: Original stories about growing up* (Vol. 1). Somerville, MA: Candlewick.

Ehrlich, A. (Ed.). (2002).*When I was your age: Original stories about growing up* (Vol. 2). Somerville, MA: Candlewick.

Engber, D. (2006, January 3). Can soldiers buy extra gear? *Slate*. Retrieved from http://www.slate.com/id/2135103/

Falvey, David, & Hutt, Julie. (2009). *Letters to a soldier*. Terrytown, NY: Marshall Cavendish Corporation.

Fershleiser, Rachel, & Smith, Larry. (Eds.). (2006). *Not quite what I was planning: Six-word memoirs by writers famous and obscure*. New York, NY: Harper.

The First Post. (2008, October 28). Pros and cons of reality TV shows. *The Week*. Retrieved from http://www.theweek.co.uk/tv/35579/pros-and-cons-reality-tv-shows

Fletcher, Ralph. (2011). My father's hands. In *Mentor author, mentor texts: Short texts, craft notes and practical classroom* (p. 29). Portsmouth, NH: Heinemann.

Furgerson, L. (2012). How to prepare a disaster contingency plan for school. eHOW Family. Retrieved from http://www.ehow.com/how_7909709_prepare-disaster-contingency-plan-school.html

Giovanni Nikki. (2007). We are Virginia Tech (Speech). Retrieved from http://www.vt.edu/remember/archive/giovanni_transcript.html

Giovanni, Nikki, & Collier, Bryan. (2007). *Rosa*. New York, NY: Square Fish.

Girl Scout Research Institute study. (2011). Real to me: Girls and reality TV. Retrieved from http://www.girlscouts.org/research/pdf/real_to_me_factsheet.pdf

Hill, Laban Carrick. (2010). *Dave the potter: Artist poet slave*. New York, NY: Little Brown Books for Young Readers.

Hooper, Meredith. (1996). *The pebble in my pocket: A history of our earth*. New York, NY: Viking.

Hoose, Phillip M. (2001). Claudette Colvin: The first to keep her seat. In *We were there, too! Young people in U.S. history* (pp. 214–217). New York, NY: Farrar, Straus & Giroux.

Hoose, Phillip M. (2001). *We were there, too! Young people in U.S. history*. New York, NY: Farrar, Straus & Giroux.

Hoose, Phillip M. (2002). *It's our world, too! Young people who are making a difference: How they do it—how you can, too!* New York, NY: Farrar, Straus & Giroux.

Hoose, Phillip M. (2010). *Claudette Colvin: Twice toward justice*. New York, NY: Square Fish.

Horgan, Denis Edward. (2007). *Flotsam: A life in debris*. Higganum, CT: Higganum Hill.

International Debate Education Association. (n.d.). Reality TV. Retrieved from http://www.idebate.org/debatabase/topic_details.php?topicID=823

Jacobson, J. (1999). Artifacts of memory. In J. Kitchen & M. P. Jones (Eds.), *In brief: Short takes on the personal* (pp. 270–272). New York, NY: W. W. Norton & Company.

Judy. (2009–2011). Cultural color. Retrieved from http://www.empower-yourself-with-color-psychology.com/cultural-color.html

Keats, Ezra Jack. (1987). *John Henry: An American legend.* New York, NY: Dragonfly Books.

Kennedy, Caroline. (2002). *Profiles in courage for our time.* New York, NY: Hyperion.

Kennedy, John F. (2006). *Profiles in courage.* New York, NY: Harper Perennial Modern Classics. (Original published in 1955)

Kerley, Barbara. (2006). *A cool drink of water.* Tampa, FL: National Geographic Books.

Kerley, Barbara. (2009). *One world, one day.* Tampa, FL: National Geographic.

Kid Nation. (2011). Wikipedia. Retrieved from http://en.wikipedia.org/wiki/Kid_Nation

Kindersley, Anabel, Kindersley, Barnabas, & UNICEF. (1995). *Children just like me: A unique celebration of children around the world.* New York, NY: DK Children's Books.

King, Martin Luther, Jr. (2007). *I have a dream* by Martin Luther King Jr. (an illustrated edition of the speech with a foreword by Coretta Scott King). New York, NY: Scholastic.

Kohl, H. The politics of children's literature: What's wrong with the Rosa Parks myth? (2011). In E. Marshall & O. Sensoy (Eds.), *Rethinking popular culture and media.* Retrieved from http://www.wou.edu/~ulvelad/courses/ED632Spring11/Assets/RosaParks.pdf

Kooser, Ted. (1996). Hands. In J. Kitchen & M. P. Jones (Eds.), *In short: A collection of brief creative nonfiction* (pp. 128–130). New York, NY: W. W. Norton.

Krull, Kathleen. (1999). *A kids' guide to America's Bill of Rights: Curfews, censorship, and the 100-pound giant.* New York, NY: HarperCollins.

Lee, L. (1996). One human hand. In J. Kitchen & M. P. Jones (Eds.), *In short: A collection of brief creative nonfiction* (pp. 293–294). New York, NY: W. W. Norton.

Lester, Julius. (1999). *John Henry.* New York, NY: Puffin.

Lester, Julius. (2008). *Let's talk about race.* New York, NY: Amistad.

Lewis, Barbara A. (1992). *Kids with courage: True stories about young people making a difference.* Minneapolis, MN: Free Spirit Publishing.

Loewen, James W. (2007). *Lies my teacher told me: Everything your American history textbook got wrong.* New York, NY: Touchstone.

Madrigal, A. (2011, May 25). Why are spy researchers building a "Metaphor Program?" *The Atlantic.* Retrieved from http://www.theatlantic.com/technology/archive/2011/05/why-are-spy-researchers-building-a-metaphor-program/239402/#slide1

McKinney, Barbara. (1998). *A drop around the world.* Nevada City, CA: Dawn Publications.

Millard, Anne. (1998). *A street through time: A 12,000-year walk through history* (A DK book). New York, NY: DK Publishing.

Miller, B. (1999). Artifacts. In J. Kitchen & M. P. Jones (Eds.), *In brief: Short takes on the personal* (pp. 244–248). New York, NY: W. W. Norton.

Minor, Horace. (1956). The body rituals among the Nacirema. *The American Anthropologist, (58)*3.

Montgomery, D. (2009, May 22). U.S. mission for sci-fi writers: Imagine that (novelists plot the future of homeland security). *Washington Post.* Retrieved from http://www.washingtonpost.com/wpdyn/content/article/2009/05/21/AR2009052104379.html

Morrison, Gordon. (2006). *A drop of water.* Boston, MA: Houghton Mifflin.

Morrison, Toni. (2008, Jan. 28). Toni Morrison's letter to Barack Obama. *New York Observer*. Retrieved from http://www.observer.com/2008/toni-morrisons-letter-barack-obama

Moutoussamy-Ashe, Jeanne. (1993). *Daddy and me: A photo story of Arthur Ashe and his daughter Camera*. New York, NY: Alfred A. Knopf.

Myers, Walter Dean. (2011). *We are American: A tribute from the heart*. New York, NY: HarperCollins.

Nelson, Scott Reynolds, & Aronson, Marc. (2007). *Ain't nothing but a man: My quest to find the real John Henry*. Tampa, FL: National Geographic Children's Press.

Niemoller, Martin. (1946). Speech addressing the German church. Retrieved from http://en.wikiquote.org/wiki/Martin_Niem%C3%B6ller

Nilsen, Anna. (2000). *Art fraud detective: Spot the difference, solve the crime!* New York, NY: Kingfisher.

NPR Books. (2010, May 16). Time flies when you're deconstructing aphorisms (Interview with Julian Baggini). Retrieved from http://www.npr.org/templates/story/story.php?storyId=126807556

Obama, Barack. (2010). *Of thee I sing: A letter to my daughters*. New York, NY: Knopf Books for Young Readers.

O'Brien, Tim. (1996). LZ Gator Vietnam, February 1994. In J. Kitchen & M. P. Jones (Eds.), *In short: A collection of brief creative nonfiction* (pp. 60–61). New York, NY: W. W. Norton.

Parks, Rosa, & Haskins, Jim. (1999). *Rosa Parks: My story*. New York, NY: Puffin.

Pitts, L., Jr. (2011, August 21). When reality goes too far someone pays. *The Miami Herald*. Retrieved from http://www.miamiherald.com/2011/08/21/2368459/when-reality-tv-goes-too-far-someone.html

Pitts, L., Jr. (2011, August 22). Reality shows have real consequences. *Columbus Dispatch*. Retrieved from http://www.dispatch.com/content/stories/editorials/2011/08/22/reality-shows-have-real-consequences.html

Rappaport, Doreen. (2007). *Martin's big words: The life of Dr. Martin Luther King Jr.* New York, NY: Hyperion.

Rappaport, Doreen. (2008). *Abe's honest words: The life of Abraham Lincoln*. New York, NY: Hyperion.

Ringgold, Faith. (2003). *If a bus could talk: The story of Rosa Parks*. Fort Worth, TX: Aladdin.

Rodriguez, A. (1996). My mother in two photographs, among other things. In J. Kitchen & M. P. Jones (Eds.), *In short: A collection of brief creative nonfiction* (pp. 138–141). New York, NY: W. W. Norton.

Rodriguez, Richard. (2004). *Hunger of memory: The education of Richard Rodriguez*. New York, NY: Dial Press.

Shetterly, R. (2008). *Americans who tell the truth*. New York, NY: Puffin.

Sis, P. (2003). *Follow the dream: The story of Christopher Columbus*. New York, NY: Knopf for Young Readers.

Sis, P. (2007). *The Wall: Growing up behind the Iron Curtain*. New York, NY: Farrar, Straus, & Giroux.

Smith, David J. (2009). *If America were a village: A book about the people of the United States*. Toronto, Canada: Kids Can Press.

Smith, David J. (2011). *If the world were a village* (2nd ed.). Toronto, Canada: Kids Can Press.

Smith, David J. (2011). *This child every child: A book about the world's children*. Toronto, Canada: Kids Can Press.

Spier, Peter (1991). *We the people: The Constitution of the United States of America.* New York, NY: Doubleday.

Strauss, Rochelle. (2007). *One well: The story of water on the earth.* Toronto, Canada: Kids Can Press.

Walker, Alice. (2008, November 5). Alice Walker open letter to Barack Obama. Retrieved from http://shiva2731.blogspot.com/2008/11/alice-walker-open-letter-to-barack.html

West, P. (1996). Borrowed time. In J. Kitchen & M. P. Jones (Eds.), *In short: A collection of brief creative nonfiction* (pp. 96–97). New York, NY: W. W. Norton.

Wick, Walter. (1997). *A drop of water: A book of science and wonder.* New York, NY: Scholastic.

Wiesel, Elie. (1986). Nobel Peace Prize acceptance speech. Nobel Prize.org. Retrieved from http://www.nobelprize.org/nobel_prizes/peace/laureates/1986/wiesel-acceptance.html

Winter, Jeanette. (2002). *Emily Dickinson's letter to the world.* New York, NY: Farrar, Straus & Giroux.

Yolen, Jane. (2009). *My uncle Emily.* New York, NY: Philomel.

Zinn, Howard. (2005). *A people's history of the United States: 1492–present.* New York, NY: HarperCollins.

Zinn, Howard, & Stefoff, Rebecca. (2007). *A Young People's History of the United States: Columbus to the Spanish-American War* (Vol. 1). New York, NY: Seven Stories Press.

Zinn, Howard, & Stefoff, Rebecca. (2007). *A Young People's History of the United States: Class struggle to the war on terror* (Vol. 2). New York, NY: Seven Stories Press.

POETRY

Angelou, Maya. (1993). *Life doesn't frighten me.* New York, NY: Stewart, Tabori, & Chang.

Angelou, Maya. (1993). *On the pulse of the morning: The inaugural poem.* New York, NY: Random House.

Angelou, Maya. (2006). *Celebrations: Rituals of peace and prayer.* New York, NY: Random House.

Burleigh, Robert. (2001). *Hoops.* Boston, MA: Sandpiper.

Carroll, Lewis, & Myers, Christopher. (2007). *Jabberwocky.* New York, NY: Hyperion.

Christian, Peggy. (2008). *If you find a rock.* Boston, MA: Sandpiper.

Collins, Billy. (2003). On turning ten. In S. M. Intrator & M. Scribner (Eds.), *Teaching with fire: Poetry that sustains the courage to teach* (p. 55). San Francisco, CA: Jossey-Bass.

Creech, Sharon. (2001). *Love that dog.* New York, NY: HarperCollins.

Creech, Sharon. (2005). *Heartbeat.* New York, NY: HarperCollins.

De Jesus, T. (2004). It makes me furious. In W. Cooling (Ed.), *Come to the great world: Poems from around the globe* (p. 37). New York, NY: Holiday House.

Frost, Robert. (2012). The road not taken (read by Robert Frost). Retrieved from http://www.poets.org/viewmedia.php/prmMID/15717

Gay, Ross. (2011). Prayer for my unborn niece or nephew (poem). Poet.Org. Retrieved from http://www.poets.org/viewmedia.php/prmMID/22600

Giovanni, Nikki. (1993). *Ego-tripping and other poems for young people*. New York, NY: Lawrence Hill Books.

Giovanni, Nikki. (Ed.). (2008). *Hip hop speaks to children: A celebration of poetry with a beat*. Naperville, IL: Sourcebooks Jabberwocky.

Goldbarth, A. (2012). *Library*. Retrieved from Poetry Daily. http://www.poetrydaily.org/special_features/library.php

Greenberg, Jan. (2001). *Heart to heart: New poems inspired by twentieth century American art*. New York, NY: Harry M. Abrams.

Greenberg, Jan. (2008). *Side by side: New poems inspired by art from around the world*. New York, NY: Harry M. Abrams.

Greenfield, Eloise. (1993). Nathaniel talking. London, England: Writers & Readers Publishing.

Grimes, Nikki. (2001). *Pocketful of poems*. New York, NY: Clarion.

Harrison, Jim, & Kooser, Ted. (2003). *Braided Creek: A conversation in poetry*. Port Townsend, WA: Copper Canyon Press.

Hopkins, Lee Bennett. (1999). *Been to yesterdays: Poems of a life*. Honesdale, PA: Boyd Mills Press.

Hughes, Langston. (1926). Dreams. Retrieved from http://www.poemhunter.com/langston-hughes/

Hughes, Langston. (1932). Dream variations. Retrieved from http://www.poemhunter.com/langston-hughes

Hughes, Langston. (1951). Dream deferred (Harlem). Retrieved from http://www.poemhunter.com/langston-hughes/

Hughes, Langston, Sims, L. S., & Voigt, D. M. (1995). *The block*. New York, NY: Metropolitan Museum of Art Books.

Intrator, S. M., & Scribner, M. (Eds.). (2003). *Teaching with fire: Poetry that sustains the courage to teach*. San Francisco, CA: Jossey-Bass.

Johnson, L. L. (1998). *Sun moon soup*. Honesdale, PA: Front Street Press.

Johnston, Tony. (1999). *My Mexico—Mexico mio*. New York, NY: Puffin.

Lantz, N. (2011). Fork with two tines pushed together. Retrieved from http://www.poets.org/viewmedia.php/prmMID/22706

Latifah, Queen. (2008). Ladies first. In N. Giovanni (Ed.), *Hip hop speaks to children: A celebration of poetry with a beat*. Naperville, IL: Sourcebooks Jabberwocky.

Lewis, J. Patrick. (2005). *Monumental verses*. Tampa, FL: National Geographic Children's Books.

Lewis, J. Patrick. (2007). *The brothers' war: Civil War voices in verse*. Tampa, FL: National Geographic Children's Books.

Lyon, G. E. (n.d.). Where I'm from. Retrieved from http://www.georgeellalyon.com/where.html

Meyer, S. (2008). *Twilight*. New York, NY: Little Brown for Young Readers. Hechette Book Group.

Myers, Walter Dean. (2009). *Here in Harlem: Poems in many voices*. New York, NY: Holiday House.

Nelson, Marilyn. (2001). *Carver: A life in poems*. Honesdale, PA: Front Street Books.

Nelson, Marilyn. (2009). *A wreath for Emmett Till*. Boston, MA: Houghton Mifflin.

Neruda, Pablo. (2003). Keeping quiet. In S. M. Intrator & M. Scribner (Eds.), *Teaching with fire: Poetry that sustains the courage to teach* (p. 103). San Francisco, CA: Jossey-Bass.

Oliver, Mary. (2003). The journey. In S. M. Intrator & M. Scribner (Eds.), *Teaching with fire: Poetry that sustains the courage to teach* (p. 59). San Francisco, CA: Jossey-Bass.

O'Neill, Mary. (1990). *Hailstones and halibut bones*. New York, NY: Doubleday Books.

Park, Linda Sue. (2007). *Tap dancing on the roof: Sijo poems*. New York, NY: Clarion.

Patz, Nancy. (2003). *Who was the woman who wore the hat?* New York, NY: Dutton Books.

Rochelle, B. (2000). *Words with wings: A treasury of African-American poetry and art*. New York, NY: HarperCollins.

Rumi. (2003). Two kinds of intelligence. In S. M. Intrator & M. Scribner (Eds.), *Teaching with fire: Poetry that sustains the courage to teach* (p. 127). San Francisco, CA: Jossey-Bass.

Rylant, Cynthia. (1994). *Something permanent*. Orlando, FL: Harcourt Children's Books.

Smith, C. R., Jr. (2008). Allow me to introduce myself. In N. Giovanni (Ed.), *Hip hop speaks to children: A celebration of poetry with a beat*. Naperville, IL: Sourcebooks Jabberwocky.

Smith, Obediah Michael. (2003). *Christmas lights*. New Providence, Bahamas: Verse Place Press.

Symborska, Wislawa. (2003). There but for the grace. In S. M., Intrator & M. Scribner (Eds.), *Teaching with fire: Poetry that sustains the courage to teach* (p. 107). San Francisco, CA: Jossey-Bass.

Thayer, Ernest L., & Bing, Christopher. (2000). *Casey at the bat: A ballad of the republic sung in the year 1888*. San Francisco, CA: Chronicle Books.

Volavkova, Hana. (Ed.). (1993). *I never saw another butterfly: Children's drawings and poems from Terezin concentration camp 1942–44*. New York, NY: Schocken Books.

Wetherford, Carole Boston. (2002). *Remember the bridge: Poems of a people*. New York, NY: Philomel.

Williams, Vera B. (2004). *Amber was brave, Essie was smart*. New York, NY: Greenwillow Books.

Williams, Willam Carlos. (1934). As the cat. Retrieved from http://www.poemhunter.com/william-carlos-williams/poems/page-3/

Williams, William Carlos. (2011). Between walls. Poetry Foundation. Retrieved from http://www.poetryfoundation.org/archive/poet.html?id=81496

Williams, Willam Carlos. (2011). The red wheelbarrow. Poetry Foundation. Retrieved from http://www.poetryfoundation.org/archive/poet.html?id=81496 (Original published in 1923)

Williams, William Carlos. (2011). Winter trees. Poetry Foundation. Retrieved from http://www.poetryfoundation.org/archive/poet.html?id=81496

Williams, William Carlos, Litz, A. Walton, & MacGowan, Christopher. (1991). *The collected poems of William Carlos Williams: Vol. 1. 1909–1939*. New York, NY: New Directions Books.

Woodson, Jacqueline. (2010). *Locomotion*. New York, NY: Speak Publishing.

Worth, Valerie. (1996). *All the small poems and fourteen more*. New York, NY: Farrar, Straus & Giroux.

Wright, Richard. (2011). *Haiku: This other world*. New York, NY: Arcade Publishing.

Yolen, Jane. (2002). *Horizons: Poems as far as the eye can see*. Honesdale, PA: Word Song/Boyd Mills Press.

Zephaniah, Benjamin. (2004). Good hope. In W. Cooling (Ed.), *Come to the great world: Poems from around the globe* (pp. 42–43). New York, NY: Holiday House.

Zephaniah, Benjamin. Good hope (poem). Retrieved from http://beltincischool
.blogspot.com/2010/12/poem-good-hope.html
Zimmer, Tracie Vaughn. (2009). *Steady hands: Poems about work.* New York, NY:
Clarion.

ELECTRONIC ADDITIONAL RESOURCES

Airline safety and contingency plans (on board the aircraft). (2006). Retrieved
from http://www.airlinetraveladvice.com/safety.shtml
American founding documents. (2001–2010). Retrieved from http://www
.foundingfathers.info/documents/ (Original documents, 1700s)
American rhetoric. (2001–2012). http://www.americanrhetoric.com/
Artcyclopedia. (2011). http://www.artcyclopedia.com/
Carol Ink GD. (2012). Psychology of color. Retrieved from http://carolinkgd
.wordpress.com/2012/01/05/psychology-of-color/
Change.org. (2012). http://www.change.org/ or http://www.change.org/start-
a-petition
Comic Life (program that creates professional-looking comics drawing from your
photographs). Available from http://plasq.com/products/comiclife/win
Comics. (2012). (Online comic strips). http://www.azcentral.com/ent/comics/
Famous paintings/art appreciation lessons for kids. (n.d.). Garden of praise.
Retrieved from http://gardenofpraise.com/art.htm
Famous speeches. (n.d.). http://www.famousquotes.me.uk/speeches/index.htm
FEMA/ready.gov (for disaster plans). http://www.ready.gov/natural-disasters
Great Quotes.com. (2011). http://www.great-quotes.com/
John F. Kennedy Presidential Library and Museum. (n.d.). Profiles in Courage Award.
http://www.jfklibrary.org/Events-and-Awards/Profile-in-Courage-Award.aspx
Johnson, M. B. (2005). *Shoes on the highway: Using visual and audio cues to inspire student
playwrights.* Retrieved from http://books.heinemann.com/shoesonthehighway/
default.aspx
Kaunakakai Multiage Primary. (2000–2001). Short poem frames and recipes. Retrieved
from http://www.k12.hi.us/~shasincl/poem_frames.html#diamante1
Legacy Project. (n.d.). www.legacyproject.org
Library of Congress. (n.d.). Prints and photographs online catalog. http://www
.loc.gov/pictures/
Need to know. (2011, January). A "lost boy" of Sudan returns to rebuild his homeland
[PBS video about Salva Dut]. http://www.pbs.org/wnet/need-to-know/
video/video-a-lost-boy-of-sudan-returns-to-rebuild-his-homeland/6249/
No Flying No Tights. [Graphic novel review website] http://www.noflying
notights.com/
Online speeches and letters related to social justice and civil rights issues. (2006–
2012). http://www.sojust.net/speeches.html & http://www.sojust.net/letters
.html
Pioch, Nicolas. (2002). Artist index. Web Museum, Paris. Retrieved from http://
www.ibiblio.org/wm/paint/auth/
Quote Mountain.com. (2010). http://www.quotemountain.com/
Quotes and Sayings. (2009). http://www.quotesandsayings.com/proverbial.htm
Rickard, D. (2008). Linda Hoyt's two word strategy. Retrieved from http://www
.worknotes.com/LA/Shreveport/DebbieRickards/OMITwo-WordStrategy.pdf

Rubin, G., & Newton, E. (Eds). Images of hate and hope—Freedom Summer. Newseum. Retrieved from http://www.newseum.org/mississippi/

Rubin, G., & Newton, E. (Eds). *The Pulitzer Prize photographs: Capture the moment*. Newseum. Retrieved from http://www.newseum.org/exhibits-and-theaters/permanent-exhibits/pulitzer/

Smith, D. J. (n.d.). Mapping.com. http://www.mapping.com/village.shtml

Smith, L. (2005–2011). Six-word memoirs. *Smith Magazine*. http://www.smithmag.net

Smithsonian Photography Initiative. (n.d). http://photography.si.edu/

Sweney, B. Z., Keeley, M., & Canalos, K. (n.d.). Artful reading [PowerPoint presentation]. Retrieved from http://www.columbusmuseum.org/monet_education/pdf/images.pdf or http://www.columbusmuseum.org/monet_education/pages/images.html

TimeLines. (n.d.). http://timelines.com/

United Citizens and Immigration Services. (2011). *A guide to naturalization*. Retrieved from http://www.uscis.gov/files/article/M-476.pdf

United Nations Development Program. (2012). Millennium development goals: Eight goals by 2015. http://www.undp.org/mdg/goal7.shtml

U.S. Constitution Online. (2011). Retrieved from http://www.usconstitution.net/const.html

Water for Sudan [Homepage of Salva Dut's nonprofit organization]. (2011). http://www.waterforsudan.org

What I Want My Words to Do to You [Video movie trailer]. Retrieved from http://www.youtube.com/watch?v=szBDN-Hp4PU [Description, study guide, lesson plans and purchase information related to this film] http://www.pbs.org/pov/whatiwant/

Zimmerman, B. (2006–2012). Make Beliefs Comix.com (Create your own comics online). http://www.makebeliefscomix.com/Comix/

Index

Adams, S., 96
After-school writing groups, 4, 163
Aging topic, 74
AIDS topic, 73
Alexander, J., 162
Analytical writing, 2, 7
Anderson, J., 173
And I Heard Them Say prompt,
    165–168
Angelou, M., 76, 77, 112, 115
Archaeologists' view of common objects
    quick write, 101
  additional resources for, 104
  background notes for, 102
  lesson outline for, 102–103
  mentor texts for, 103
  quick write possibilities for, 103
  sharing mentor texts and, 102–103
  writer's notebook and, 103
  See also Close observation topics
Argumentative writing, 5
Aronson, M., 44
Artful Reading and Writing
    prompt, 77–82
Artifacts. *See* Archaeologists' view of
    common objects quick write
Art-inspired reading/writing
    quick write, 77
  additional resources for, 81–82
  background notes for, 77–78
  lesson outline for, 78–79
  mentor texts for, 79–81
  quick write possibilities for, 79
  sharing mentor texts and, 78–79
  See also Close observation topics
Authentic writing, 3–4, 5
Autobiographies, 19, 29

Baylor, B., 41
Belenky, M. F., 35
Best, D., 184
The Bill of Rights prompt, 140–143
Bing, C., 178
Boroditsky, L., 108
Bosak, S. V., 59, 61
Bryant, J., 110, 170, 171
Bunting, E., 52, 73
Burleigh, R., 171, 178
Burnett, F. H., 126

Calkins, L. M., 6
Campbell, E., 184
Carroll, L., 176, 178
Cartoons. *See* Comics/cartoons
    quick write
Celebrations. *See* Special events
    remembrance/celebration quick write
Change. *See* Writing for world change
    topics
Charlip, R., 48
Christensen, L., 173
Christian, P., 41
Citizenship. *See* Defining Americans quick
    write; Recognition of noteworthy
    people/action quick write
Clean Water Act of 1972, 139
Clinchy, B. M., 35
Clinton, H. R., 89
Close observation topics, 63
  archaeologists' view of common
      objects, 101–104
  art-inspired reading/writing, 77–82
  effects/costs of decisions, 91–93
  essential objects in lives, 93–97
  horizons/limits in life, 74–77

metaphors, 107–110
misconceptions about history, 97–101
photo-inspired writing, 82–87
proverbs/sayings analysis, 88–91
questioning object's nature/
    uses/owner, 67–71
reality television programs, 104–107
seeing common objects, 63–67
shocking statements, 71–74
See also Quick writes
Collected objects quick write, 37
additional resources for, 41–42
background notes for, 37–38
lesson outline for, 38–39
mentor texts for, 39–41
quick write possibilities for, 39
sharing mentor texts and, 38
writer's notebook and, 38–39
See also Personal knowledge/
    memory topics; *See*ing common
    objects quick write
Collier, B., 99
Collins, B., 76, 77, 158
Columbus Area Writing Project,
    ix, 2, 179, 193
Comic Life software, 184, 185
Comic Lives prompt, 182–185
Comics/cartoons quick write, 182
additional resources for, 185
background notes for, 183
graphic novels, 184
lesson outline for, 183–184
mentor texts for, 184–185
picture stories, 184–185
quick write possibilities for, 184
sharing mentor texts and, 183–184
See also Writing craft/conventions topics
Coming together of people/groups
    quick write, 120
additional resources for, 122–123
background notes for, 120–121
lesson outline for, 121–122
mentor texts for, 122
quick write possibilities for, 122
sharing mentor texts and, 121
See also Writing for world change topics
Common Core. *See* New Common Core
    College and Career Readiness Anchor
    Standards for Writing

Communities topic, 31–32, 74
Constitutional rights quick write, 140–141
additional resources for, 143
background notes for, 141
lesson outline for, 142–143
mentor texts for, 143
quick write possibilities for, 142–143
sharing mentor texts and, 142
writer's notebook and, 142
See also Writing for world change topics
Contingency Plans prompt, 144–147
Conversations in writing quick write, 165
additional resources for, 168
background notes for, 165–166
dialogue in, 167–168
lesson outline for, 166–168
mentor texts for, 168
quick write possibilities for, 167–168
sharing mentor texts and, 166
writer's notebook and, 166–167
See also Genre experimentation topics
Cooling, W., 160
Craft/conventions. *See* Writing craft/
    conventions topics
Creative writing, 5
Creech, S., 158, 161
Crew, G., 165
Critical analysis, xi, 2, 7
Cronin, D., 143
Cumulative Poems prompt, 171–175
Cuomo, M., 116

Death topic, 74
Decisions. *See* Effects/costs of
    decisions quick write
Deeper writing, xi, 1
after-school writing groups and, 4
alternative perspectives and, 1, 2
authentic writing and, 3–4, 5
conscious attention and, 2–3
constant composition, state of, 194
description of, 1–4
existential definition activity and, 6
insight, development of, 2, 3
instructional scaffolding, mini-lessons
    and, 6–7
literature/student writing
    linkage and, 7
prompts, quick writes and, 5–7

rich texts and, 2
risk-taking and, 4
struggling writers and, 5–6, 7
types of writing, 5
writing curriculum and, 6–7
writing practice opportunities and, 4–5
writing techniques, charting of, 10
writing-what-you-know
        approach and, 6
See also Quick writes
Defining Americans quick write, 151
    additional resources for, 154–155
    background notes for, 151–152
    lesson outline for, 152–153
    mentor texts for, 154
    quick write possibilities for, 153
    sharing mentor texts and, 152–153
    See also Writing for world change topics
de Jesus, T., 160
Descriptive writing, 63
Diamante short form, 179, 181 (figure)
    See also Short form writing quick write
Diaz, J., 169
Dickens, C., 47, 48
Divorce/separation topic, 734
Draper, S. M., 126
Dreams quick write, 58
    additional resources for, 61–62
    background notes for, 58–59
    lesson outline for, 59–60
    mentor text for, 61
    quick write possibilities for, 60
    sharing mentor texts and, 59
    writer's notebook and, 59–60
    See also Magical powers in lives quick
        write; Personal knowledge/
        memory topics
Dut, S., 138

Earliest memories quick write, 17–18
    additional resources for, 22–23
    background notes for, 18–19
    lesson outline for, 19–21
    mentor texts for, 21–22
    quick write possibilities for, 20–21
    sharing mentor texts and, 19
    writer's notebook and, 20
    See also Personal knowledge/
        memory topics

Effects/costs of decisions
        quick write, 91
    background notes for, 91–92
    lesson outline for, 92–93
    quick write possibilities for, 92
    sharing mentor texts and, 92
    writer's notebook and, 92
    See also Close observation topics
Encounters prompt, 120–123
Essential objects in lives quick write, 93
    additional resources for, 97
    background notes for, 93–94
    lesson outline for, 94–96
    mentor texts for, 96
    quick write possibilities for, 96
    sharing mentor texts and, 94–95
    writer's notebook and, 95–96
    See also Close observation topics
Existential definition activity, 6
Explanatory writing, 5

The Face of Reality prompt, 103–107
Falvey, D., 95, 96
Family homes topic, 30–31, 32–33
Family secrets topic, 74
    See also Secrets in lives quick write
Family stories/tall tales quick write, 42
    additional resources for, 45–46
    background notes for, 42–43
    lesson outline for, 43–45
    mentor texts for, 45
    quick write possibilities for, 44–45
    sharing mentor texts and, 43–44
    writer's notebook and, 44
    See also Personal knowledge/
        memory topics
Feinson, R., 24
Fershleiser, R., 181
Flash fiction, 179
    See also Short form writing quick write
Fletcher, R., 68, 128
For Better or For Worse prompt, 46–49
FRIED (facts/reasons/incidents/
        evidence) information, 54–55
Frost, R., 92

Genre experimentation topics, 157
    conversations in writing, 165–168
    genre selection, 162–165

introducing mentor texts, 157–161
origins of writing piece, 169–171
See also Quick writes; Writing craft/
conventions topics
Genre selection quick write, 162
background notes for, 162–163
lesson outline for, 163–164
mentor texts for, 164–165
quick write possibilities for, 163–164
sharing mentor texts and, 163
writer's notebook and, 163
See also Genre experimentation topics;
Short form writing quick write
Giovanni, N., 21, 43, 45, 99, 112,
113, 116, 158
Global connectedness/
interdependence quick write, 130
additional resources for, 137
background notes for, 130–135,
132–134 (figures)
lesson outline for, 135–136
mentor text for, 136–137
quick write possibilities for, 136
sharing mentor texts and, 135–136
writer's notebook and, 136
See also Writing for world
change topics
Goldbarth, A., 66
Goldberger, N. R., 35
Good times/bad times quick write, 46
background notes for, 46–47
lesson outline for, 47–48
mentor texts for, 48–49
quick write possibilities for, 48
sharing mentor texts and, 47–48
writer's notebook and, 48
See also Personal knowledge/
memory topics
Graphic organizers, 7
Graves, D. H., 4, 6, 194
Guided reading texts, 7

Haiku, 179
See also Short form writing
quick write
Hamilton, V., 56
Hands as windows on self
quick write, 126

additional resources for, 129–130
background notes for, 127
lesson outline for, 127–128
mentor texts for, 128–129
quick write possibilities for, 128
sharing mentor texts and, 127–128
See also Writing for world change topics
Harrison, J., 182
Haskins, J., 99
Hayes, T., 191
Head Swivelers prompt, 71–74
Hellman, L., 77
Henrichon, N., 184
Hill, L. C., 127, 129
History topics, 99–101
The History We Know prompt, 97–101
Holland, R., ix
Home. *See* Family homes topic; Home/
important places quick write
Home/important places quick write, 27
background notes for, 27–28
lesson outline for, 28–30
mentor texts for, 30–33
quick write possibilities for, 29–30
sharing mentor texts and, 28–29
writer's notebook and, 28
See also Personal knowledge/
memory topics
Hooper, M., 41
Hoose, P., 100, 150
Hopkins, L. B., 73
Horizons/limits in life quick write, 74
background notes for, 74–75
lesson outline for, 75–77
mentor texts for, 77
quick write possibilities for, 76–77
sharing mentor texts and, 75–76
writer's notebook and, 76
See also Close observation topics
Horizons prompt, 74–77
Horton, A., 188
Hoyt, L., 179, 182
Hughes, L., 158, 170
Hutt, J., 95, 96

If That's a Poem: Introducing Mentor
Texts prompt, 157–161
I Know What I Know prompt, 34–37

Intelligence Advanced Research Projects Activity (IARPA), 108
Intrator, S. M., 37, 52, 77, 93
Introducing mentor texts quick write, 157
   additional resources for, 161
   background notes for, 157–159
   lesson outline for, 159–160
   mentor text for, 161
   quick write possibilities for, 159–160
   sharing mentor texts and, 159
   See also Genre experimentation topics
It Was a Very Good Year prompt, 52–55

Johnson, S. T., 178
Journal writing, 6, 99, 100 (figure)

Keats, E. J., 44, 45
Kennedy, C., 148, 149, 150
Kennedy, J. F., 147, 148, 149, 150
Kinney, J., 169
Knowledge. *See* Personal knowledge/memory topics; Ways of knowing quick write
Koertge, R., 78
Kooser, T., 128, 182

Laminack, L., 166, 168
Landowne, Y., 188
Lantz, N., 66
Lawrence, J., 166
Lee, L.-Y., 128
Leedy, L., 103
Less is Better prompt, 178–182
Lester, J., 37, 44, 45, 56
Lewis, B. A., 150
Life evaluation. *See* Horizons/limits in life quick write; Personal knowledge/memory topics; Year/time period evaluation quick write
Limitations. *See* Horizons/limits in life quick write
Lipster, M., 65
Literature. *See* Resources
Litz, A. W., 182
Lyon, G. E., 158

Macaulay, D., 103
MacGowan, C., 182

Magical powers in lives quick write, 55–56
   background notes for, 56
   lesson outline for, 56–57
   mentor texts for, 57–58
   quick write possibilities for, 57
   sharing mentor texts and, 56–57
   See also Dreams quick write; Personal knowledge/memory topics
MakeBeliefsComix.com, 184, 185
Mandated reporting, 72
Masterson, D., 79
McGovern, A., 189
McNaughton, C., 110
Memoir writing, 19, 29, 178
Memory. *See* Earliest memories quick write; Personal knowledge/memory topics
Mental images, 2
Mentor texts, 7, 8, 9–10
   See also Introducing mentor texts quick write; Resources
The Metaphor Program, 108
Metaphors, 2, 64
Metaphors quick write, 107
   additional resources for, 110
   background notes for, 107–108
   lesson outline for, 108–110
   mentor texts for, 110
   quick write possibilities for, 109–110
   sharing mentor texts and, 108–109
   writer's notebook and, 109
   See also Close observation topics
Metaphors: Seeing the World In Other Words prompt, 107–110
Meyer, S., 47, 49
Millennium Development Goals, 138
Mini-lessons, 6–7
Minor, H., 102, 103
Misconceptions about history quick write, 97
   additional resources for, 101
   background notes for, 97–98
   lesson outline for, 98–99
   mentor texts for, 99–101
   Quad Entry Journal for Nonfiction and, 99, 100 (figure)
   quick write possibilities for, 99

sharing mentor texts and, 98–99
writer's notebook and, 99
See also Close observation topics
Modeling writing. *See* Mentor texts
Morrison, T., 76, 77
Mosley, W., 24, 26, 56
Moss, S., 181
My Big Words prompt, 115–119
Myers, C., 152, 154, 176, 178
Myers, W. D., 152, 153, 154

Nagin, C., 4
Name power/pain quick write, 23
    additional resources for, 26
    background notes for, 24–25
    lesson outline for, 25–26
    mentor texts for, 26
    quick write possibilities for, 25–26
    sharing mentor texts and, 25
    writer's notebook and, 25
    See also Personal knowledge/
        memory topics
Narrative writing, 5
National Council of Teachers of English
    (NCTE), 169, 172, 173, 188
National Writing Project, ix, 4, 172, 173
Nelson, G. L., 35
Nelson, M., 162, 164, 192
Nelson, S. R., 44
Neruda, P., 51
Neumeyer, P. F., 166, 168
New Common Core College and Career
    Readiness Anchor Standards for
    Writing, 5
Niemöller, M., 50
Numbering Our Village prompt,
    130–137

Obama, B. H., 148, 149, 150
Objects. *See* Archaeologists' view of
    common objects quick write; Close
    observation topics; Collected objects
    quick write; Essential objects in lives
    quick write; Questioning object's
    nature/uses/owner quick write;
    Seeing common objects quick write
O'Brien, T., 94, 95, 96
Observation. *See* Close observation topics

Of Thee I Sing prompt, 147–151
O'Neill, M., 189
Opportunity Costs prompt, 91–93
Origins of writing piece quick write, 169
    background notes for, 169–170
    lesson outline for, 170–171
    mentor texts for, 171
    quick write possibilities for, 171
    sharing mentor texts and, 170
    writer's notebook and, 170–171
    See also Genre experimentation topics
Ourselves. *See* Personal knowledge/
    memory topics

Parks, L. S., 138, 139, 182
Parks, R., 97, 98, 99
Paterson, K., 146
Patz, N., 70
Personal knowledge/memory
    topics, 17
    collected objects, 37–42
    dreams, 58–62
    earliest memories, 17–23
    family stories/tall tales, 42–46
    good times/bad times in life, 46–49
    home/important places, 27–33
    magical powers in lives, 55–58
    names, power/pain of, 23–26
    silence/keeping quiet, 49–52
    types of writing and, 17
    ways of knowing, 34–37
    year/time period evaluation,
        52–55
    See also Quick writes
Persuasive writing, 5
Phelps, T. D., 172
Philipsen, G., 102
Photographs, 84–86
Photo-inspired writing quick write, 82
    additional resources for, 84–86
    background notes for, 82–84
    lesson outline for, 84
    mentor texts for, 86–87
    quick write possibilities for, 84
    sharing mentor texts and, 84
    See also Close observation topics
Pinkney, M. C., 189
Pinkney, S. L., 189

Pitts, L., 105
Planning for the unexpected
    quick write, 144
    additional resources for, 147
    background notes for, 144–145
    lesson outline for, 145–146
    mentor texts for, 146–147
    quick write possibilities for, 146
    sharing mentor texts and, 145–146
    writer's notebook and, 145
    See also Writing for world change topics
Poetry Daily website, 66
Polacco, P., 124, 126
Practice opportunities, 4–5
Prelutsky, J., 110
Profiles in Courage Award, 150, 151
Prompts, ix, 5–7
    See also Quick writes; Quick writes
        development process
Proverbially Speaking: Words to Live By
    prompt, 88–91
Proverbs/sayings analysis
    quick write, 88
    additional resources for, 90–91
    background notes for, 88–89
    lesson outline for, 90
    quick write possibilities for, 90
    sharing mentor texts and, 90
    writer's notebook and, 90
    See also Close observation topics

Quad Entry Journal for Nonfiction,
    99, 100 (figure)
Questioning object's nature/
    uses/owner quick write, 67
    additional resources for, 71
    background notes for, 68
    lesson outline for, 68–70
    mentor text for, 70
    quick write possibilities for, 70
    sharing mentor texts and, 68–70
    See also Close observation topics
Quick writes, ix–x, xii, 1
    constant composition, state of, 194
    definition of, 7
    development of, 5–7, 187–188
    framework for, 7–9
    guided reading texts and, 7

mentor texts and, 8, 9–10
overview listing of, 13–15
prewriting preparation and, 8
purpose of, 3, 7
quick write lesson components and, 8
read-arounds, shared student writing
    and, 10–11
reading aloud and, 9–10
reflective response writing and, 7
resources for, 8, 197–208
suggestions/possibilities for, 8, 9
teacher groups, trial quick
    writes and, 9
topic/concept context, teacher
    presentation of, 7–8
writing practice opportunities
    and, 4–5, 7
See also Close observation topics; Deeper
    writing; Genre experimentation
    topics; Personal knowledge/
    memory topics; Quick writes
    development process; Writing
    craft/conventions topics; Writing
    for world change topics
Quick writes development
    process, 187–188
    alternative/multiple perspectives
        and, 193–194
    constant composition, state of, 194
    content of writing and, 190–192
    contexts of writing and, 188–190
    extension of ideas and, 187–188
    genre selection and,
        192–193, 193 (figure)
    initial ideas and, 187
    quick write possibilities
        and, 189–190
    See also Quick writes
Quiet. See Silence/keeping
    quiet quick write

Racial topics, 74
Ray, K. W., 158
Read-alouds, 5, 7, 9–10
Read-arounds, 10–11
Reality television programs
    quick write, 104
    background notes for, 104–105

lesson outline for, 105–106
mentor texts for, 106–107
quick write possibilities for, 106
sharing mentor texts and, 105–106
See also Close observation topics
Recognition of noteworthy people/action
quick write, 147
background notes for, 147–149
lesson outline for, 149–150
mentor texts for, 150–151
quick write possibilities for, 150
sharing mentor texts and, 149–150
writer's notebook and, 149
See also Writing for world
change topics
Reflective writing, xi, 1, 3
existential definition activity and, 6
journal writing and, 6
quick writes and, 7
See also Deeper writing
The Remains of the Day prompt,
101–104
Resources:
electronic resources, 207–208
graphic novels, 200
information books/nonfiction,
200–204
novels/fiction, 199–200
picture books, 197–199
poetry books, 204–207
Rich texts, 2
Ringgold, F., 99
Risk-taking, 4
Rites and Righteous Celebrations:
Celebrating Events in
Our Lives With Special Words
prompt, 111–115
Rodriquez, L., 190
Romano, T., 35
Rumi, J., 35

Safe Drinking Water Act (SDWA)
of 1974, 139
Sapphire, 50
Satrapi, M., 184
Scaffolded lessons, 6–7
School topic, 110
Schotter, R., 110, 117, 118

Schribner, M., 37, 52, 77, 93
Science & Technology Stakeholders
Conference, 145
Secrets in lives quick write, 123
background notes for, 124–125
lesson outline for, 125–126
mentor texts for, 126
quick write possibilities for, 126
sharing mentor texts and, 125
writer's notebook and, 125–126
See also Writing for world change topics
Secrets prompt, 123–126
Seeing common objects quick write, 63–64
additional resources for, 66–67
background notes for, 64
lesson outline for, 64–66
mentor texts for, 66
quick write possibilities for, 66
sharing mentor texts and, 64–65
See also Close observation topics;
Collected objects quick write
Seeing Things and Having New Eyes
prompt, 63–67
Self-knowledge. *See* Personal
knowledge/memory topics
Selznick, B., 185
Sendak, M., 164
Sentence stalking, 172
Sentence structure improvement
quick write, 171
additional resources for, 174–175
background notes for, 171–173
cumulative sentence
examples, 174–175
lesson outline for, 173–174
quick write possibilities for, 174
sharing mentor texts and, 173–174
See also Writing craft/
conventions topics
Shared student writing, 10–11
Shetterly, R., 152, 153, 154
Shiga, J., 184
Shocking statements quick write, 71
background notes for, 71–72
lesson outline for, 72–73
mandated reporting obligation and, 72
mentor texts for, 73–74
quick write possibilities for, 73

sharing mentor texts and, 72
writer's notebook and, 72–73
See also Close observation topics
Shore, S. Z., 162
Short form writing quick write, 178
    additional references for, 182
    background notes for, 179–180
    less is better forms, 179
    mentor texts for, 181–182
    quick write possibilities for, 181
    sharing mentor texts and, 180
    short forms reference chart,
        180, 180–181 (figure)
    two word strategy, 179, 182
    See also Genre selection quick write;
        Writing craft/conventions topics
Sibling rivalry topic, 73
Silence/keeping quiet quick write, 49–50
    additional resources for, 52
    background notes for, 50–51
    lesson outline for, 51–52
    mentor text for, 52
    quick write possibilities for, 51–52
    sharing mentor texts and, 51
    See also Personal knowledge/
        memory topics
Similes, 64
Sis, P., 101, 121, 122, 185
Six-word memoirs, 179
    See also Short form writing quick write
Smith, D. J., 110, 130, 136, 137
Smith, J., 184
Smith, L., 110, 181
Smith, O. M., 181
Snapshots: Capture the Moment
    prompt, 82–87
Special events remembrance/
    celebration quick write, 111–112
    additional resources for, 115
    background notes for, 112–113
    lesson outline for, 113–114
    quick write possibilities for, 114
    sharing mentor texts and, 113–114
    writer's notebook and, 114
    See also Writing for world change topics
Speigelman, A., 184
Stevens, J., 146
Stones in My Pocket prompt, 37–42

The Story of My Story prompt, 169–171
Storytelling. *See* Family stories/
    tall tales quick write
Strauss, R., 139
Struggling writers, 5–6, 7
Student Writing Project, 64, 65
Symborska, W., 92

Take Five short form, 179, 181 (figure)
    See also Short form writing quick write
Tall tales. *See* Family stories/tall tales
    quick write
Tan, S., 165, 185
Tarule, J. M., 35
Television programming. *See* Reality
    television programs quick write
Thayer, E. L., 178
Thibodeau, P., 108
The Things They Carried prompt, 93–97
Thompson, N. B., 102
Timelines.com, 55
Time periods. *See* Year/time period
    evaluation quick write
Tran, I., 44, 46
Truth, S., 113
Twitter poetry/fiction, 179
Two words strategy, 179, 182
    See also Short form writing quick write

U.S. Department of Homeland
    Security, 145
Unexpected events. *See* Planning
    for the unexpected quick write
United Nations Millennium
    Summit (2000), 138

Van Allsburg, C., 184
Vender Zee, R., 126
Verb usage quick write, 175
    background notes for, 176
    lesson outline for, 176–178
    mentor texts for, 178
    quick write possibilities for, 177–178
    sensory detail list example,
        177, 177 (figure)
    sharing mentor texts and, 176–177
    writer's notebook and, 177
    See also Writing craft/conventions topics

Violence topic, 74
Viorst, J., 48
Visual art topic, 81–82

Walker, A., 76, 77
Water availability/usage quick
    write, 137
  additional resources for, 140
  background notes for, 137–138
  lesson outline for, 138–139
  mentor texts for, 139
  quick write possibilities for, 139
  sharing mentor texts and, 138–139
  See also Writing for world change topics
Watering Our World prompt, 137–140
Ways of knowing quick write, 34
  additional resources for, 37
  background notes for, 34–35
  lesson outline for, 36
  mentor text for, 37
  quick write possibilities for, 36
  sharing mentor texts and, 36
  writer's notebook and, 36
  See also Personal knowledge/
    memory topics
We Are America prompt, 151–155
Weatherford, C. B., 164
Well-chosen words as power
    quick write, 115
  additional resources for, 118–119
  background notes for, 116–117
  lesson outline for, 117–118
  mentor texts for, 118
  quick write possibilities for, 117–118
  sharing mentor texts and, 117
  writer's notebook and, 117
  See also Writing for world
    change topics
What Container Will Hold My Words
    prompt, 162–165
What Dreams May Come prompt, 58–62
What's in a Name prompt, 23–26
What You Know First prompt, 17–23
Wheeler, D. K., 145
When I Was Magic prompt, 55–58
When I Was Silent prompt, 49–52
Where Do You Live prompt, 27–33

Where the Action Is prompt,
    175–178
Who Wore the Hat prompt,
    67–71
Wiesel, E., 51, 190
Wild, M., 164
Williams, W. C., 158, 170, 171, 182
Wilson, J., 164
Woodson, J., 166, 168
The Work of Our Hands
    prompt, 126–130
World change. *See* Writing
    for world change topics
Worth, V., 64, 182
Wright, R., 181
Writing craft/conventions
    topics, 157
  comics/cartoon writing,
    182–185
  sentence structure improvement,
    171–175
  short form writing, 178–182
  verb usage, 175–178
  See also Genre experimentation topics;
    Quick writes
Writing for world change topics, 111
  coming together of people/
    groups, 120–123
  constitutional rights, 140–143
  defining Americans, 151–155
  global connectedness/
    interdependence, 130–137
  hands as windows on self, 126–130
  planning for the unexpected, 144–147
  recognition of noteworthy people/
    actions, 147–151
  secrets in lives, 123–126
  special events remembrance/
    celebration, 111–115
  water availability/usage, 137–140
  well-chosen words as
    power, 115–119
  See also Quick writes
Writing Stories and Boasting Poems
    prompt, 42–46
Writing-what-you-know
    approach, 6

Year/time period evaluation quick write, 52–53
  additional resources for, 55
  background notes for, 53–54
  lesson outline for, 54–55
  mentor texts for, 55
  quick write possibilities and, 54–55
  sharing mentor texts and, 54

writer's notebook and, 54
  See also Personal knowledge/
    memory topics
Yolen, J., 75, 77, 101, 121, 122, 171, 184

Zephaniah, B., 160
Zimmer, T. V., 128, 129
Zinn, H., 98

CORWIN

A SAGE Company

The Corwin logo—a raven striding across an open book—represents the union of courage and learning. Corwin is committed to improving education for all learners by publishing books and other professional development resources for those serving the field of PreK–12 education. By providing practical, hands-on materials, Corwin continues to carry out the promise of its motto: **"Helping Educators Do Their Work Better."**